W9-BZB-576

Othello

William Shakespeare

Shane Barnes Aidan Coleman

insight

insight

Othello by Shane Barnes & Aidan Coleman
Insight Shakespeare Plays

Copyright © 2011 Insight Publications Pty Ltd

First published in 2010 by
Insight Publications Pty Ltd
ABN 57 005 102 983
89 Wellington Street
St Kilda VIC 3182
Australia
Tel: +61 3 9523 0044
Fax: +61 3 9523 2044
Email: books@insightpublications.com
Website: www.insightpublications.com

This edition published 2011 in the United States of America by
Insight Publications Pty Ltd, Australia.

ISBN-13: 978-192-1-088-54-4

Library of Congress Control Number: 2011932016

Cover image: Lenny Henry and Conrad Nelson in the 2009
Northern Broadsides' production of *Othello* / Nobby Clark / ArenaPAL

Printed in the United States of America by Lightning Source
10 9 8 7 6 5 4 3 2 1

Contents

Contents

Contents

Support materials

History and criticism

The Turkish threat	40
What did Othello look like?	63
Iago and the Devil	98
Shakespeare's clowns	100
A soldier's life	104
Women, marriage and society	152
Othello as tragedy	202

Shakespeare's themes & techniques

Thinking about Othello and race	24
Introducing imagery: animal imagery	33
Thinking about conflict and antithesis	41
A word about soliloquies and asides	51
Introducing similes, metaphors and conceits	62
A word about pathetic fallacy and foreshadowing	74
Thinking about characters' fatal flaws	79
Introducing dramatic irony	81
Annotating a soliloquy	92
A word about puns	103
A word about hyperbole	116
More about imagery	127
The deterioration of Othello's language	146
Thinking about the conflict between illusion and reality	164
A word about repetition in *Othello*	171
Props as symbols in *Othello*	179
Performing Act 5 Scene 2	189
Othello's final speech	191

About the authors

Shane Barnes BA Dip Ed is currently Deputy Principal at Craigmore Christian School, Adelaide. He has contributed several chapters to *Great Ideas for English in the Senior Years* (SAETA, 2001) and has presented at numerous SAETA and VATE workshops. Shane has been on marking and moderation panels for senior secondary level English and Tourism, and was nominated for a National Excellence in Teaching Award in 2007.

Aidan Coleman BA Dip Ed teaches English at Cedar College, Adelaide. In 2004, he attended the prestigious Prince of Wales Shakespeare School at Stratford-upon-Avon, and in 2005 his poetry collection *Avenues & Runways* was short-listed for the New South Wales Premier's Literary Award. Aidan has been awarded the ASG Community Merit Medal and a 2006 National Excellence In Teaching Award.

Acknowledgements

The authors wish to thank the following people:

The South Australian English Teachers' Association, for their ongoing and generous support.

Dave McGillivray, who has appeared in many Shakespearean productions (including the State Theatre Company of South Australia), for many insights into the language and performability of Shakespeare.

Abbie Thomas, Walford Anglican School for Girls, for her helpful comments and suggestions on the manuscript.

Tess Coleman for proofreading.

The staff at Insight Publications, especially Iris Breuer and Catherine Lewis, for their sound advice and willingness to listen to our ideas, as well as Robert Beardwood and Anni Dillon for their meticulous editing and intelligent suggestions.

Our families, for their infinite patience, understanding, excitement and support.

Insight Publications thanks the University of Birmingham for permission to reproduce the image of *Abd el-Ouahed ben Messaoud ben Mohammed Anoun, Moorish Ambassador to Queen Elizabeth I, 1600*.

Introduction

Who was Shakespeare?

Shakespeare was neither a king nor a lord, and this is the reason we know little about him. While historians and writers made an effort to record the details of the lives of those born into noble families (kings, queens, ladies and lords), they were not generally interested in the important details of other people's lives. In his time Shakespeare was a famous playwright, but perhaps no more famous than some other London playwrights like Ben Jonson or Christopher Marlowe. Little effort was made to record the details of his life until some 50 years after his death.

The Chandos Portrait of William Shakespeare

Did Shakespeare write Shakespeare?

Nearly all scholars agree that we have enough evidence to confirm that William Shakespeare, the man born in Stratford-upon-Avon, was the author of the plays and poems attributed to him. However, a few other theories exist as to who wrote the plays. Some authors that have been suggested include Edward de Vere, the Seventeenth Earl of Oxford; Christopher Marlowe (a talented playwright who died in 1593 but who conspiracy theorists claim may have faked his own death); Francis Bacon (a philosopher and scientist); and even Queen Elizabeth I.

There are a number of problems with all of these theories and very little evidence to support them. No one doubted Shakespeare was the author of the plays and poems until 200 years after his death and these theories are usually based on the argument that Shakespeare was not university-educated.

1564	He was baptised on 26 April 1564; it is likely that he was born three days before this on 23 April (St George's Day).
1560s	William's parents, John and Anne, were possibly both illiterate (they couldn't read or write). His father, John Shakespeare, was a glove maker and was involved in a number of other business activities. He became a member of the town council when Shakespeare was very young.
	Shakespeare was John and Anne's third child. He had seven brothers and sisters but only five of them survived to adulthood.
1571	It is believed that Shakespeare entered the King's New Grammar School in Stratford around the age of seven. Shakespeare's school days would have begun at six in the morning in summer and seven in winter and they would have finished at five in the evening (Monday to Saturday). The school would have been very strict and students could have expected to be beaten for misbehaving or showing any signs of laziness.
1578	Shakespeare probably left school at 14 or 15. His father owed quite a few people money by this time, and, for this reason, William was unable to attend university.
1582	At age 18, he married 26-year-old Anne Hathaway. They had three children – Susanna, and twins, Judith and Hamnet (Hamnet died when he was only eleven).
1590s	We are unsure what Shakespeare did in his early twenties. There are stories of his being employed by a rich landowner in the north of England. It is possible that he joined a travelling company of actors. We do know that by the early 1590s he was a popular playwright in London; in 1594 he invested in the acting company of which he was a member (The Lord Chamberlain's Men), becoming a part-owner.
	Through the 1590s Shakespeare wrote a number of poems and many of his most popular plays including *Richard III*, *A Midsummer Night's Dream* and *Romeo and Juliet*. He acted in some of his own plays and those of other playwrights.
	In 1596 Shakespeare obtained a coat of arms for his father, which meant that he would be officially regarded as a gentleman. In the following year, Shakespeare bought New Place, the second largest house in Stratford-upon-Avon.
1600s	The first decade of the 1600s was his most productive period, when he wrote most of his greatest plays, including *Hamlet*, *Othello*, *Macbeth* and *King Lear*.
	In 1603 Shakespeare's company became the King's Men and regularly performed at Court before King James from this time. During this decade he bought more properties around London and the Stratford area and became very wealthy.
1613	In 1613 Shakespeare returned to Stratford-upon-Avon but still travelled to London occasionally to look after his business interests.
1616	He died on his 52nd birthday (23 April 1616) and was buried at Holy Trinity Church in Stratford.

Jacobean England

Portrait of James I by an unknown artist; c.1604

Upon her death, Queen Elizabeth I was childless and it was widely accepted that her second cousin, James, already the King of Scotland, was the best candidate to replace her. James I of England came to the throne in 1603, and ruled both England and Scotland until his death in 1625. Historians refer to this period (1603–1625) as 'Jacobean'.

Most English people were pleased to finally have a man on the throne because they believed it would lead to greater stability. King James was intelligent and knowledgeable, but with no real practical sense, and this earned him the reputation of being 'the wisest fool in Christendom'. He was very opinionated, and wrote books and pamphlets on such diverse topics as politics, tobacco and witchcraft.

James was not as diplomatic as Elizabeth in dealing with the English Parliament and he promoted the doctrine of the Divine Right of Kings, which argued that kings received their power from God and could not, therefore, be challenged. James was instinctively conservative and, despite replacing many of the English courtiers with Scottish favourites, made few changes to the government of the realm. Early in his reign, James secured a lasting peace treaty with Spain, and tried to introduce a union between England and Scotland. Although the union was not achieved in James' lifetime, the flag he introduced still flies today as the British Union Jack.

The kingdom James inherited was thriving with confidence and patriotic feeling. This was the high point of the period often described as the English Renaissance. The modern scientific method was being developed, based on observation and experiment, and new discoveries were being made, particularly in the areas of anatomy, mathematics and astronomy. It was also a time of great achievement in the arts. At the centre were the English theatres, attracting audiences of around 20 000 per week.

When James came to power, Shakespeare had already written many of his most famous plays, including *Romeo and Juliet* and *Hamlet*. James was quick to name Shakespeare's company of actors the King's Men. This new title allowed Shakespeare's company to march in processions and to play before the King, which they did on many occasions. In the next few years Shakespeare wrote some of his most profound plays, including *Othello*, *King Lear* and *Macbeth*.

Unlike today, when the people of England vote for a government, England was ruled by a monarch, James I, and his advisors. Jacobean society was divided into two broad groups: the 'gentle', the two to five per cent of the population who governed the country (including earls, lords, ladies and gentlemen), and the 'base' or 'knaves', who made up most of the population. People were born into a certain class and marriages between people of different classes were reasonably rare. While the 'gentle' were generally wealthy, some businessmen of lower rank were also beginning to make their fortunes during this time. The practice of knighting or even ennobling a person of lesser rank became more common under James; people usually paid for this privilege and James saw this as another source of income.

In the early 1600s, virtually everyone believed in a God who created and controlled the universe. Jacobeans believed in a divine order called the Great Chain of Being. In this way of seeing the world, God ruled the universe and below Him were a number of angels. The King was the highest earthly rank in the Chain of Being; beneath him were nobles and lesser lords, and below them the majority of the population. This Chain extended further to the animal and then the plant kingdom. Such an idea was used to reinforce the class system: everything had its place in the chain and people believed that upsetting this order in any way would cause chaos. A person's social class was even made clear through the clothing they wore, which was governed by strict laws.

Jacobeans were quite superstitious. Many of them believed in fairies and witches, whom they blamed for unexplained mishaps, although many educated people were becoming sceptical. A Jacobean would worry if a black cat crossed her path, and would avoid walking beneath ladders

Illustration from 1579 of the Great Chain of Being (artist unknown)

The New Globe Theatre

because this was considered bad luck. The Earth was generally believed to be the centre of the universe, and it was thought that in their motion around the Earth, the planets produced musical notes that together formed a perfect harmony. Jacobeans also believed that the constellations and other heavenly bodies, including the moon, influenced human events and held clues for the future.

At the beginning of the sixteenth century, England, like most other European countries, was Roman Catholic. Under Henry VIII, the country broke away from the Roman Catholic Church and formed the Protestant Church of England. Although England briefly became Catholic again under Queen Mary, the country remained Protestant throughout the reigns of Elizabeth and James. This meant James I was the head of the Church of England. Catholicism was illegal when James came to the throne and English Catholics hoped that their new king would change this. The King's wife, Anne of Denmark, was a Catholic and James had made some remarks as King of Scotland that suggested he might introduce a limited tolerance towards Catholics. The early years of James' reign were a disappointment for some, and in 1605 a group of radical Catholics attempted to assassinate James and the ruling elite by blowing up the Houses of Parliament. The scheme, known as the Gunpowder Plot, failed and everyone involved was executed.

Many Protestants, known sometimes as Puritans, appealed to James to reform the Church of England and make it more distinct from the Catholic Church. James ignored their appeals on most points, except their request for a new translation of the Bible. The now famous *King James Bible* was produced early in James' reign (1611) by a committee of Greek and Hebrew scholars. Many consider it the most poetic translation of the Bible into English. Like Shakespeare's plays, the *King James Bible* has had a profound effect on the development of the English language.

A day at the theatre, London 1605

Imagine you could go back to London on a Saturday afternoon in September 1605. It is a warm sunny day with a slight breeze blowing in from the country. You decide to avoid the crowds flowing over London Bridge, choosing instead to be rowed across the River Thames (pronounced *Temz*) in one of the many water taxis. There are dozens of similar boats making their way across the river from the main city to Southwark.

Southwark is a poor, overcrowded suburb filled with hastily built houses and flats. This is where immigrants from other parts of England or overseas come to live when they first arrive in London because it's cheap and no one asks questions. It is full of workshops and young apprentices and you notice an overly high number of beggars. It is also the location for five of London's prisons, including that most notorious prison: the Clink.

Panorama of London by Claes Van Visscher, 1616

More importantly, Southwark is London's entertainment district. This is largely because it is outside the control of the city officials and their strict laws. The streets are packed with bowling alleys, brothels and taverns, where you can drink, or gamble illegally on dice, backgammon or cards. Here you can see all sorts of professional entertainers, from acrobats and clowns to musicians and puppeteers. You can also see some sickeningly violent entertainment. In the bear-baiting rings you are likely to see a bear or bull being attacked by vicious dogs. But you haven't crossed the river to see any of these things. You are here to see a play.

As you near the theatre, it is the smells you notice: roasting meats and pies mingle with the ever-present stench of horse dung, human sweat and sewage. Then you turn a corner, and there it is, standing thirty metres high: the Globe Theatre. The building is almost round in shape and white, criss-crossed with timbers. Above the brown thatched roof a white flag ripples in the breeze.

Today's play is *Othello*. You've heard that it was a hit at court when it was performed before the King. It costs just a penny to enter. This is about a tenth of the average worker's daily wage, which makes it cheaper than a movie today. As you pass beneath the entrance you read the words *Totus mundus agit histrionem*: the whole world is a playhouse.

Inside, three tiers of gallery seating wrap around the stage. If you pay another penny, you can buy yourself a seat in one of the lower tiers, or for sixpence you can purchase one of the best seats in the upper galleries. This is where the upper classes sit: the gentlemen, lords and ladies.

The stage is raised about one and a half metres above the ground. Like the seats in the galleries, the performance area is covered. The ceiling, which they call the heavens, is painted with stars. You notice there are very few props of any sort and no backdrops or scenery: just a curtain at the back of the stage, and above this three balcony areas that face the audience. These are the most expensive seats in the house, where people sit to be seen.

The Globe is now almost full with 3000 noisy people. You find a place off to the side of the stage. You'll have to stand for two or three hours but you've done that before at plenty of concerts. There are no toilets, and you will need to keep a careful eye on your bag.

The audience around you are poorer Londoners, the groundlings. You'll find they're a lot like a crowd at the football but rougher. They will eat, drink and talk throughout the performance and will shout out or boo if they don't like what's happening.

When the actors come on you'll find they speak very quickly, but you'll be able to hear them clearly where you are. If you look very closely you may even notice something strange about the female characters. All of the parts are played by men, and female characters, like Desdemona and Emilia, are played by boys whose voices have not yet broken. Theatre companies are considered too dangerous for women, and they won't be permitted onstage for another 60 years.

Anyway, it's almost 2 o'clock and the performance is about to begin …

Interior of the New Globe Theatre

Dates and sources

Shakespeare probably finished writing *Othello* in 1604. The first known registered performance was in November of that year before King James I at Whitehall. *Othello* was first published in 1622 as a Quarto (the Jacobean equivalent of a paperback today). One year later, it was included in a book that attempted to collect all of Shakespeare's plays, a book we now refer to as the First Folio.

In writing *Othello*, Shakespeare used 'The Story of Disdemona of Venice and the Moorish Captain' from a book of 110 short stories, published in 1565 by the Italian writer and professor of philosophy, Giovanni Battista Giraldi, commonly known as Cinthio. Shakespeare's *Othello* shares many of the basic details of this story but is much more expansive and complex. In Cinthio's story, the Moor (Othello in Shakespeare's play) remains unnamed, as does the evil Ensign (Iago).

In the original story, the Ensign is in love with Desdemona but Shakespeare makes Iago's motivations far more ambiguous. The narratives of Cinthio and Shakespeare also differ greatly in their endings. In Cinthio's story, the Ensign is caught after murdering Desdemona with the Moor's consent. The story ends with the Ensign dying miserably and the Moor being sent into exile. Shakespeare's resolution, however, sees Othello murdering Desdemona and then committing suicide.

Settings

Venice: Act 1

The opening act of *Othello* is set in Venice, a city in northern Italy consisting of a number of islands in the centre of a lagoon. Locals who were fleeing from barbarian invaders founded the city in the final years of the Roman Empire. As the Roman Empire dissolved, Italy broke up into a number of smaller states. During the Middle Ages, Venice became one of the most powerful and wealthy city-states in Italy.

Because it was built in the middle of a lagoon, Venice's streets were (and still are) canals and most Venetians moved about the city in long, narrow boats called gondolas. Not surprisingly, Venetian wealth and military power was due primarily to its large fleet of ships. Venice dominated trade between the Middle East and Europe, mainly in such luxury items as silks and spices. Through her naval power, Venice also added a number of islands, including Corfu, Crete and Cyprus, and significant areas of the Balkans to her territory in mainland Italy. The Venetians won their greatest naval victory, over the Ottoman Turks at the Battle of Lepanto, in 1571, shortly after the time in which *Othello* is set.

Venice was a republic, which meant it was governed by the people rather than by a monarch. In reality, a rich aristocratic class held power and elected a Duke (called the Doge), often for life. After 1229, a Senate of 60 members assisted the Doge in running the Republic. We see the Senate in action in Act 1 Scene 3.

Venetian law was considered to be fairly liberal or tolerant compared with other European nations. While the majority of Venetians were practising Roman Catholics, heretics (people who deviated from the orthodox faith) were rarely persecuted. In the minds of many Europeans, Venice was associated with luxury and decadence. It was already famous in Shakespeare's time for its courtesans (prostitutes) and for massive spending on art and architecture. Venetians were quick to adopt the printing press and established the paperback format. By the late fifteenth century, Venice was a leader in European publishing.

The signs of Venice's decline were already apparent in Shakespeare's day. The ongoing war with the Ottoman Empire proved very costly, and Venice's problems were compounded by various international developments, including Christopher Columbus' discovery of the Americas (1492) and Portugal's discovery of a sea route to India (1498). These events, together with the rising naval power of Holland and England, broke Venice's monopoly on trade. Venice's decline continued and by the end of the seventeenth century, she was only a second-rate power.

Cyprus: Acts 2–5

The final four acts of *Othello* are set in Cyprus, an island located in the Eastern Mediterranean, off the coast of Syria. The island generally experiences hot and dry summers, and productions of *Othello* usually emphasise this climate.

Cyprus truly fits Cassio's description as 'this warlike isle'. Today, the mountainous landscape is still dominated by the imposing castles and forts left by the island's various conquerors. Before the Venetians took charge in 1473, the island had been ruled by Assyrians, Egyptians, Persians, Greeks, Romans, Arabs, Byzantine Greeks and Crusaders. *Othello* is set at a time when the island was still ruled by the Venetians but was coming under increasing threat from the Ottoman Turks. The Turks conquered the island in 1570, when Shakespeare was six years old, with a force of 60 000 troops, and ruled in Cyprus until the mid-nineteenth century.

The island is also associated with romantic love. In classical mythology, the goddess Aphrodite (Venus to the Romans) first came ashore on

Cyprus, after being born out of the sea-foam. Aphrodite was the goddess of beauty, love and sexual desire and, for this reason, Cyprus is often called the Island of Love. When Othello and Desdemona come ashore, they certainly are passionately in love, but Iago's schemes will render the island's title highly ironic.

Shakespeare's language

Shakespeare wrote with an astonishing command of the English language. His lines are packed with puns, metaphors and ironies. He often uses words and phrases that sound strange to a modern reader, and some words have shifted in meaning since Shakespeare's time. Sometimes he uses a different word-order from what you might be used to, and his characters often speak in poetry. Shakespeare's language can, at times, be challenging, but the reward is in the challenge.

Below are some tips on how to read the text and some of the main features to look out for. At this stage in your schooling, you should be relatively confident with terms like **iambic pentameter** and **rhyming couplet**. Even so, practise reading the text aloud and enjoy the sound of the language.

Tips for reading

It is vital not to pause at the end of a line if a thought or an idea continues on to the next line. The following example from *Othello* illustrates this point. Try reading it aloud, pausing at the end of each line.

[Context: Iago plots to use Desdemona's handkerchief as a way to poison Othello's thoughts with jealousy.]

IAGO	I will in Cassio's lodging lose this napkin,	
	And let him find it. Trifles light as air	
	Are to the jealous confirmations strong	
	As proofs of holy writ. This may do something.	
	The Moor already changes with my poison;	(Act 3 Scene 3)

The most natural place in these lines to pause is where you see a punctuation mark such as a full stop (.), comma (,) or semi-colon (;). In this case, it is natural to pause at the full stops after 'it' and 'writ', at the comma after 'napkin' and at the semi-colon after 'poison'.

Read the lines again, this time pausing at punctuation marks rather than at the end of each line. You will notice that the lines flow much more smoothly now and that the meaning of the lines is clearer. Pause for a little longer after 'it' and 'writ' than after 'napkin', as a comma does not require as long a breath as a full stop. The key point to remember is to pause in your reading only at punctuation marks, the same way you would when reading a novel.

The dash

In this version of Shakespeare's *Othello,* the dash (–) is a specific punctuation mark. It is used to indicate **interruptions** to the flow of conversation in several ways.

a Alternating between speaking to one character and then another

[Context: Brabantio questions Roderigo as to the whereabouts of his daughter, Desdemona. Interrupting his questioning of Roderigo, Brabantio issues commands to his servants.]

BRABANTIO	… What said she to you? – Get more tapers;	
	Raise all my kindred – Are they married, think you?	(Act 1 Scene 1)

b Becoming sidetracked during a conversation

[Context: While Brabantio questions Roderigo as to the whereabouts of his daughter, his anxiety is indicated by the dashes in the text, showing that his thoughts are jumbled and interrupted.]

BRABANTIO	… Now, Roderigo,	
	Where didst thou see her? – O unhappy girl! –	
	With the Moor, say'st thou? – Who would be a father! –	
	How didst thou know 'twas she? – O she deceives me	
	Past thought! …	(Act 1 Scene 1)

c Interrupting another character's dialogue

[Context: Desdemona tries to defend the reputation of Cassio before Othello, her husband. Othello's interruptions, obsessing over Desdemona's handkerchief, are indicated by dashes in the text.]

DESDEMONA	You'll never meet a more sufficient man –	
OTHELLO	The handkerchief!	
DESDEMONA	I pray, talk me of Cassio –	
OTHELLO	The handkerchief!	(Act 3 Scene 4)

The meaning of the dash (–) in the text is indicated by the context of the dialogue. In all cases in this edition of *Othello*, it signals an interruption of some sort.

Language features

a Blank verse and iambic pentameter

Most of Shakespeare's plays are written in **blank verse**, which is unrhymed poetry written in a regular rhythm or meter known as **iambic pentameter**. The majority of *Othello* is written in blank verse, so we will start with this aspect in order to understand the rhythm of the text. For example:

> OTHELLO It gives me wonder great as my content
> To see you here before me. O my soul's joy! (Act 2 Scene 1)

Set out like a poem (verse) rather than a novel (prose), there is something else you might notice about these lines, besides the fact that they do not rhyme. Take a moment to read them aloud. Can you hear the rhythm in the words? Read the lines aloud once more. Can you hear the regular heartbeat repeating itself in each line?

te-DUM, te-DUM, te-DUM, te-DUM, te-DUM ...

Shakespeare generally uses ten beats per line, divided into what are called **iambs**. Each iamb contains one unstressed beat and one stressed beat (te-DUM). As each line has five iambs, this forms the rhythm called **iambic pentameter** ('penta' relates to a group of five, as in <u>penta</u>gon, which is a five-sided shape).

This pattern is made clearer below, where the CAPITALISED letters are a stressed or strong beat. They should be emphasised a little more than the weaker beats:

> IAGO I'll POUR this PEST-i-LENCE in-TO his EAR. (Act 2 Scene 3)

Not only does Shakespeare's iambic pentameter (five te-DUMs per line) work **across** words ('his EAR', as written above) and **within** words (as in 'PEST-i-LENCE' and 'in-TO' above), but also **across speakers**:

> OTHELLO O my fair warrior!
> DESDEMONA My dear Othello! (Act 2 Scene 1)

Shakespeare emphasises the bond between Othello and Desdemona by having Desdemona complete Othello's line of iambic pentameter. This is shown in the text by indenting Desdemona's lines. Whoever reads the part of Desdemona in this case should speak immediately after Othello to complete the rhythm of the line. In this way, the heart of the play does not stop beating.

You will not necessarily be able to pick this rhythm straight away, but the more you read Shakespeare, the more you will develop a feel for blank verse, and especially for the all-important iambic pentameter.

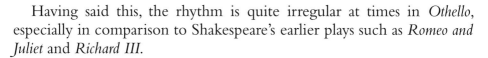

Having said this, the rhythm is quite irregular at times in *Othello*, especially in comparison to Shakespeare's earlier plays such as *Romeo and Juliet* and *Richard III*.

b Rhyme

Despite the importance of blank verse (unrhymed iambic pentameter) in Shakespeare's plays, some lines in *Othello* are actually written in **rhyming verse**. There are two different forms of rhyming verse used throughout the play.

i Rhyming couplets

IAGO	I have't! It is engendered! Hell and night
	Must bring this monstrous birth to the world's light. (Act 1 Scene 3)

Sometimes a rhyming couplet (two consecutive lines that rhyme) helped the audience to know it was the end of the scene, and that they could fidget a little. It might also have been a cue to the actors that they were soon due on stage for the next scene. Structurally, it ties up a speech neatly and makes a point memorable, as in the example above. Note, too, that the rhyming couplet is still in iambic pentameter.

At other times, Shakespeare uses rhyming couplets to signal a shift in tone in the midst of a scene; this is particularly notable in *Othello*. By way of illustration, when Brabantio reports Othello to the Duke for supposedly abusing Desdemona, the tension of the scene is relaxed when the Duke responds to Brabantio in rhyming couplets:

DUKE	The robbed that smiles steals something from the thief;
	He robs himself that spends a bootless grief.
BRABANTIO	So let the Turk of Cyprus us beguile;
	We lose it not, so long as we can smile. (Act 1 Scene 3)

The Duke seems to trivialise Brabantio's complaint, and Brabantio's overly polite reply to the Duke perhaps reflects this lighter tone. Iago's use of rhyming couplets in Act 2 Scene 1, in which he publicly invents a number of witty proverbs for Desdemona, also contributes to a trivial, more light-hearted tone, and serves as a useful contrast to his privately aired thoughts of jealousy and malice.

ii Songs

At key moments in *Othello*, Shakespeare's characters share their thoughts by means of song (italicised in this edition), using different rhyming schemes from the previously mentioned rhyming couplets. Iago's drinking songs (Act 2 Scene 3) seem particularly appropriate in establishing a sense of realism; his colloquial wording and simple rhymes create an atmosphere of mischief as he deliberately causes Cassio to become drunk.

A quite different tone is produced later in the play when Desdemona shares her pain and confusion over Othello's transformation with Emilia indirectly, via a song:

> DESDEMONA   *The poor soul sat sighing by a sycamore tree,*
> *Sing all a green willow;*
> *Her hand on her bosom, her head on her knee,*
> *Sing willow, willow, willow.*   (Act 4 Scene 3)

In this instance, Desdemona's song is a useful dramatic device that prompts the audience to reflect on the characters and their actions; it also slows the pace of the play before the action hurtles into the painfully tragic conclusion.

c Prose

While most of Shakespeare's plays are written in verse, he sometimes chooses to have his characters speak in prose. This is the sort of writing found in novels; it is how we naturally speak and think, and it does not necessarily have a consistent rhythm.

> IAGO   O villainous! I have looked upon the world for four times seven years, and since I could distinguish betwixt a benefit and an injury, I never found a man that knew how to love himself. Ere I would say I would drown myself for the love of a guinea-hen, I would change my humanity with a baboon.   (Act 1 Scene 3)

In many of Shakespeare's plays, prose indicates that a character is of a lower class or is engaging in 'low' or casual behaviour. This is certainly the case when Cassio is drunk (Act 2 Scene 3), and likewise for the dialogue of the Herald (Act 2 Scene 2), Clown (Act 3 Scene 1) and Bianca the prostitute (Act 4). However, prose in *Othello* often has more to do with the context and nature of what the characters are saying than their class. In fact, most characters in the play are able to shift with relative ease from verse to prose. Iago, for example, often speaks at length in prose (e.g. Act 1 Scene 3), perhaps as a means of luring Roderigo into trusting him. Of particular note is the way that the characters' shifting from verse to prose also signifies a shift in the tone of a scene, evident in Act 1 Scene 3, when the Duke changes focus from Brabantio's concerns about Desdemona to the war against the Turks. Conversely, Iago shifts from prose when speaking with other characters on stage to verse in his soliloquies (which we can take to be his private thoughts). This highlights his duplicitous character.

d Dramatic pauses

An aspect of *Othello* that you are sure to notice is the frequent occurrence of lines that do not strictly adhere to Shakespeare's typical use of iambic pentameter. For example, Shakespeare sometimes leaves a line of iambic pentameter incomplete, breaking the rhythm of the text:

OTHELLO	Now do I see 'tis true. Look here, Iago:
	All my fond love thus do I blow to heaven.
	'Tis gone. (Act 3 Scene 3)

These irregular lines are constructed on purpose by Shakespeare to highlight aspects such as dramatic tension. Leaving the line with fewer than the usual ten beats allows time for the characters to pause or perhaps to do something during the moment of silence. Here it allows time for Othello to contemplate the supposed loss of Desdemona's faithfulness, before he launches into an angry outburst. The pause in the dialogue adds discord or tension to the scene.

DESDEMONA	Then would to God that I had never seen't!
OTHELLO	Ha! Wherefore?
DESDEMONA	Why do you speak so startingly and rash?
OTHELLO	Is't lost? Is't gone? Speak: is it out o' the' way?
DESDEMONA	Heaven bless us!
OTHELLO	Say you? (Act 3 Scene 4)

This more irregular rhythm is an essential feature of *Othello*, similar to the abundance of rhythmical disruption found in *Macbeth*. When Iago deliberately poisons Othello's mind with jealousy, the resulting chaos is arguably reflected in the disrupted rhythm of the characters' language. A further irregularity in rhythm is noticeable in *Othello*:

IAGO	'Faith, that he did … I know not what he did.
OTHELLO	What? What?
IAGO	Lie …
OTHELLO	With her?
IAGO	With her, on her; what you will. (Act 4 Scene 1)

The lines above are examples of Iago's masterful art of manipulation. He carefully and subtly hints to Othello of Desdemona's unfaithfulness without directly accusing her. Instead, he deliberately begins a thought and trails off, leading Othello to 'fill in the blanks'. While the use of a series of dots (…) typically indicates *ellipsis*, or that words are missing from an original quote, in this edition of the play it designates that Iago's words trail off and that he purposely leaves a sentence unfinished. This breaking of the rhythm of the text contributes further to the dramatic tension of the scene.

e Contractions and accents

Shakespeare frequently uses **contractions** in order to preserve the rhythm of iambic pentameter. Contractions are shortened words. You use contractions such as don't (do not) and haven't (have not) in everyday speech. In each of these examples, an apostrophe indicates that something is missing, that the word has been shortened:

'tis (it is)   'sblood (by His blood)   o'er (over)   'twas (it was)

At other times, Shakespeare <u>adds</u> a syllable or a beat to a word to make it fit the iambic pentameter. This is indicated in the text by an accent mark to create an extra syllable:

raisèd [RAIS-ed] (two beats instead of one)
despisèd [de-SPIS-ed] (three beats instead of two)

Be on the lookout for the variety of language forms throughout the play: blank verse, rhyming couplets in iambic pentameter, and even songs. And remember, the rich variety of language is used by Shakespeare to show the range of characters, and the shifting relationships and often ambiguous emotions that make up the world of *Othello*.

Important vocabulary

Shakespeare's works include an incredibly wide vocabulary; some scholars have estimated that his plays and poems make use of up to 15 000 different words. You can enjoy Shakespeare without understanding every word, but it is still a good idea to learn the words that are used regularly throughout the play. Some of the words like 'wit' and 'dote' are still used today, and others like 'ere' or 'ay' are rarely employed.

You might like to begin a vocabulary list of your own. Here are some examples of words that occur frequently throughout *Othello*.

Abroad: About the place; freely at large
Beseech: Beg; forcefully request (entreat)
Censure: Severe criticism
Chide / chid: Criticise or tell someone off
Conceit: Thought, idea or imagination (also a technical term for an extended metaphor)
Cuckold: A man whose wife has been sexually unfaithful
Fie: An exclamation of annoyance, disapproval or disgust
Honest: Honourable or chaste (sexually pure), as well as truthful, as it means today
Knave: Troublemaker or trickster
Moor: Someone of north African origin (Othello is a Moor)
Noble: Dignified and brave; of the upper-class
Prithee: Used to introduce a request (short for 'I pray thee …')
Suit: A petition or request to someone in authority
Thou: You
Thy: Your
Wherefore: Why

The characters

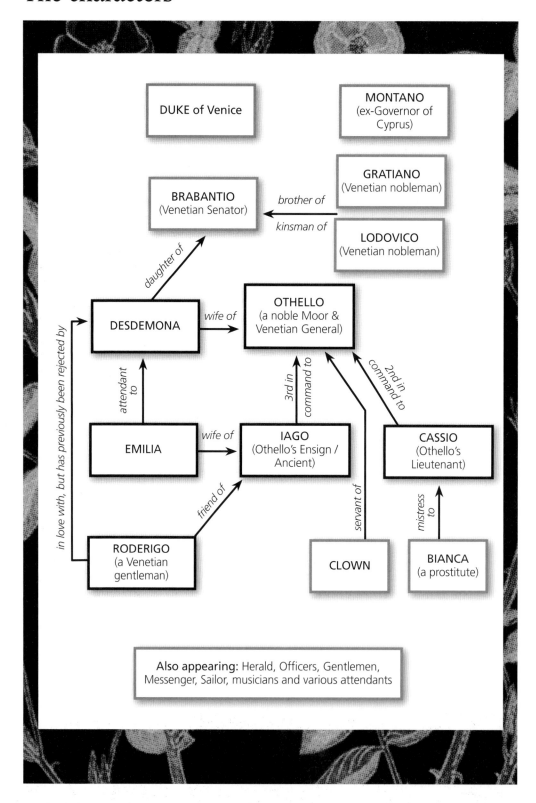

DUKE of Venice

MONTANO
(ex-Governor of
Cyprus)

GRATIANO
(Venetian nobleman)

BRABANTIO
(Venetian Senator)

brother of

kinsman of

LODOVICO
(Venetian nobleman)

daughter of

DESDEMONA

wife of

OTHELLO
(a noble Moor &
Venetian General)

in love with, but has previously been rejected by

attendant to

3rd in command to

2nd in command to

EMILIA

wife of

IAGO
(Othello's Ensign /
Ancient)

CASSIO
(Othello's
Lieutenant)

friend of

servant of

mistress to

RODERIGO
(a Venetian
gentleman)

CLOWN

BIANCA
(a prostitute)

Also appearing: Herald, Officers, Gentlemen,
Messenger, Sailor, musicians and various attendants

Act summaries for *Othello*

Act 1

The play opens in Venice with a conversation between a soldier, Iago, and a rich nobleman, Roderigo. We learn that Iago hates his General, Othello, who has overlooked him for promotion and instead has chosen Cassio as his Lieutenant. Roderigo, too, dislikes Othello, having recently learned of the General's secret marriage to Desdemona, a young woman he also loves. Despite it being the middle of the night, the pair wake Desdemona's father, Brabantio, who sets off with some of his servants and Roderigo to find his daughter. They confront Othello, who is on his way to answer an urgent call from the Senate. Brabantio accuses Othello of stealing his daughter, and both parties agree to go to the Senate to resolve the dispute. The Senate breaks off from its discussion about the Turkish threat to Cyprus to hear the case. Othello informs the Senate how he won Desdemona's love by telling her the story of his life. When Desdemona appears, she confirms her love for Othello. A bitter Brabantio accepts the marriage but suggests that Othello should keep an eye on his bride, who has so easily deceived her father. The Senate decides that Othello must defend the island of Cyprus, and it is agreed that Desdemona will accompany him on the campaign. Although Roderigo is upset by recent events, Iago easily persuades him to go to Cyprus in disguise. When alone, Iago reveals that he is formulating a plan to take Cassio's position.

Act 2

A storm destroys the Turkish fleet and Othello and Desdemona arrive safely on the island of Cyprus. That night the islanders and the Venetian army celebrate both the victory and Othello's wedding. When Othello and Desdemona retire to bed, Cassio is left in charge. Iago encourages Cassio to get drunk and then orchestrates a brawl. The alarm raises Othello from bed and, after hearing Iago's selective retelling of events, he dismisses Cassio from the position of Lieutenant. Cassio is ashamed of his behaviour but Iago comforts him with the plan that he appeal to Othello's wife, Desdemona, to help him recover his position. Privately, Iago reveals his strategy, which is to suggest to Othello that Desdemona and Cassio are having an affair.

Act 3

Cassio appeals to Desdemona and she promises to do all she can for him. Iago's wife, Emilia (who is employed as Desdemona's handmaid), is also very supportive. When Desdemona pleads for Cassio, Othello is not unsympathetic but decides against immediately reappointing Cassio. When Iago and Othello are alone together, Iago subtly suggests that Cassio and Desdemona are having an affair. He advises Othello to delay Cassio's reappointment, and to observe Desdemona's behaviour in response to this. Othello behaves strangely when he next meets Desdemona, and complains of a headache. In trying to soothe Othello's pain, Desdemona loses her handkerchief, which Emilia picks up and gives to Iago. When he next sees Othello, Iago makes bolder claims about Desdemona's infidelity and says that he has seen Cassio with her handkerchief. Othello swears revenge and instructs Iago to kill Cassio, then makes him his new Lieutenant. Othello asks to see Desdemona's handkerchief, and when she attempts to distract him by pleading for Cassio's reinstatement, Othello becomes enraged and storms off. When Cassio meets his mistress, Bianca, he gives her the handkerchief he has recently acquired (planted by Iago in his lodgings) and requests that she make a copy of the beautiful embroidery.

Act 4

Iago continues to give Othello false information, which causes him to suffer an epileptic fit, and then contrives a situation where Othello can partially overhear his conversation with Cassio. Iago and Cassio are actually discussing Cassio's affair with Bianca, but Othello believes Cassio's comments concern Desdemona. Bianca enters with the handkerchief and accuses Cassio of having an affair. After Cassio leaves to chase after Bianca, Othello emerges from his hiding-place and vows vengeance on his wife and Cassio. It is agreed that Iago will kill Cassio and Othello will strangle Desdemona. Letters from Venice arrive with Lodovico, recalling Othello home and replacing him with Cassio. Othello strikes and insults Desdemona in front of Lodovico before storming off. In the presence of Emilia, Othello questions Desdemona but does not reveal exactly what is tormenting him. Iago arranges for Roderigo to ambush Cassio. Before Desdemona retires to bed, she confides her situation to Emilia, and they discuss unfaithful wives.

Act 5

Roderigo botches his attempt to kill Cassio, and Iago only manages to wound Cassio's leg. Roderigo is also injured and their cries draw other people to the scene. Iago pretends he has just arrived and takes control of the situation, stabbing Roderigo and binding Cassio's wounds. When Bianca arrives, Iago accuses her of plotting to kill Cassio. Othello enters Desdemona's bedroom determined to kill her. She awakes terrified and attempts to persuade him to spare her life. When Othello reveals his suspicions, Desdemona protests her innocence, but he smothers her with a pillow. Emilia, bringing news of the attack on Cassio, discovers Othello with Desdemona's murdered body, and raises the alarm. When Emilia reveals the truth about the handkerchief, Iago stabs her and tries to escape. Emilia climbs onto the bed to die beside Desdemona. Othello stabs himself and dies, after which Iago is taken away to be tortured.

Quick questions!

Questions

Spend a few minutes answering these questions in pairs or as a class.

1   Where is the opening act of *Othello* set?

2   Who is unhappy about being passed over for promotion?

3   Who is unhappy at Desdemona and Othello's recent marriage?

4   Whom has Othello made his Lieutenant?

5   Who is Brabantio's daughter?

6   Why is the Senate meeting late at night?

7   How does Othello say he won Desdemona's love?

8   Why does Brabantio suggest that Othello should keep an eye on his bride?

9   How are the Turks defeated?

10   What two things are celebrated in Act 2?

11   Who is left in charge when Othello retires to bed?

12   Why does Cassio lose his position?

13   What strategy does Iago suggest for Cassio to recover his position?

14   Why does Iago give this advice?

15   Who is Iago's wife?

16   How is she employed?

17   What does Iago tell Othello he suspects?

18   What advice does he give Othello?

19   How does Desdemona lose her handkerchief?

20   How does Iago get hold of the handkerchief?

21   Whom does Iago claim he has seen with Desdemona's handkerchief?

22   Whose responsibility is it to kill Cassio?

23   About whom are Cassio and Iago talking when Othello overhears their conversation?

24   Why does Bianca return the handkerchief?

25 What do the letters from Venice command?

26 How does Othello mistreat Desdemona in front of the messenger?

27 Which character does Iago set up to ambush Cassio?

28 How is Cassio injured?

29 How does Iago betray Roderigo?

30 How does Othello murder Desdemona?

31 Who is the first character to discover the murder?

32 Which characters die in the play's conclusion?

33 What happens to Iago?

Freeze-frames

The recommended time allocation for this task (preparation and performance) is approximately 50–60 minutes in total.

Present the play in five freeze-frames (one for each act) in groups of five to seven students.

Instructions

- Read carefully through the summaries for each act.

- Work out how you will present the action of each act in a single 'frozen' pose.

- You may choose to represent a character, an event or even an idea. You may strike a pose where you are doing two things at once.

- Your teacher will tell you to present Act 1 and then instruct you to CHANGE and then FREEZE for your representation of Act 2. This will continue until you have represented all five acts.

- You shouldn't take longer than 15 seconds between acts, so make sure you practise your changeovers before you present your freeze-frames to the class.

- Make sure you can explain what you represent, who you are or what you are doing when you present your freeze-frames to the class.

Characters

Iago
Roderigo
Brabantio

In a nutshell

Othello has recently married Desdemona. Roderigo, who is in love with Desdemona, questions why Iago, who claims to hate Othello, still appears to be loyal to him. Iago assures him that he hates Othello because he has overlooked him for promotion, choosing Cassio instead as his second-in-command. The two of them call loudly and wake Desdemona's father, Brabantio, describing his daughter's marriage in particularly gross terms. After Iago leaves Roderigo, Brabantio appears in the street with servants, ready to search for Desdemona.

Before you read

- In this play, the highest military rank is referred to as General or Captain. This position belongs to Othello, who is not a white Venetian but a Moor, a northern African with dark skin. While Cassio has been promoted to the position of Lieutenant (second-in-command), Iago has remained third-in-command as Ensign or Ancient. An Ensign would carry the standard or regimental flag into battle, and would be noted for his bravery and honesty. As Ensign, Iago is disgusted that a man of study, like Cassio, has been promoted ahead of him.

- Keep in mind that the action in this scene occurs late at night, when all respectable citizens of Venice are asleep. Perhaps this might add to our understanding of Iago's character. It also explains why Brabantio cannot see Iago and Roderigo but can only hear their voices. Finally, Brabantio has just been woken from sleep, so the person reading his lines might consider whether this would create confusion or anger or both.

Tush:	Rubbish
'Sblood:	God's blood (an oath appropriate for a rough soldier)
Abhor:	Hate
Spinster:	An old woman
Knave:	Troublemaker
Profess:	Declare publicly
Kinsmen:	Relatives
Vexation:	Exasperation or worry
Wherefore:	Why

Thinking about Othello and race

Othello, the tragic hero of Shakespeare's play, is black. His colour and appearance are described throughout the play as 'black', 'sooty', 'dark' and 'coal black'. The skin colour of this Venetian General, who originated from northern Africa, is central to our understanding of the story, particularly the notion of racial prejudice.

It is important to remember that Shakespeare's London audience was white, and that they probably would have seen few dark-skinned people. Queen Elizabeth I herself, in 1601, issued a royal proclamation stating that 'those kind of people' should be 'sent out of the land' or expelled from Britain. Some of the attitudes that led to later colonialism and the British slave trade were in their infancy at this point in history.

Additionally, the dominant white Elizabethan and subsequent Jacobean culture viewed those with dark skin primarily in one of two ways, both of which are easily identifiable in Shakespeare's *Othello*. First of all, to seventeenth-century audiences, a Moor or African conjured up images of exotic strangeness, of something unknown and dangerous, something fundamentally 'other'. In the opening scenes of the play, Othello is introduced as a foreigner to Venice, an outsider with an exotic African past. While Shakespeare's white English audience might well have responded with a degree of awe, wonder and even 'delight' at this unusual stranger, the character of Iago plays upon the entrenched cultural prejudice: the association of the colour black with moral darkness, with something 'evil', 'unnatural', 'monstrous' and even 'devilish' – something 'to fear and not to delight' (Act 1 Scene 2, line 71).

Before *Othello*, playwrights created stereotypical black characters to represent evil. Black souls of the damned in the Coventry Mystery Cycle, and even Shakespeare's bloodthirsty and immoral villain, Aaron the Moor in *Titus Andronicus*, typify these wicked characterisations. Shakespeare introduces a radical departure from such racial stereotypes, by creating a noble General, described by Coleridge as 'a high and chivalrous Moorish chief'.

These ideas, thematically linked to the notion of Othello's dark skin colour, are reinforced throughout the play by Shakespeare's use of three particular literary devices:

Imagery of darkness
Much of the play is set at night (as you will notice in the opening scene), and the physical darkness suitably parallels the moral darkness that dominates the story.

Contrast of black and white
Othello, and all that his dark skin implied to Shakespeare's white audience, is repeatedly contrasted with the other characters' perceptions of 'honest Iago' and the 'fair' (white) Desdemona, who is presented as virginal and pure. See the box on conflict or antithesis (page 41) for more on this point.

Act 1 Scene 1 A street in Venice, late at night.

[RODERIGO and IAGO enter]

RODERIGO	Tush! Never tell me; I take it much unkindly	
	That thou, Iago, who hast had my purse	
	As if the strings were thine, shouldst know of this.	
IAGO	'Sblood, but you will not hear me.	
	If ever I did dream of such a matter,	5
	Abhor me.	
RODERIGO	Thou told'st me thou didst hold him in thy hate.	
IAGO	Despise me, if I do not. Three great ones of the city,	
	In personal suit to make me his Lieutenant,	
	Off-capped to him; and, by the faith of man,	10
	I know my price: I am worth no worse a place;	
	But he, as loving his own pride and purposes,	
	Evades them, with a bombast circumstance	
	Horribly stuffed with epithets of war;	
	And, in conclusion,	15
	Nonsuits my mediators, for, 'Certes,' says he,	
	'I have already chose my officer.'	
	And what was he?	
	Forsooth, a great arithmetician,	
	One Michael Cassio, a Florentine,	20
	A fellow almost damned in a fair wife;	
	That never set a squadron in the field,	
	Nor the division of a battle knows	
	More than a spinster, unless the bookish theoric,	
	Wherein the togèd consuls can propose	25
	As masterly as he. Mere prattle without practice	
	In all his soldiership. But he, sir, had the election;	
	And I, of whom his eyes had seen the proof	

	At Rhodes, at Cyprus and on other grounds	
	Christian and heathen, must be be-leed and calmed	30
	By debitor and creditor. This counter-caster,	
	He, in good time, must his Lieutenant be,	
	And I – God bless the mark! – his Moorship's Ancient.	
RODERIGO	By heaven, I rather would have been his hangman.	
IAGO	Why, there's no remedy; 'tis the curse of service:	35
	Preferment goes by letter and affection,	
	And not by old gradation, where each second	
	Stood heir to the first. Now, sir, be judge yourself,	
	Whether I in any just term am affined	
	To love the Moor.	
RODERIGO	I would not follow him then.	40
IAGO	O, sir, content you;	
	I follow him to serve my turn upon him.	
	We cannot all be masters, nor all masters	
	Cannot be truly followed. You shall mark	
	Many a duteous and knee-crooking knave,	45
	That, doting on his own obsequious bondage,	
	Wears out his time, much like his master's ass,	
	For nought but provender, and when he's old, cashiered.	
	Whip me such honest knaves. Others there are	
	Who, trimmed in forms and visages of duty,	50
	Keep yet their hearts attending on themselves,	
	And, throwing but shows of service on their lords,	
	Do well thrive by them and when they have lined their coats	
	Do themselves homage. These fellows have some soul,	
	And such a one do I profess myself. For, sir,	55
	It is as sure as you are Roderigo,	
	Were I the Moor, I would not be Iago:	
	In following him, I follow but myself.	
	Heaven is my judge, not I for love and duty,	
	But seeming so, for my peculiar end;	60
	For when my outward action doth demonstrate	
	The native act and figure of my heart	
	In compliment extern, 'tis not long after	
	But I will wear my heart upon my sleeve	
	For daws to peck at. I am not what I am.	65
RODERIGO	What a full fortune does the thicklips owe	
	If he can carry't thus!	
IAGO	Call up her father:	
	Rouse him, make after him, poison his delight,	
	Proclaim him in the streets; incense her kinsmen,	
	And, though he in a fertile climate dwell,	70
	Plague him with flies; though that his joy be joy,	
	Yet throw such changes of vexation on't,	

	As it may lose some colour.	
RODERIGO	Here is her father's house; I'll call aloud.	
IAGO	Do, with like timorous accent and dire yell	75
	As when, by night and negligence, the fire	
	Is spied in populous cities.	
RODERIGO	What, ho, Brabantio! Signior Brabantio, ho!	
IAGO	Awake! What, ho, Brabantio! Thieves! Thieves! Thieves!	
	Look to your house, your daughter and your bags!	80
	Thieves! Thieves!	

[BRABANTIO appears above, at a window]

BRABANTIO	What is the reason of this terrible summons?	
	What is the matter there?	
RODERIGO	Signior, is all your family within?	
IAGO	Are your doors locked?	
BRABANTIO	Why, wherefore ask you this?	85
IAGO	'Zounds, sir, you're robbed; for shame, put on your gown;	
	Your heart is burst, you have lost half your soul;	
	Even now, now, very now, an old black ram	
	Is tupping your white ewe. Arise, arise;	
	Awake the snorting citizens with the bell,	90
	Or else the devil will make a grandsire of you.	
	Arise, I say.	
BRABANTIO	What, have you lost your wits?	
RODERIGO	Most reverend signior, do you know my voice?	
BRABANTIO	Not I; what are you?	
RODERIGO	My name is Roderigo.	
BRABANTIO	The worser welcome:	95
	I have charged thee not to haunt about my doors;	
	In honest plainness thou hast heard me say	
	My daughter is not for thee; and now, in madness,	
	Being full of supper and distempering draughts,	
	Upon malicious knavery, dost thou come	100
	To start my quiet.	
RODERIGO	Sir, sir, sir —	
BRABANTIO	But thou must needs be sure	
	My spirit and my place have in them power	
	To make this bitter to thee.	
RODERIGO	Patience, good sir.	
BRABANTIO	What tell'st thou me of robbing? This is Venice;	105
	My house is not a grange.	
RODERIGO	Most grave Brabantio,	
	In simple and pure soul I come to you.	
IAGO	'Zounds, sir, you are one of those that will not serve God,	
	if the devil bid you. Because we come to do you service	
	and you think we are ruffians, you'll have your daughter	

	covered with a Barbary horse; you'll have your nephews
	neigh to you; you'll have coursers for cousins and
	gennets for germans.
BRABANTIO	What profane wretch art thou?
IAGO	I am one, sir, that comes to tell you your daughter and
	the Moor are now making the beast with two backs.
BRABANTIO	Thou art a villain.
IAGO	You are a senator.
BRABANTIO	This thou shalt answer; I know thee, Roderigo.
RODERIGO	Sir, I will answer anything. But, I beseech you,
	If't be your pleasure and most wise consent,
	As partly I find it is, that your fair daughter,
	At this odd-even and dull watch o' the night,
	Transported, with no worse nor better guard
	But with a knave of common hire, a gondolier,
	To the gross clasps of a lascivious Moor –
	If this be known to you and your allowance,
	We then have done you bold and saucy wrongs;
	But if you know not this, my manners tell me
	We have your wrong rebuke. Do not believe
	That, from the sense of all civility,
	I thus would play and trifle with your reverence:
	Your daughter, if you have not given her leave,
	I say again, hath made a gross revolt;
	Tying her duty, beauty, wit and fortunes
	In an extravagant and wheeling stranger
	Of here and everywhere. Straight satisfy yourself:
	If she be in her chamber or your house,
	Let loose on me the justice of the state
	For thus deluding you.
BRABANTIO	Strike on the tinder, ho!
	Give me a taper! Call up all my people!
	This accident is not unlike my dream;
	Belief of it oppresses me already.
	Light, I say! Light!

[BRABANTIO exits, above]

IAGO	Farewell, for I must leave you:
	It seems not meet, nor wholesome to my place,
	To be produced – as, if I stay, I shall –
	Against the Moor: for, I do know, the state,
	However this may gall him with some check,
	Cannot with safety cast him, for he's embarked
	With such loud reason to the Cyprus wars,
	Which even now stand in act, that, for their souls,

Line numbers: 110, 115, 120, 125, 130, 135, 140, 145

	Another of his fathom they have none,	150
	To lead their business: in which regard,	
	Though I do hate him as I do hell-pains.	
	Yet, for necessity of present life,	
	I must show out a flag and sign of love,	
	Which is indeed but sign. That you shall surely find him,	155
	Lead to the Sagittary the raisèd search;	
	And there will I be with him. So, farewell.	

[IAGO exits]

[BRABANTIO and Servants with torches enter below]

BRABANTIO   It is too true an evil: gone she is;
             And what's to come of my despisèd time
             Is nought but bitterness. Now, Roderigo,   160
             Where didst thou see her? – O unhappy girl! –
             With the Moor, say'st thou? – Who would be a father! –
             How didst thou know 'twas she? – O she deceives me
             Past thought! – What said she to you? – Get more tapers;
             Raise all my kindred – Are they married, think you?   165
RODERIGO   Truly, I think they are.
BRABANTIO   O heaven! How got she out? O treason of the blood!
             Fathers, from hence trust not your daughters' minds
             By what you see them act. Is there not charms
             By which the property of youth and maidhood   170
             May be abused? Have you not read, Roderigo,
             Of some such thing?
RODERIGO   Yes, sir, I have indeed.
BRABANTIO   Call up my brother – O, would you had had her! –
             Some one way, some another – Do you know
             Where we may apprehend her and the Moor?   175
RODERIGO   I think I can discover him, if you please,
             To get good guard and go along with me.
BRABANTIO   Pray you, lead on. At every house I'll call;
             I may command at most – Get weapons, ho!
             And raise some special officers of night –   180
             On, good Roderigo: I'll deserve your pains.

[All exit]

Text notes

10   **Off-capped:** Took off their caps or hats as a sign of respect.

13–17   **Evades them ... 'chose my officer':** Iago is saying that Othello avoids answering their
        appeal by using 'bombast' (pompous or inflated language) and military jargon ('epithets of
        war'), while he also 'non-suits' or refuses their request ('suit').

| 16 | **Certes:** Certainly. |

20 **Florentine:** Someone from Florence, a powerful and wealthy Italian city.

21 **A fellow almost damned in a fair wife:** Iago implies that Cassio is a womaniser, almost to the point of damnation.

25 **Togèd consuls:** Consuls or senators wearing their togas (loose flowing robes). Consuls were the heads of state in ancient Rome. Here Iago adds to his view of Cassio as a politician rather than a soldier.

28–31 **And I, of whom ... counter-caster:** Iago asserts that Othello would have witnessed his abilities at Rhodes, Cyprus and other places, and therefore cannot believe he has been given a lower rank than the book-keeper ('counter-caster'), Cassio.

31–33 **And I – God bless the mark! – his Moorship's Ancient:** Iago expresses his anger at remaining Ancient or Ensign of Othello's force. The phrase 'God bless the mark!' is roughly equivalent to 'God save us'. Iago probably uses the term 'Moorship' sarcastically, perhaps as a pun on 'Lordship'.

39 **Affined:** Bound to someone or something.

44–48 **You shall mark ... he's old, cashiered:** A paraphrase of this might read: you shall see many servants who suck up to their masters wear themselves out like donkeys for their daily food and drink ('provender') and are sacked ('cashiered') when they grow old ('Obsequious' = fawning and overly submissive).

49–55 **Others there are ... I profess myself:** Iago says that others (himself included) appear to serve their masters while, in fact, they are looking after themselves ('visage' = face).

61–65 **For when my outward ... For daws to peck at:** Iago confesses to being deceptive, stating that if he outwardly revealed his real thoughts, he would expose himself to criticism ('daws' = jackdaws, a type of bird thought to be very stupid). It is thought that the saying about wearing your heart on your sleeve, based on a medieval saying, was first recorded in this play.

67–73 **Call up her father ... may lose some colour:** Iago instructs Roderigo to wake Desdemona's father, Brabantio, by shouting about the marriage in the streets, thus worrying and angering Brabantio and all of Desdemona's family ('incense' = anger; 'vexation' = exasperation and worry).

75–77 **Do, with like timorous accent ... in populous cities:** A paraphrase of this might read: cry out like people do when they see a fire burning out of control ('timorous' means nervous today, but in Shakespeare's day its meaning was more like frightening).

89 **Tupping:** Copulating or having sex with.

91 **The devil will make a grandsire of you:** The devil will make you a grandfather. Here, Iago associates the devil with the colour black, in keeping with some European traditions.

99–101 **Being full of supper ... To start my quiet:** Brabantio is suggesting they are making noise and hurling insults because they are drunk. Remember, it is the middle of the night and the citizens of Venice are asleep.

106 **A grange:** A farmhouse. Brabantio is insisting that the city of Venice and his house are well-ordered; the imagery he uses could be a response to the bestial insults that Iago and Roderigo are calling out.

110–12 **You'll have your daughter ... gennets for germans:** Iago suggests here that Desdemona and Othello will produce animals, more specifically horses, instead of human children. These insults are crude and provocative, designed to make Brabantio react ('Barbary horse' = a horse from northern Africa, Othello's region of origin; 'coursers' = racehorses; 'gennets' = Spanish horses; 'germans' = close family).

113 **Profane:** Blasphemous or foul-mouthed.

118 **Beseech:** Beg or forcefully request.

121–24 **At this odd-even … a lascivious Moor:** Roderigo reports that Desdemona has travelled at this late hour virtually unprotected into the hands of the lustful Othello. Roderigo uses particularly grotesque language to present Othello as a shady and lustful character. A 'gondolier' is a person who propels a gondola through the waters of Venice. Roderigo is suggesting that such a person is unfit to transport Desdemona safely. Gondolas are long, narrow boats, still used to taxi people around the city of Venice.

126 **Saucy:** Insolent; insulting.

128 **Rebuke:** Criticism or insult.

129 **Civility:** Manners or proper behaviour.

134 **An extravagant and wheeling stranger:** Roderigo is playing on the fact that Othello is not a Venetian, suggesting that he is a wanderer, likely to be disloyal or unfaithful.

138–39 **Strike on the tinder, ho! / Give me a taper:** Brabantio calls for lights and torches ('taper' = candle).

143 **Meet:** Appropriate; fitting.

144–45 **To be produced … Against the Moor:** Iago is pointing out that if he stays any longer, he will be found stirring things up against his General, Othello.

146–51 **However this may gall … To lead their business:** A paraphrase might read: although this will probably cause him some annoyance, the Venetian state doesn't have any other people of his calibre to lead us, so they will not get rid of him.

156 **Sagittary:** The name of an inn or a pub.

169–71 **Charms …May be abused:** Brabantio is suggesting that Othello has used some kind of dark magic on Desdemona. This assumption is based on Othello's being an exotic stranger.

181 **I'll deserve your pains:** I will reward your service.

Questions

1 What is Roderigo's concern about Iago early in this scene?

2 What reason does Iago give for hating Othello ('the Moor')?

3 What do you think Iago is implying when he describes Cassio as 'a great arithmetician' and a 'bookish theoric' (lines 19 and 24)?

4 In line 65 Iago says, 'I am not what I am'. What does he mean by this?

5 Describe the tactics Iago and Roderigo use to stir up or agitate Brabantio.

6 In this scene, the picture Iago presents of the sexual act is in stark contrast to what a love poet may present:

 a Quote a particularly gross image from this scene.

 b Why do you think Iago uses this kind of imagery?

7 Quote some evidence from the text that shows Brabantio's opinion of Roderigo.

8 What strategies does Brabantio think Othello has used to win Desdemona's love?

9 What picture do we have of Othello based on the dialogue in this scene?

10 To what extent do you think Roderigo has good reason to distrust Iago?

Extend   **1**   What do you think Iago means when he describes Othello as 'loving his own pride and purposes'?

2   Copy and complete the following table:

Speaker	Quote	Meaning
	'thou, Iago, who hast had my purse / As if the strings were thine'	
	'... preferment goes by letter and affection, / And not by old gradation'	
Iago		Iago is deceptive.

3   Iago says to Roderigo, 'I must show out a flag and sign of love, / Which is indeed but sign.' How does this language play on Iago's position in the Venetian military? (See **Before you read** for further assistance.)

4   Copy and complete the following table to show your understanding of the various language devices that Shakespeare uses to present Brabantio's anxiety in lines 158–81.

Language device	Quotes / examples	Line number
Short sentences		
Exclamation marks		
Interrupted train of thought		
Exaggeration		

5   What is Iago implying about Desdemona when he shouts, 'Thieves! Thieves! Thieves!' (line 79)?

6   The opening lines of *Othello* are rhythmically very rough (they do not strictly follow regular iambic pentameter). What might Shakespeare be suggesting about the characters by writing this way? What mood or atmosphere is established?

Discuss   What impression would the audience have of the character of Othello, based solely on the evidence in the opening scene?

Press PLAY   **Oliver Parker: DVD Chapter 1**

1   Make a list of strategies that the director (Oliver Parker) uses to make Shakespeare's text accessible or easy to understand for a modern audience.

2   How does Parker use a range of cinematic techniques (e.g. props, lighting, camera work and music) to create a sinister atmosphere at the beginning of the film?

3   In what ways does Parker present Roderigo as a bitter yet purposeful character? How accurate is this characterisation of Roderigo in relation to Shakespeare's text?

Introducing imagery: animal imagery

When writers use words to form pictures in our minds, perhaps comparing one thing with another, this is known as using **imagery**. These word pictures typically involve our five senses: sight (visual imagery), sound (auditory imagery), touch (tactile imagery), taste (gustatory imagery) and smell (olfactory imagery).

Shakespeare's plays contain an abundance of powerful imagery. In *Othello*, these images gain their power through frequent repetition and from the way they interweave in distinct patterns throughout the play.

Images relating to animals are a dominant feature of *Othello*, especially noticeable in Act 1; they effectively assist in characterisation and craft powerful connections with the play's central themes and ideas.

1   Characterisation of Iago

Every mention of animals in Act 1 is made by Iago: an ass (Scene 1, line 47; Scene 3, lines 377–81), jackdaws (Scene 1, line 65), sheep (Scene 1, lines 88–89), a horse (Scene 1, lines 110–12), a beast (Scene 1, line 115), a baboon (Scene 3, lines 307–10), and even cats and blind puppies (Scene 3, lines 325–27).

Q How do you think Shakespeare's association of Iago with animals assists in characterising him as the villain of the play?

Q Read Scene 1, lines 86–89 and 108–15. Iago reduces the sexual union of Othello and Desdemona to animals rutting or humping. In what ways does Iago's use of gross sexual imagery reinforce our opinion of him as a villain?

2   Reinforcement of themes and ideas

Animal images are regularly and deliberately associated with some of the major themes and ideas of the play, especially in the opening scenes.

a   Racism

Iago's hatred of the Moor is seen clearly when Iago labels Othello as an 'old black ram', a 'Barbary horse' and an 'ass'. In these instances, it is no accident that Shakespeare uses what we might describe as image clustering: images of animals are also connected with images of black and white, or darkness and light.

Q How does Shakespeare employ image clusters to present Iago's racist attitudes toward Othello in Scene 1, lines 86–89 and Scene 3, lines 377–81?

b Illusion versus reality

Q Read Scene 1, lines 42–65 and Scene 3, lines 377–81. Publically, Iago only <u>pretends</u> to love and respect Othello. How does Iago's use of animal imagery strengthen this notion?

c Human nature

Note in Scene 3, lines 306–50 that Iago discusses his self-absorbed and pessimistic view of humanity in bestial (relating to animals) terms.

As you read the rest of *Othello*, watch for the way Shakespeare characterises Iago and highlights the various ideas of the play through distinct images – not just of animals, but also of plants, the sea, darkness and light, and even poison.

Act 1 Scene 2

Characters

Othello
Brabantio
Iago
Cassio
1ST Officer
Roderigo

In a nutshell

Iago attempts to unsettle Othello by warning him of Brabantio's rage. Cassio enters with news that the Duke seeks Othello to lead the Venetians into battle against the Turks. When Brabantio finds them, he verbally abuses Othello for corrupting his daughter and threatens a fight. Othello calms everybody and, after a brief discussion, both parties agree to bring their dispute before the Duke.

Before you read

- In the previous scene, Iago and Roderigo have depicted Othello as a bragging, lustful conman. Brabantio too, shocked by the news of his daughter's marriage, assumes Othello has employed some kind of black magic to win her over. In this scene, the audience meets Othello for the first time and they will make their own judgements about his character.

- Whoever reads the part of Brabantio (especially lines 62–81) needs to remember that he is extremely angry with Othello, whom he believes to be an untrustworthy foreigner who has corrupted his daughter. This anger should be expressed in the way his lines are read.

- Iago swears by Janus in this scene. Janus was the Roman god associated with doors and gates and was depicted as having two faces. You might consider how it is particularly appropriate that Iago swears by this god.

Iniquity:	Wrong-doing
Prated:	Prattled or talked rubbish
Forbear:	Tolerate; put up with

Signiory:	Venetian government
Promulgate:	Make something widely known
Galleys:	Venetian ships
Consuls:	Ancient Roman heads of state (rhymes with *tonsils*)
Senate:	The government
Pagan:	Anyone who is not Christian (in Shakespeare's time)
Manifest:	Show

Act 1 Scene 2   Another street.

[OTHELLO, IAGO and Attendants with torches enter]

IAGO   Though in the trade of war I have slain men,
              Yet do I hold it very stuff o' the conscience
              To do no contrived murder: I lack iniquity
              Sometimes to do me service. Nine or ten times
              I had thought to have yerked him here under the ribs.   5
OTHELLO   'Tis better as it is.
IAGO   Nay, but he prated,
              And spoke such scurvy and provoking terms
              Against your honour
              That, with the little godliness I have,
              I did full hard forbear him. But, I pray you, sir,   10
              Are you fast married? Be assured of this,
              That the magnifico is much beloved,
              And hath in his effect a voice potential
              As double as the Duke's. He will divorce you,
              Or put upon you what restraint and grievance   15
              The law, with all his might to enforce it on,
              Will give him cable.
OTHELLO   Let him do his spite:
              My services which I have done the signiory
              Shall out-tongue his complaints. 'Tis yet to know
              (Which, when I know that boasting is an honour,   20
              I shall promulgate), I fetch my life and being
              From men of royal siege, and my demerits
              May speak unbonneted to as proud a fortune
              As this that I have reached: for know, Iago,
              But that I love the gentle Desdemona,   25
              I would not my unhousèd free condition
              Put into circumscription and confine
              For the sea's worth. But, look! What lights come yond?
IAGO   Those are the raisèd father and his friends:
              You were best go in.

OTHELLO	Not I; I must be found.	30
	My parts, my title and my perfect soul	
	Shall manifest me rightly. Is it they?	
IAGO	By Janus, I think no.	

[CASSIO and several Officers with torches enter]

OTHELLO	The servants of the Duke, and my Lieutenant.	
	The goodness of the night upon you, friends!	35
	What is the news?	
CASSIO	The Duke does greet you, General,	
	And he requires your haste-post-haste appearance,	
	Even on the instant.	
OTHELLO	What is the matter, think you?	
CASSIO	Something from Cyprus as I may divine;	
	It is a business of some heat: the galleys	40
	Have sent a dozen sequent messengers	
	This very night at one another's heels,	
	And many of the consuls, raised and met,	
	Are at the Duke's already: you have been hotly called for;	
	When, being not at your lodging to be found,	45
	The Senate hath sent about three several quests	
	To search you out.	
OTHELLO	'Tis well I am found by you.	
	I will but spend a word here in the house,	
	And go with you.	

[OTHELLO exits]

CASSIO	Ancient, what makes he here?	
IAGO	'Faith, he tonight hath boarded a land carrack;	50
	If it prove lawful prize, he's made for ever.	
CASSIO	I do not understand.	
IAGO	He's married.	
CASSIO	To whom?	
IAGO	Marry, to — *[OTHELLO re-enters]*	
	Come, Captain, will you go?	
OTHELLO	Have with you.	
CASSIO	Here comes another troop to seek for you.	
IAGO	It is Brabantio. General, be advised:	55
	He comes to bad intent.	

[BRABANTIO, RODERIGO and Officers with torches and weapons enter]

OTHELLO	Holla! Stand there!	
RODERIGO	Signior, it is the Moor.	
BRABANTIO	Down with him, thief!	

[They draw swords on both sides]

IAGO	You, Roderigo! Come, sir; I am for you.
OTHELLO	Keep up your bright swords, for the dew will rust them.
	Good signior, you shall more command with years 60
	Than with your weapons.
BRABANTIO	O thou foul thief, where hast thou stowed my daughter?
	Damned as thou art, thou hast enchanted her;
	For I'll refer me to all things of sense,
	If she in chains of magic were not bound, 65
	Whether a maid so tender, fair and happy,
	So opposite to marriage that she shunned
	The wealthy curlèd darlings of our nation,
	Would ever have, to incur a general mock,
	Run from her guardage to the sooty bosom 70
	Of such a thing as thou, to fear, not to delight.
	Judge me the world, if 'tis not gross in sense
	That thou hast practised on her with foul charms,
	Abused her delicate youth with drugs or minerals
	That weaken motion. I'll have't disputed on; 75
	'Tis probable and palpable to thinking.
	I therefore apprehend and do attach thee
	For an abuser of the world, a practiser
	Of arts inhibited and out of warrant.
	Lay hold upon him; if he do resist, 80
	Subdue him at his peril.
OTHELLO	Hold your hands,
	Both you of my inclining, and the rest;
	Were it my cue to fight, I should have known it
	Without a prompter. Where will you that I go
	To answer this your charge?
BRABANTIO	To prison, till fit time 85
	Of law and course of direct session
	Call thee to answer.
OTHELLO	What if I do obey?
	How may the Duke be therewith satisfied,
	Whose messengers are here about my side,
	Upon some present business of the state 90
	To bring me to him?
1ST OFFICER	'Tis true, most worthy signior;
	The Duke's in council and your noble self,
	I am sure, is sent for.
BRABANTIO	How? The Duke in council?
	In this time of the night? Bring him away;
	Mine's not an idle cause. The Duke himself, 95
	Or any of my brothers of the state,
	Cannot but feel this wrong as 'twere their own:
	For if such actions may have passage free,
	Bond-slaves and pagans shall our statesmen be.

[All exit]

1–5   **Though in the trade … under the ribs:** Iago claims that, although he is a soldier who has slain men in battle, he lacks the evil ('iniquity') to carry out murder. He admits that he thought of stabbing Roderigo nine or ten times during their conversation ('yerked' = thrust at).

7   **Scurvy:** Insulting.

11   **Fast married:** Quickly or definitely married.

12   **Magnifico:** A Venetian nobleman (Brabantio).

14–17   **He will divorce you … give him cable:** Brabantio will make things very difficult for you, as much as the law will allow him, like a dog going as far as its lead ('cable') will allow.

21–24   **I shall promulgate … I have reached:** A paraphrase of this might read: I shall make it known that I am descended from royalty only when it is honourable to do so, and this will justify my current position ('siege' = rank; 'demerits' = deserts; 'unbonneted' = without wearing a hat: on equal terms).

26–28   **I would not my unhousèd … the sea's worth:** Othello asserts that, in marrying Desdemona, he has given up his freedom (something he valued highly and would not have traded for the sea's worth before he met her).

31–32   **My parts, my title … manifest me rightly:** Othello claims that his natural qualities ('parts'), his rank and clear conscience will show him to be innocent.

37   **Haste-post-haste:** As quickly as possible.

39   **As I may divine:** As I may guess.

41   **Sequent:** One after the other (in sequence).

50–51   **'Faith, he tonight … he's made for ever:** A 'carrack' is a treasure ship. Iago uses this metaphor to suggest that Othello captured a ship full of treasures (Desdemona) and that he will be rich forever if the law allows him to keep it.

53   **Marry:** A mild oath used here as an expression of surprise. In Renaissance England, the word was used as an abbreviation for swearing by the Virgin Mary.

59   **Keep up your bright swords, for the dew will rust them:** Othello asks them to put away their swords. This could be a joke, suggesting that the swords will rust through being held out for so long or, more threateningly, that they will be killed and the morning dew will rust their swords.

67–71   **So opposite to marriage … of such a thing as thou:** Brabantio asserts that Desdemona was opposed to the idea of marriage and disapproved of the wealthy, frivolous people who married. This, Brabantio argues, makes the idea that Desdemona would run away with Othello ridiculous.

72–75   **That thou hast practised … weaken motion:** Brabantio accuses Othello of using magic and poisons ('minerals') to weaken Desdemona's strength to resist him.

78–79   **A practiser … out of warrant:** More accusations of practising magic ('arts inhibited').

85–87   **To prison … thee to answer:** To prison until your trial.

98–99   **For if such actions … our statesman be:** Brabantio declares that if the rulers of Venice allow this marriage to go ahead, they might as well throw out everything Christian and become pagans, like Othello. 'Pagan' in Shakespeare's time related to any religion other than Christianity. Brabantio is assuming that Othello, who is a Christian convert, will always be a pagan.

1 Why has the Duke sent for Othello?

2 Of what sort of practices and acts does Brabantio accuse Othello?

3 What sort of picture does Brabantio present of his daughter?

4 How is Iago dishonest or deceptive in this scene?

5 Find a quote from Othello's lines that suggests the following:

Quality	Line
That he is polite	
That he loves Desdemona	
That he is open and honest	
That he is not unnecessarily violent	
That he is of noble birth	
That he is calm and confident	

6 How does the way Othello is presented in this scene contrast to the way he was described in the opening scene?

Extend

1 Why do you think Iago advises Othello to hide (line 30)? What might Iago's motivation be for doing this?

2 In what way(s) are Iago's words in lines 6–8 ironic?

3 How does Othello's view of women contrast with that of Iago, judging it from the following comments? In your response, discuss the ideas presented and the language they use.

Othello: … for know, Iago, / But that I love the gentle Desdemona.	**Iago:** 'Faith, he tonight hath boarded a land carrack; / If it prove lawful prize, he's made forever (see **Text note** for lines 50–51).

4 The way Shakespeare begins this scene suggests that Iago and Othello are already part of the way through a conversation. What dramatic purpose do you think this serves? How is this effective?

5 Copy and complete the following table to demonstrate your understanding of how Shakespeare uses language devices to convey Brabantio's anger toward and low opinion of Othello (lines 62–81).

Language Device	Quote(s)
Repetition of words/phrases	
Use of second person ('thou')	'Thou foul thief'
Harsh sounding words	
Insulting words	
Imagery associated with witchcraft	'chains of magic'
Contrast to Desdemona's beauty and innocence	

Discuss What is your impression of Othello in this scene? Has your opinion of him changed from the previous scene?

Press PLAY **Oliver Parker: DVD Chapters 2 and 3**

1 How does Parker present the conflict between Brabantio and Othello? Discuss various cinematic and dramatic devices such as camera work, body language, gestures, lighting and music.

2 Parker chooses to present the back-story of Othello and Desdemona's love by means of a voiceover by Othello. How effective is Parker's choice of music, lighting and camera work in presenting the characters' love and gentleness? How might he have created this atmosphere differently?

Against the general enemy Ottoman
The Turkish threat

When Shakespeare wrote *Othello,* the Ottoman Empire was still arguably the most powerful empire in the world, ruling vast territories in Europe, North Africa and the Middle East. The Ottoman Empire had a population of roughly 30 million at that time, compared with England's population of just over four million.

Some of the peoples of Turkish Anatolia formed a powerful fighting force in the fourteenth century under the leadership of Osman I (from whom the name 'Ottoman' is derived). In the two centuries following Osman's death, the Ottoman Turks conquered most of the Byzantine or Eastern Roman Empire and made Constantinople, formerly the greatest city in the Christian world, their new capital (it was renamed Istanbul in 1930).

The Ottoman Empire controlled the trade routes between Europe and the Middle East, India and China and their ruler, the Sultan, was famous for his great wealth and absolute power. While the Ottoman Empire held vast territories in Europe, including the Balkans, modern Greece, Bulgaria and Hungary, it was an Islamic empire, and Shakespeare's audience would have viewed the Turks with more suspicion than their Christian neighbours.

Shakespeare's principal source for *Othello,* 'The Story of Disdemona of Venice and the Moorish Captain' by Cinthio, was published in 1565. At that time, Venice was almost perpetually at war with the Ottoman Empire, with many naval battles taking place in the Eastern Mediterranean: the islands of Rhodes, Crete and Cyprus were all among the disputed territories.

Thinking about conflict and antithesis

Playwright and critic George Bernard Shaw once said, 'The essence of drama is conflict'. The essence of *Othello* is Shakespeare's creation of a series of sustained oppositions that manifest themselves on multiple levels throughout the play.

1 Turkish invasion of Cyprus

Providing the structural foundation of the narrative of *Othello* is the historical conflict between the 'Christian' city-state of Venice and the 'barbarian' Ottoman Empire. The geographical and political invasion of Venetian property (Cyprus) by the Turks is a public, physical opposition in the opening scenes of the play, which Shakespeare consequently uses to establish conflicts of a more private and potentially dangerous nature.

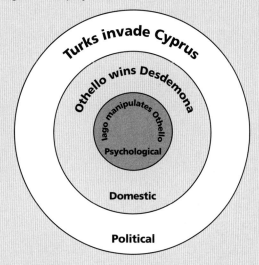

2 Othello's 'conquest' of Desdemona

Much has been said by recent critics of the structural parallels between the Turkish seizure of the Venetian property of Cyprus and Othello's 'conquest' of Brabantio's 'property': his daughter, Desdemona (Act 1 Scene 1, line 170). Brabantio passionately accuses Othello of being a 'foul thief' (Act 1 Scene 1, line 62), who has 'stol'n' his precious 'jewel' from him (Act 1 Scene 3, lines 60 and 194).

A further clash of opposites in this regard is the contrast between Othello and Iago's view of women. Note carefully the conflict between the near spiritual dimension of Othello and Desdemona's poetic declarations of love (Act 1 Scene 3 and Act 2 Scene 1) and Iago's insistence that love is 'carnal … merely a lust of the blood' (Act 1 Scene 3, lines 321 and 324), no more than animals mating. In the opening scenes, Iago and Roderigo crudely refer to Othello and Desdemona's marriage union, both in these bestial terms and as a military invasion by an alien (foreign) force.

3 Iago's infiltration of Othello's mind

Structurally, conflict in *Othello* progresses from external wars to domestic disputes to the intensely private battleground of Othello's mind, psychologically invaded by the villainous Iago. While following Othello's psychological and linguistic disintegration, which culminates in the tragic murder of Desdemona on their marriage bed, Shakespeare presents a host of binary oppositions to draw our attention to the persistent notion of conflict within the play. Note in your reading the many potent examples of antithesis: black and white, night and day, male and female, man and beast, good and evil, love and jealousy, reality and illusion.

Yet, as noted in the discussion of **Othello and race** (page 24), Shakespeare deliberately complicates the simplistic Jacobean cultural dualities of black/evil/man and white/good/woman with the ambiguous characters of Othello and Iago.

- The black-skinned military commander, Othello, is the Christian protector of 'fair' Venice against 'dark' Turks.
- Eloquent Othello possesses moral integrity, nobility and manly gentleness, whereas the psychopathic white male, Iago, is the one who is morally 'blackened'.
- Clearly paralleling the invasion of 'civilised' Cyprus by the 'barbarous' Turks, poisonous Iago invades Othello's mind with the 'green-eyed monster' of jealousy (Act 2 Scene 3, lines 318–24).
- Finally, Shakespeare's masterful employment of antithesis, the contrast between the external appearance of 'honest Iago' and the inner reality of his corrupt nature, sustains the conflict of the play until its painfully terrible conclusion.

Act 1 Scene 3 (Part 1)

Characters

Othello
Duke
Brabantio
1ST Senator
Desdemona
2ND Senator
1ST Officer
Messenger
Sailor

In a nutshell

The Senate, meeting to discuss the threatened Turkish invasion of Cyprus, hears Brabantio's complaint against Othello. When questioned by the Senate, Othello tells how Brabantio invited him into his house where, by recounting his life-story, he won Desdemona's love. When Desdemona arrives, she confirms that she freely married Othello.

Before you read

- The first two pages of this scene are amongst the most difficult in the play, but you should not worry about trying to understand every word. In summary, the Senate is meeting late at night to discuss the threat of the Turkish invasion of Rhodes and Cyprus. The reports about the numbers of ships in the invading fleet differ, and the Duke resolves that Cyprus is the more likely destination for the invasion. News arrives in this scene by a system of messengers crying, 'What ho!'.

- Listen carefully to Othello's speeches. Brabantio accuses him of using witchcraft and, while this proves a baseless and even racist assumption, there is a kind of magic or beauty in Othello's language. One critic, Wilson Knight, calls this 'the Othello music'.

- The galleys that the Senate discuss in the opening lines are single-decked naval vessels with sails and oars, used by the Turks and Venetians. The Ottoman galleys were rowed by slaves; the Venetian galleys by free men.

Disproportioned:	Inconsistent
Ottomites:	Ottoman Turks
Aught:	Anything
Ay:	Yes
Err:	Make an error
Vouch:	Guarantee or warrant
Sagittary:	An inn
Woo:	Win someone over romantically

Act 1 Scene 3 (Part 1)   A council-chamber.

[The DUKE OF VENICE and Senators are sitting at a table; Officers are attending]

DUKE　　　　　There is no composition in these news
　　　　　　　That gives them credit.
1ST SENATOR　　　　　　　　　　　Indeed, they are disproportioned;
　　　　　　　My letters say a hundred and seven galleys.
DUKE　　　　　And mine, a hundred and forty.
2ND SENATOR　　　　　　　　　　　　　And mine, two hundred.
　　　　　　　But though they jump not on a just account　　　　　5
　　　　　　　(As in these cases, where the aim reports,
　　　　　　　'Tis oft with difference), yet do they all confirm
　　　　　　　A Turkish fleet, and bearing up to Cyprus.
DUKE　　　　　Nay, it is possible enough to judgment;
　　　　　　　I do not so secure me in the error,　　　　　　　10
　　　　　　　But the main article I do approve
　　　　　　　In fearful sense.
SAILOR　　　　*[Within]*　　　What, ho! What, ho! What, ho!
1ST OFFICER　　A messenger from the galleys.

[SAILOR enters]

DUKE　　　　　　　　　　　　　　Now, what's the business?
SAILOR　　　　The Turkish preparation makes for Rhodes;
　　　　　　　So was I bid report here to the state　　　　　　15
　　　　　　　By Signior Angelo.
DUKE　　　　　How say you by this change?
1ST SENATOR　　　　　　　　　　　This cannot be,
　　　　　　　By no assay of reason: 'tis a pageant,
　　　　　　　To keep us in false gaze. When we consider
　　　　　　　The importancy of Cyprus to the Turk,　　　　　20

	And let ourselves again but understand,	
	That as it more concerns the Turk than Rhodes,	
	So may he with more facile question bear it,	
	For that it stands not in such warlike brace,	
	But altogether lacks the abilities	25
	That Rhodes is dressed in. If we make thought of this,	
	We must not think the Turk is so unskillful	
	To leave that latest which concerns him first,	
	Neglecting an attempt of ease and gain,	
	To wake and wage a danger profitless.	30
DUKE	Nay, in all confidence, he's not for Rhodes.	
1ST OFFICER	Here is more news.	

[MESSENGER enters]

MESSENGER	The Ottomites, reverend and gracious,	
	Steering with due course towards the isle of Rhodes,	
	Have there injointed them with an after fleet.	35
1ST SENATOR	Ay, so I thought. How many, as you guess?	
MESSENGER	Of thirty sail, and now they do restem	
	Their backward course, bearing with frank appearance	
	Their purposes toward Cyprus. Signior Montano,	
	Your trusty and most valiant servitor,	40
	With his free duty recommends you thus,	
	And prays you to believe him.	
DUKE	'Tis certain, then, for Cyprus.	
	Marcus Luccicos: is not he in town?	
1ST SENATOR	He's now in Florence.	45
DUKE	Write from us to him. Post-post-haste dispatch!	
1ST SENATOR	Here comes Brabantio and the valiant Moor.	

[BRABANTIO, OTHELLO, IAGO, RODERIGO and Officers enter]

DUKE	Valiant Othello, we must straight employ you	
	Against the general enemy Ottoman –	

[To BRABANTIO]

	I did not see you; welcome, gentle signior.	50
	We lacked your counsel and your help tonight.	
BRABANTIO	So did I yours. Good your grace, pardon me;	
	Neither my place nor aught I heard of business	
	Hath raised me from my bed, nor doth the general care	
	Take hold on me, for my particular grief	55
	Is of so flood-gate and o'erbearing nature	
	That it engluts and swallows other sorrows	
	And it is still itself.	
DUKE	Why, what's the matter?	
BRABANTIO	My daughter! O, my daughter!	

DUKE & 1ST SENATOR	Dead?	
BRABANTIO	Ay, to me.	
	She is abused, stol'n from me, and corrupted	60
	By spells and medicines bought of mountebanks;	
	For nature so preposterously to err,	
	Being not deficient, blind, or lame of sense,	
	Sans witchcraft could not.	
DUKE	Whoe'er he be that in this foul proceeding	65
	Hath thus beguiled your daughter of herself	
	And you of her, the bloody book of law	
	You shall yourself read in the bitter letter	
	After your own sense, yea, though our proper son	
	Stood in your action.	
BRABANTIO	Humbly I thank your grace.	70
	Here is the man, this Moor, whom now, it seems,	
	Your special mandate for the state-affairs	
	Hath hither brought.	
DUKE & 1ST SENATOR	We are very sorry for't.	
DUKE	*[To OTHELLO]* What, in your own part, can you say to this?	
BRABANTIO	Nothing, but this is so.	75
OTHELLO	Most potent, grave, and reverend signiors,	
	My very noble and approved good masters,	
	That I have ta'en away this old man's daughter,	
	It is most true; true, I have married her.	
	The very head and front of my offending	80
	Hath this extent, no more. Rude am I in my speech,	
	And little blessed with the soft phrase of peace;	
	For since these arms of mine had seven years' pith,	
	Till now some nine moons wasted, they have used	
	Their dearest action in the tented field,	85
	And little of this great world can I speak,	
	More than pertains to feats of broil and battle,	
	And therefore little shall I grace my cause	
	In speaking for myself. Yet, by your gracious patience,	
	I will a round unvarnished tale deliver	90
	Of my whole course of love; what drugs, what charms,	
	What conjuration and what mighty magic,	
	For such proceeding I am charged withal,	
	I won his daughter.	
BRABANTIO	A maiden never bold;	
	Of spirit so still and quiet, that her motion	95
	Blushed at herself; and she, in spite of nature,	
	Of years, of country, credit, everything,	
	To fall in love with what she feared to look on!	
	It is a judgment maimed and most imperfect	
	That will confess perfection so could err	100

	Against all rules of nature, and must be driven	
	To find out practices of cunning hell,	
	Why this should be. I therefore vouch again	
	That with some mixtures powerful o'er the blood,	
	Or with some dram conjured to this effect,	105
	He wrought upon her.	
DUKE	To vouch this, is no proof,	

DUKE   To vouch this, is no proof,
Without more wider and more overt test
Than these thin habits and poor likelihoods
Of modern seeming do prefer against him.

1ST SENATOR But, Othello, speak.   110
Did you by indirect and forcèd courses
Subdue and poison this young maid's affections?
Or came it by request and such fair question
As soul to soul affordeth?

OTHELLO   I do beseech you,
Send for the lady to the Sagittary,   115
And let her speak of me before her father.
If you do find me foul in her report,
The trust, the office I do hold of you,
Not only take away, but let your sentence
Even fall upon my life.

DUKE   Fetch Desdemona hither.   120

OTHELLO Ancient, conduct them; you best know the place.

[IAGO and several Attendants exit]

And, till she come, as truly as to heaven
I do confess the vices of my blood,
So justly to your grave ears I'll present
How I did thrive in this fair lady's love,   125
And she in mine.

DUKE   Say it, Othello.

OTHELLO Her father loved me, oft invited me,
Still questioned me the story of my life,
From year to year, the battles, sieges, fortunes,
That I have passed.   130
I ran it through, even from my boyish days,
To the very moment that he bade me tell it;
Wherein I spake of most disastrous chances,
Of moving accidents by flood and field,
Of hair-breadth scapes i' the imminent deadly breach,   135
Of being taken by the insolent foe
And sold to slavery, of my redemption thence
And portance in my travels' history;
Wherein of antres vast and deserts idle,
Rough quarries, rocks and hills whose heads touch heaven   140

It was my hint to speak (such was the process),
And of the Cannibals that each other eat,
The Anthropophagi and men whose heads
Do grow beneath their shoulders. This to hear
Would Desdemona seriously incline,   145
But still the house-affairs would draw her thence,
Whichever as she could with haste dispatch,
She'd come again, and with a greedy ear
Devour up my discourse; which I observing,
Took once a pliant hour, and found good means   150
To draw from her a prayer of earnest heart
That I would all my pilgrimage dilate,
Whereof by parcels she had something heard,
But not intentively. I did consent,
And often did beguile her of her tears,   155
When I did speak of some distressful stroke
That my youth suffered. My story being done,
She gave me for my pains a world of sighs;
She swore, in faith, 'twas strange, 'twas passing strange,
'Twas pitiful, 'twas wondrous pitiful.   160
She wished she had not heard it, yet she wished
That heaven had made her such a man. She thanked me,
And bade me, if I had a friend that loved her,
I should but teach him how to tell my story,
And that would woo her. Upon this hint I spake: 165
She loved me for the dangers I had passed,
And I loved her that she did pity them.
This only is the witchcraft I have used.
Here comes the lady; let her witness it.

[DESDEMONA, IAGO and Attendants enter]

DUKE	I think this tale would win my daughter too. 170
	Good Brabantio,
	Take up this mangled matter at the best;
	Men do their broken weapons rather use
	Than their bare hands.
BRABANTIO	I pray you, hear her speak:
	If she confess that she was half the wooer, 175
	Destruction on my head, if my bad blame
	Light on the man! – Come hither, gentle mistress.
	Do you perceive in all this noble company
	Where most you owe obedience?
DESDEMONA	My noble father,
	I do perceive here a divided duty: 180
	To you I am bound for life and education;
	My life and education both do learn me

How to respect you. You are the lord of duty,
I am hitherto your daughter, but here's my husband,
And so much duty as my mother showed   185
To you, preferring you before her father,
So much I challenge that I may profess
Due to the Moor, my lord.

BRABANTIO   God be wi' you! I have done –
Please it your grace, on to the state affairs;
I had rather to adopt a child than get it –   190
Come hither, Moor.
I here do give thee that with all my heart
Which, but thou hast already, with all my heart
I would keep from thee – For your sake, jewel,
I am glad at soul I have no other child,   195
For thy escape would teach me tyranny,
To hang clogs on them – I have done, my lord.

DUKE   Let me speak like yourself, and lay a sentence,
Which, as a grise or step, may help these lovers
Into your favour.   200
When remedies are past, the griefs are ended
By seeing the worst, which late on hopes depended.
To mourn a mischief that is past and gone
Is the next way to draw new mischief on.
What cannot be preserved when fortune takes   205
Patience, her injury a mockery makes.
The robbed that smiles steals something from the thief;
He robs himself that spends a bootless grief.

BRABANTIO   So let the Turk of Cyprus us beguile;
We lose it not, so long as we can smile.   210
He bears the sentence well that nothing bears
But the free comfort which from thence he hears,
But he bears both the sentence and the sorrow
That, to pay grief, must of poor patience borrow.
These sentences, to sugar, or to gall,   215
Being strong on both sides, are equivocal.
But words are words; I never yet did hear
That the bruised heart was piercèd through the ear.
I humbly beseech you, proceed to the affairs of state.

Text notes

1–2   **There is no composition … gives them credit:** The Duke finds the reports he receives do
       not add up and, therefore, has trouble believing them ('composition' = agreement).

9–12   **Nay, it is possible … In fearful sense:** In essence, the Duke says that he will not argue
       about the details.

18–19 **By no assay of reason … in false gaze:** This does not make reasonable sense; it is a trick
       to distract us.

23–26 **So may he with more facile … Rhodes is dressed in:** The Senator stresses the importance of Cyprus compared with Rhodes and adds that Cyprus is less fortified and ready, and is, therefore, less trouble for the Turks to capture.

26–30 **If we make thought … wage a danger profitless:** The Senator is saying that the Turks conduct their wars wisely and so are unlikely to give their most important objective (Cyprus) such a low priority. They are unlikely to take any risks for something that is near worthless ('profitless') such as Rhodes.

37–39 **Of thirty sail … purposes toward Cyprus:** Thirty ships have retraced ('re-stemmed') their course and are now heading straight for Cyprus.

40 **Servitor:** Servant.

46 **Post-post-haste dispatch:** Deal with it or dispatch the task as quickly as possible.

55–58 **For my particular grief … is still itself:** Brabantio is asserting that his kind of grief distracts from all other griefs, making them seem insignificant.

61 **Mountebanks:** Travelling con-men or dodgy doctors.

64 **Sans witchcraft could not:** Her decision could not be explained without witchcraft ('sans' = a French word meaning without).

83–89 **For since these arms … In speaking for myself:** A paraphrase might read: for since I was seven (apart from the last nine months) I have been involved in battle, and have lived in military camps; the military life is all I know, so my speech might be lacking in certain graces.

91–94 **What drugs, what charms … I won his daughter:** Othello declares that he did not use the drugs, charms, conjuring or magic that Brabantio is charging him with, but won Desdemona fairly.

95–96 **That her motion / Blushed at herself:** Desdemona blushed at her own movement or impulses, according to Brabantio. He is making the point that she is very shy.

96–97 **In spite of nature … she feared to look on:** Brabantio points out the differences in their ages, nationality, status and wealth. Given these factors, he finds her love for Othello improbable, especially as she never seems to look at him.

103–06 **I therefore vouch … wrought upon her:** Brabantio once again accuses Othello of using some magic potion to work on Desdemona's blood ('dram' = small amount of spirits; 'wrought' = worked).

107–09 **Without more wider … do prefer against him:** The Duke is simply stating that Brabantio's accusations are baseless and he needs more substantial evidence ('overt' = open and obvious).

111 **Indirect and forcèd:** Deviously or by force.

113–14 **Or came it by request … soul affordeth:** The Duke is asking if Othello gained Desdemona's affections by 'request' (consent) and by one to one conversation ('soul to soul').

123 **Vices:** Morally bad qualities.

135 **Of hair-breadth scapes i' the imminent deadly breach:** Escaping from death by a hair's breadth or very narrowly.

138 **Portance:** Conduct.

139 **Antres:** Caves.

143 **Anthropophagi:** Cannibals (from the Greek *anthropos*: man; *phagein*: to eat).

149 **Discourse:** Usually a conversation; a story in this case.

150 **Pliant hour:** Convenient time.

152–54 **That I would all my … But not intentively:** Othello expands upon ('dilates') the details of his journey ('pilgrimage'), explaining that Desdemona would hear them in small instalments ('parcels') but did not stop purposefully to listen (not 'intentively').

172–74 **Take up this mangled … their bare hands:** Try to mend this bad situation. It is better to use a broken weapon than no weapon at all.

184 **Hitherto:** Up until now.

190   **I had rather to adopt a child than get it:** Brabantio says that he wishes he had adopted a child than be the natural father of one. This is an insult suggesting that Desdemona is acting unnaturally or against her family.

196–97   **For thy escape … clogs on them:** Brabantio is glad he has no other daughters; Desdemona's actions would cause him to be so cruel as to lock them up to prevent them escaping ('clogs' = blocks of wood that were attached to someone's feet to prevent them from escaping).

198   **Let me speak like yourself:** Let me speak like you would if you were feeling more fatherly.

199   **Grise:** Stair.

201–02   **When remedies are past … on hopes depended:** When it is too late for solutions ('remedies'), the grief ends by giving up on emptiness and realising that things cannot get worse.

205–06   **What cannot be preserved … a mockery makes:** The Duke reminds Brabantio that 'Fortune' is unpredictable and can quickly take things from them. He urges him to be patient and, in doing so, mock the 'injury'.

207–08   **The robbed that smiles … spends a bootless grief:** The Duke further urges Brabantio to be stoic or less passionate, claiming that if a person robbed can smile he steals something from the thief, but that if he adds grief to his loss, he robs himself further ('bootless' = useless).

209–16   **So let the Turk … are equivocal:** Brabantio is not convinced by the Duke's judgment. He responds using proverbs, and points out that words do not offer much comfort. He relates his situation to Venetian politics, presenting the view that the Venetians would not be smiling if they were robbed of Cyprus by the Turks.

Questions

1   For what island does the Senate decide that the Turkish attack is heading?

2   Why does Brabantio assume that Desdemona would not marry Othello of her own free will? What reasons does he give?

3   How did Othello win Desdemona's affection?

4   Brabantio mentions that Desdemona feared to 'look upon' Othello and takes this as proof of her disgust; can you think of another interpretation of her reaction?

5   How does Desdemona present her decision to marry Othello in a favourable light? In what way(s) does her speech show confidence and intelligence?

6   Before Desdemona enters the Senate, Brabantio has already spoken about her. How does the reality of Desdemona's behaviour and speech contradict his portrait of her?

7   Do you think the Venetian Duke is a competent and fair judge? Find some evidence for your answer.

8   In lines 127–169 Othello speaks in lyrical poetry that creates a sense of nobility and grandeur about him. Quote examples of the following from this speech:

Alliteration	
Poetic repetition	
Exotic names	
Highly descriptive words and phrases	
Lyrical rhythm or flow of words	
Quote the phrase or line you judge to be most lyrical.	

Extend

1. In what way(s) do you think Shakespeare creates an atmosphere of urgency at the beginning of this scene?

2. What major theme of the play is foreshadowed by the behaviour of the Turkish fleet?

3. What does the Duke initially assume has happened to Brabantio's daughter? What dramatic effect does this achieve?

4. Othello recalls that when he told his life story to Desdemona, 'she wished / That heaven had made her such a man'. How is this statement ambiguous? Explain two possible interpretations.

5. When the Duke attempts to comfort Brabantio and advises him to reconcile with his daughter and her new husband, he speaks in rhyming couplets and regular iambic rhythm. Do you think these poetic features make the Duke's speech more or less convincing?

Discuss

1. How different might the Senate's decision on the marriage have been:
   a. in a time of peace?
   b. if Othello were not a great general?

2. Do you think a father's reaction in the twenty-first century to this kind of hasty marriage would be similar to Brabantio's?

A word about soliloquies and asides

Picture this: you don't go to school one day and you end up watching *Days of Our Lives*. Besides the rather predictable plot and the abundance of plastic surgery, you notice that sometimes the characters express their thoughts aloud to themselves when nobody else is around! Actually, this is not as strange as it sounds – Shakespeare had his characters doing this hundreds of years ago and it is known as a **soliloquy** (so-*li*-lo-kwee).

A soliloquy involves a character talking when he or she is alone. Shakespeare uses this theatrical device to help the audience understand the mind of the character who is speaking and their motives for what they are doing or planning to do. We talk to ourselves all the time as we are thinking (try thinking without language!) and soliloquies reflect this practice.

Some playwrights before Shakespeare used the device, but he is generally considered the first writer to genuinely capture the inner workings of the human mind. At the end of Act 1 Scene 3, Iago speaks his mind, vocalising his hatred of Othello and revealing the beginnings of his 'monstrous' plan to bring about Othello's destruction. No one else is around and we, as an audience, catch a glimpse of his scheming, malicious character.

It is interesting in *Othello* that Shakespeare does not employ soliloquy as a key device in presenting the mind of the noble central character, which is a salient feature of plays such as *Hamlet* and *Macbeth*. When Othello actually does begin to speak when alone (Act 3 Scene 3, lines 244–45), Iago is the one who interrupts him. Not until the play hurtles towards its unstoppable tragic conclusion (Act 5 Scene 2) does Othello finally engage in soliloquy, speaking his thoughts aloud before the sleeping Desdemona. Until that time, it is solely Iago who soliloquises, differentiating him from the other characters, allowing the audience to gain valuable insight into his often ambiguously presented motives, and consequently serving to increase the audience's antipathy for 'this demi-devil'.

Similar in some ways to soliloquies, **asides** (generally indicated by [aside] in the stage directions) also occur occasionally in *Othello*. Whereas soliloquies are quite lengthy and are delivered with no one else on the stage, asides are usually quite brief and allow a character to speak his or her thoughts without other characters hearing them. Again, it is Iago (especially in Act 2) who speaks in asides, although Othello does speak his mind whilst hiding and spying on Cassio and Desdemona in Act 4.

While Iago hides his malicious scheming from most of the other characters, Shakespeare has the play's 'hellish villain' reveal his plans to the audience. He uses soliloquies and asides to emphasise this deception, increasing the sense of dramatic irony, thus tension, experienced by the audience. Many of the play's most famous lines are found in Iago's soliloquies and asides, which is yet further evidence of the effectiveness of this essential theatrical device in conveying Shakespeare's archetypal characters and universal themes.

Act 1 Scene 3 (Part 2)

Characters

Iago
Othello
Duke
Desdemona
Roderigo
Brabantio
1ST Senator

In a nutshell

Othello is ordered to head immediately for Cyprus, and the Duke grants Desdemona's request to accompany him. When left alone with Iago, Roderigo threatens suicide, believing he has lost Desdemona forever. Iago quickly persuades Roderigo to go to Cyprus as well, assuring him that the marriage will not last. Once Roderigo exits, Iago reveals his true nature and his plan to take Cassio's position as Lieutenant.

Before you read

- Consider Desdemona's behaviour before the powerful Venetian Senate. She is confident and measured in her speech. Previously, in Desdemona's absence, Brabantio (her father) spoke of a shy, blushing girl, but her behaviour before the Senate presents a stark contrast to this image.

- Othello requests, in this scene, that Desdemona be provided with accommodation befitting her 'levels of breeding'. You can read more about the class system in England at the front of this book, under the heading

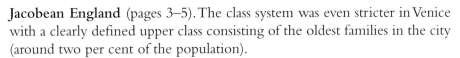

Jacobean England (pages 3–5). The class system was even stricter in Venice with a clearly defined upper class consisting of the oldest families in the city (around two per cent of the population).

- Iago repeats the phrase 'put money in thy purse', or variations of this, throughout the latter part of this scene. In short, he is encouraging Roderigo to bring lots of money to Cyprus and, therefore, make an investment in the venture to win Desdemona. Iago tells the audience at the end of this scene that he is using Roderigo for his own financial gain.

Fortitude:	Strength (and in this case, the fortifications)
Alacrity:	Speed
Disposition:	Arrangements
Prosperous:	Wealthy (perhaps also generous)
Charter:	Permission
Visage:	Face
Bereft:	Without or lacking
Bounteous:	Generous

Act 1 Scene 3 (Part 2) A council-chamber.

DUKE   The Turk with a most mighty preparation makes for Cyprus. Othello, 220
the fortitude of the place is best known to you; and though we have
there a substitute of most allowed sufficiency, yet opinion, a sovereign
mistress of effects, throws a more safer voice on you. You must,
therefore, be content to slubber the gloss of your new fortunes
with this more stubborn and boisterous expedition.   225

OTHELLO   The tyrant custom, most grave senators,
Hath made the flinty and steel couch of war
My thrice-driven bed of down. I do agnise
A natural and prompt alacrity
I find in hardness, and do undertake   230
These present wars against the Ottomites.
Most humbly, therefore, bending to your state,
I crave fit disposition for my wife.
Due reference of place and exhibition,
With such accommodation and besort   235
As levels with her breeding.

DUKE   If you please,
Be't at her father's.

BRABANTIO   I'll not have it so.

OTHELLO   Nor I.

DESDEMONA   Nor I; I would not there reside,
To put my father in impatient thoughts

	By being in his eye. Most gracious Duke,	240
	To my unfolding lend your prosperous ear;	
	And let me find a charter in your voice,	
	To assist my simpleness.	
DUKE	What would you, Desdemona?	
DESDEMONA	That I did love the Moor to live with him,	245
	My downright violence and storm of fortunes	
	May trumpet to the world; my heart's subdued	
	Even to the very quality of my lord:	
	I saw Othello's visage in his mind,	
	And to his honour and his valiant parts	250
	Did I my soul and fortunes consecrate.	
	So that, dear lords, if I be left behind,	
	A moth of peace, and he go to the war,	
	The rites for which I love him are bereft me,	
	And I a heavy interim shall support	255
	By his dear absence. Let me go with him.	
OTHELLO	Let her have your voice.	
	Vouch with me, heaven; I therefore beg it not,	
	To please the palate of my appetite,	
	Nor to comply with heat (the young affects	260
	In me defunct) and proper satisfaction,	
	But to be free and bounteous to her mind.	
	And heaven defend your good souls, that you think	
	I will your serious and great business scant	
	For she is with me. No, when light-winged toys	265
	Of feathered Cupid seal with wanton dullness	
	My speculative and officed instruments,	
	That my disports corrupt and taint my business,	
	Let housewives make a skillet of my helm,	
	And all indign and base adversities	270
	Make head against my estimation.	
DUKE	Be it as you shall privately determine.	
	Either for her stay or going: the affair cries haste,	
	And speed must answer it.	
1ST SENATOR	You must away tonight.	
OTHELLO	With all my heart.	275
DUKE	At nine i' the morning here we'll meet again.	
	Othello, leave some officer behind,	
	And he shall our commission bring to you,	
	With such things else of quality and respect	
	As doth import you.	
OTHELLO	So please your grace, my ancient:	280
	A man he is of honest and trust.	
	To his conveyance I assign my wife,	
	With what else needful your good grace shall think	

| DUKE | To be sent after me. |
| | Let it be so. |

DUKE   To be sent after me.

                                     Let it be so.

Good night to every one.

[To BRABANTIO]   And, noble signior,   285

If virtue no delighted beauty lack,

Your son-in-law is far more fair than black.

1ST SENATOR   Adieu, brave Moor; use Desdemona well.

BRABANTIO   Look to her, Moor, if thou hast eyes to see:

               She has deceived her father, and may thee.   290

[DUKE OF VENICE, Senators, Officers, etc, exit]

OTHELLO   My life upon her faith! – Honest Iago,

               My Desdemona must I leave to thee.

               I prithee, let thy wife attend on her,

               And bring them after in the best advantage.

               Come, Desdemona: I have but an hour   295

               Of love, of worldly matters and direction,

               To spend with thee. We must obey the time.

[OTHELLO and DESDEMONA exit]

RODERIGO   Iago?

IAGO   What say'st thou, noble heart?

RODERIGO   What will I do, thinkest thou?   300

IAGO   Why, go to bed, and sleep.

RODERIGO   I will incontinently drown myself.

IAGO   If thou dost, I shall never love thee after. Why, thou silly gentleman!

RODERIGO   It is silliness to live when to live is torment; and then have

               we a prescription to die when death is our physician.   305

IAGO   O villainous! I have looked upon the world for four times

               seven years, and since I could distinguish betwixt a benefit

               and an injury, I never found man that knew how to love

               himself. Ere I would say I would drown myself for the love

               of a guinea-hen, I would change my humanity with a baboon.   310

RODERIGO   What should I do? I confess it is my shame to be so fond,

               but it is not in my virtue to amend it.

IAGO   Virtue! A fig! 'Tis in ourselves that we are thus or thus.

               Our bodies are our gardens, to the which our wills are

               gardeners; so that if we will plant nettles, or sow lettuce,

               set hyssop and weed up thyme, supply it with one   315

               gender of herbs, or distract it with many, either to have it

               sterile with idleness, or manured with industry, why, the

               power and corrigible authority of this lies in our wills. If

               the balance of our lives had not one scale of reason to poise

               another of sensuality, the blood and baseness of our natures

               would conduct us to most preposterous conclusions. But we   320

               have reason to cool our raging motions, our carnal stings,

our unbitted lusts, whereof I take this that you call love to
be a sect or scion.

RODERIGO   It cannot be.

IAGO   It is merely a lust of the blood and a permission of
the will. Come, be a man. Drown thyself? Drown
cats and blind puppies. I have professed me   325
thy friend and I confess me knit to thy deserving with
cables of perdurable toughness. I could never better
stead thee than now. Put money in thy purse; follow
thou the wars; defeat thy favour with an usurpèd
beard – I say, put money in thy purse. – It cannot be
that Desdemona should long continue her love to the
Moor – put money in thy purse – nor he his to   330
her. It was a violent commencement, and thou shalt
see an answerable sequestration – put but money in
thy purse. – These Moors are changeable in their wills
– fill thy purse with money – the food that to him
now is as luscious as locusts, shall be to him shortly
as bitter as coloquintida. She must change for youth:
when she is sated with his body, she will find the   335
error of her choice. She must have change, she must;
therefore put money in thy purse. If thou wilt needs
damn thyself, do it a more delicate way than drowning.
– Make all the money thou canst – if sanctimony
and a frail vow betwixt an erring barbarian and a
supersubtle Venetian be not too hard for my wits and
all the tribe of hell, thou shalt enjoy her – therefore,   340
make money. – A pox of drowning thyself! It is clean out
of the way. Seek thou rather to be hanged in compassing
thy joy than to be drowned and go without her.

RODERIGO   Wilt thou be fast to my hopes, if I depend on the issue?

IAGO   Thou art sure of me – Go, make money –
I have told thee often, and I   345
re-tell thee again and again: I hate the Moor.
My cause is hearted; thine hath no less reason.
Let us be conjunctive in our revenge against him; if
thou canst cuckold him, thou dost thyself a pleasure,
me a sport. There are many events in the womb of
time which will be delivered. Traverse! Go, provide
thy money. We will have more of this tomorrow. Adieu.   350

RODERIGO   Where shall we meet i' the morning?

IAGO   At my lodging.

RODERIGO   I'll be with thee betimes.

IAGO   Go to; farewell. Do you hear, Roderigo?

RODERIGO   What say you?   355

IAGO	No more of drowning, do you hear?
RODERIGO	I am changed.
IAGO	Go to. Farewell – put money in thy purse!
RODERIGO	I'll sell all my land!

[RODERIGO exits]

IAGO   Thus do I ever make my fool my purse: 360
        For I mine own gained knowledge should profane,
        If I would time expend with such a snipe
        But for my sport and profit. I hate the Moor:
        And it is thought abroad, that 'twixt my sheets
        He's done my office. I know not if't be true,   365
        But I, for mere suspicion in that kind,
        Will do as if for surety. He holds me well;
        The better shall my purpose work on him.
        Cassio's a proper man. Let me see now:
        To get his place and to plume up my will   370
        In double knavery – How? How? – Let's see:
        After some time, to abuse Othello's ear
        That he is too familiar with his wife.
        He hath a person and a smooth dispose
        To be suspected, framed to make women false.   375
        The Moor is of a free and open nature,
        That thinks men honest that but seem to be so,
        And will as tenderly be led by the nose
        As asses are.
        I have't! It is engendered! Hell and night   380
        Must bring this monstrous birth to the world's light.

[Exit]

Text notes

222   **A substitute of most allowed sufficiency:** The Governor is capable (but obviously not as capable as Othello).

223–25   **You must therefore ... and boisterous expedition:** The Duke commands Othello to head off to war – making dirty ('slubbering') the gloss of his marriage ('new fortune').

226–28   **The tyrant custom ... thrice-driven bed of down:** Othello says that he is used to war and sleeping in rough, uncomfortable conditions.

228–31   **I do agnise ... against the Ottomites:** A paraphrase of this might read: I recognise in myself a natural desire to go with speed to the hardship of war; it is the same with this situation now ('alacrity' = speed).

232–36   **Most humbly, therefore ... levels with her breeding:** Othello asks the Senate to arrange for his wife some accommodation that is appropriate for someone of her social status or 'breeding'.

242   **Charter:** Favour.

249–52 **I saw Othello's visage ... and fortunes consecrate:** Desdemona states that she saw Othello's face ('visage') in her mind, and his good qualities made her pledge her love to him.

254–56 **The rites for which I love ... Let me go with him:** Desdemona claims that as she has married Othello their time apart would be a heavy burden for her and so asks permission to go with him to Cyprus.

258–62 **Vouch with me, heaven ... bounteous to her mind:** Othello swears that he does not need Desdemona to go with him as his sexual partner, because his age means he is in better control of his sexual desire. Othello wants Desdemona to accompany him for her general company and conversation.

264 **Scant:** Neglect.

265–71 **No, when light-winged toys ... against my estimation:** Othello makes it clear that his new love for Desdemona's company will not cause him to neglect his military duty. If this does happen, he promises that housewives can use his helmet ('helm') as a saucepan ('skillet'), and that he will resign from being a soldier.

282 **Conveyance:** Escort.

286–87 **If virtue no delighted ... far more fair than black:** The Duke proclaims that if virtue is beautiful ('fair'), Brabantio's new son-in-law, Othello, is more fair than black. In saying this, he is associating the colour black with evil, and white with good.

302 **Incontinently:** Immediately.

305 **Physician:** Doctor.

309 **Guinea-hen:** This is a derogatory term for a woman, almost as strong as prostitute.

315 **Hyssop:** A bushy green herb; **thyme:** another herb.

317 **Corrigible:** Corrective.

318–22 **If the balance of our lives ... love to be a sect or scion:** Iago argues that reason counteracts the more base qualities such as lust, to prevent people from doing stupid things. He dismisses Roderigo's love as a 'sect or scion' – a cutting or offshoot of love that should be easily dealt with.

326 **Perdurable:** Everlasting.

328 **Usurpèd beard:** A false beard.

331–32 **An answerable sequestration:** A divorce in answer.

333–34 **The food that to him now ... as bitter as coloquintida:** Locusts are carobs (a sweet Mediterranean fruit), while a 'coloquintida' is a bitter type of apple.

335 **Sated:** Usually means satisfied; in this case, sick of something or someone.

337 **If thou wilt needs damn thyself:** Most people in Shakespeare's day believed that those who committed suicide damned themselves to hell.

338 **Sanctimony:** The holiness of their marriage vows.

341 **A pox of drowning thyself:** Iago is disdainful of Roderigo's desire to drown himself ('pox' = a sexually transmitted disease).

347 **Be conjunctive:** Work together.

347–48 **If thou canst cuckold him ... me a sport:** Iago suggests that seducing Desdemona will be pleasurable for Roderigo and entertaining for him. A 'cuckold' is a man whose wife has been sexually unfaithful, and Iago uses the word as a verb here. If Roderigo can successfully seduce Desdemona, he will be cuckolding Othello.

349 **Traverse:** Turn about and march (a military term).

361–63 **For I mine own gained ... for my sport and profit:** For Iago, it would be an insult to his experience to suggest that he would hang about with Roderigo simply for his friendship.

He uses Roderigo for his money, entertainment and as a pawn in the schemes he devises ('snipe' = a marsh bird with a long beak).

364–67 **And it is thought abroad … Will do as if for surety:** Iago implies that some people such as Othello have slept with his wife (performing his 'office' or duty). While Iago only suspects this, he will act as if he is certain ('abroad' = about the place).

370–71 **To get his place … In double knavery:** A rough paraphrase might read: to attain his position (Lieutenant) and achieve my plans in tricking both Othello and Cassio.

380 **Engendered:** Conceived. Iago extends this metaphor in the rest of the couplet, describing his plan as a 'monstrous birth'.

Questions

1 Why does Desdemona ask to go Cyprus with Othello? What qualities does she demonstrate in making this request before the Senate?

2 What evidence can you find in this section of the play that Othello trusts Iago absolutely?

3 Why is it ironic that Othello describes Iago as 'honest' (lines 281 and 291)?

4 In what sort of mood is Brabantio before he exits? What advice does he give to Othello?

5 What does Roderigo threaten to do? Why does he threaten this?

6 How does Iago view romantic love? Quote some phrases from this scene as evidence.

7 What reason does Iago give for Roderigo to go on living rather than committing suicide?

8 Summarise Iago's plan for Roderigo.

9 Carefully read Iago's soliloquy beginning: 'Thus do I ever make my fool my purse' (lines 360–381).

   a What is Iago's true opinion of Roderigo?

   b What reason does Iago give for hating Othello?

   c How does he intend to cause a falling out between Othello and Cassio?

10 Find a quote to justify the following propositions:

Proposition	Quote
That Iago suspects his wife has slept with Othello	
That Iago is using Roderigo for his own amusement and financial gain	
That Cassio is popular with women	
That Othello has a very trusting nature	

11 Do you find the reasons Iago gives for hating Othello in Act 1 convincing? What seems to be his strongest motivation in your opinion?

Extend **1** When Othello seconds Desdemona's request that she should accompany him to Cyprus, he takes pains to make his motivations clear to the Senate. In the table below, indicate what Othello says:

is <u>not</u> his reason?	
i<u>s</u> his reason?	
about how her company will affect the way he performs his duty?	

2 Find a quote from this scene indicating that Othello is no longer young.

3 What is the Senate's opinion of Othello? Include some quotes in your answer.

4 Read the following dialogue in lines 289–91 and then, referring back to the Act summaries, answer the questions below:

> BRABANTIO   Look to her, Moor, if thou hast eyes to see:
> She has deceived her father, and may thee.
> OTHELLO   My life upon her faith!

a How do you think this exchange will be important to the rest of the play?

b What event(s) might this exchange be foreshadowing?

5 What do you think Iago means when he describes Desdemona as 'supersubtle'? Does this description match what the audience has already seen of her?

6 How does Othello's character provide a contrast to the characters of Iago and Roderigo? Perhaps you could create a table of your own to illustrate how they differ.

7 Copy and complete the following table in your notes to show your understanding of Shakespeare's use of prose (rather than iambic pentameter). What might each instance of prose indicate about the subject matter or perhaps the characters themselves?

Use of strict iambic pentameter	Use of prose	Significance of prose
At the end of Act 1 Scene 3 (Part 1), the characters discuss Othello and Desdemona's relationship	Lines 220–25: the Duke discusses 'the affairs of the state' (the Turkish invasion of Cyprus)	
In this scene, Othello and Desdemona discuss their relationship	Lines 298–359: Iago and Roderigo scheme together	

8   Iago and Roderigo's dialogue (lines 298 onwards) contains four images relating to animals.

    a   List these images.

    b   What is Iago trying to suggest about other characters by using these images?

    c   What do you think Shakespeare is suggesting about the character of Iago by having him use so many animal images?

Discuss

1   What is your opinion of Iago's speeches on the role of the will and human reason? Do you agree with the views he expresses?

2   If you were given the role of director of this scene, how would you present lines 369–81, during which Iago is devising a plan by which he can deceive Othello? In particular, discuss how you might direct the character playing Iago when delivering lines such as: 'Let me see now … How? How? Let's see … I have't!' Consider such aspects as facial expressions, movement, gestures, etc.

Press PLAY Oliver Parker: DVD Chapter 6 ('I hate the Moor')

In small groups, discuss how effective you believe Parker's choices of cinematic and dramatic devices are in presenting Iago's famous 'I hate the Moor' soliloquy. Draw up and complete the following table as part of your discussion.

Cinematic or dramatic device chosen by Parker	How effective is this device?	How else might Parker have used the device in this scene?
Actor's voice (e.g. soft, trembling, pauses)		
Camera work (e.g. close-up, actor looking directly at camera)		
Music		
Props (e.g. chess pieces)		
Lighting (e.g. flash of lightning)		

Introducing similes, metaphors and conceits

If you have ever called someone hot, a pig, a gun, a dog or even a legend, then you have used a metaphor. A **metaphor** is not literally true but it makes a powerful comparison that is true in a deeper sense. If, for example, you call your brother a *pig*, you know that he is not literally a pig, but you might be communicating something about his manners or perhaps how much he eats. If you describe a shot on the soccer pitch as a *rocket*, you know it's not literally a rocket, but you are saying something about the shot's speed and power. Again, you might describe someone attractive as *hot*. Clearly, you are not discussing their temperature!

Similes work in much the same way, but whereas a metaphor is a direct statement of equivalence (my brother <u>is</u> a pig), similes make clear that one thing is being compared to another (my brother is <u>like</u> a pig). Similes make the nature of the comparison clear but are less direct than metaphors. In the opening speech of this play, Iago uses a rare comparison when he advises Roderigo to 'call aloud … as when … the fire / Is spied in populous cities'. Similes are fairly infrequent in the opening act of *Othello*, perhaps because of the urgency that permeates the entire act.

However, in the opening scene, Iago, in particular, uses gross and crude **metaphors** to describe Othello, aiming to 'poison' Brabantio's 'delight'. For instance, Iago refers to Othello as a 'Barbary horse' and describes the sexual union as 'making the beast with two backs'. In Act 1 Scene 2, Iago tells Cassio that Othello 'hath boarded a land carrack' or a treasure ship. Again, this is not literally true but a metaphor. The crudeness and directness of these metaphors are appropriate to Iago's character.

Conceits are extended metaphors, which were very popular with poets and playwrights in Shakespeare's time. Shakespeare regularly employs them in his plays and sonnets. The Metaphysical poets, like John Donne, whose career began towards the end of Shakespeare's career, filled their poetry with conceits. The device remains popular with contemporary poets and songwriters. The Ben Lee song *Cigarettes Will Kill You* is a popular example today. The song compares a bad relationship to cookery: 'You throw me in a pan / You cook in a can … You love to watch me bake / You serve me up with cake … You left burned and seared … You had to try dessert'. This extended metaphor or conceit is explored throughout the entire song.

In Act 1 Scene 1 of *Othello*, Iago uses a conceit when he compares Othello with a Barbary horse, then continues the metaphor to include a fanciful image of Othello and Desdemona's offspring: 'You'll have your nephews neigh at you'. Towards the end of Act 1 Scene 3, Iago uses a lengthy conceit again when he compares men with gardeners tending the gardens of their desires (lines 313–22). Conceits demonstrate Iago's frightening intelligence and assist him to smooth over his more implausible or unlikely arguments, making them sound more convincing to Roderigo.

For a contemporary poet who makes good use of conceits, see the Scottish poet Don Paterson, especially poems such as 'Imperial' and 'An Elliptical Stylus'. Be warned, Paterson can at times use strong language. You can listen to *Cigarettes Will Kill You* by Ben Lee on Grooveshark (www.grooveshark.com).

... black as my own face
What did Othello look like?

Theatre companies generally dressed non-European characters, such as Moors, in lavish and exotic costumes that bore little relation to the dress codes of their societies. In the sixteenth century, black masks and wigs were used to portray such characters but by the seventeenth century more subtle black make-up was employed for these roles. There is a famous account of James I's Catholic Queen, Anne of Denmark, and some of her ladies, wearing black make-up to perform their own play in 1605. Could they have been inspired by a performance of *Othello* at the court? The great actor Richard Burbage (who was white) is believed to be the first actor to play the part of Othello and it is assumed he wore similar make-up for his performances.

In Jacobean England the term 'moor' was used very loosely and could have meant anything from an Ethiopian to a person of Middle Eastern appearance, with much lighter skin. Many historians think that the character Othello was inspired by the visit of the Moorish ambassador from the north African Kingdom of Barbary, late in the reign of Queen Elizabeth I. England and Barbary were already trading partners, and the ambassador was sent to England to discuss the possibility of an armed alliance against the Spanish Empire. The ambassador and his entourage were a striking spectacle around the streets of London, one that was sure to capture a playwright's attention.

Abd el-Ouahed ben Messaoud ben Mohammed Anoun, Moorish Ambassador to Queen Elizabeth I, 1600 – painted by an unknown artist

Characters

Cassio
Iago
Desdemona
Othello
Montano
1ST – 4TH Gentlemen
Emilia
Voices (one or two people)
Narrator (Optional, or someone to cry 'a sail, a sail')

In a nutshell

The setting shifts to Cyprus, where a fierce storm has delivered the Venetians victory over the Turks. Cassio arrives and praises Desdemona's beauty to the islanders. A large party of Venetians enters, including Iago and Desdemona. Everyone awaits Othello's safe arrival, and Iago recites some rhymes and riddles to pass the time. When Othello finally arrives, he and Desdemona speak of their love and happiness.

Before you read

- Many of Iago's rhymes are enigmatic or mysterious, and students often find them confusing. These rhymes or riddles are of little importance for your understanding of the play. They do, however, establish Iago's public persona. By referring to 'black and white', Shakespeare's audience would usually assume a character is discussing brunettes and blondes, but Iago's joking has a further resonance in a play that is charged with racial prejudice.

- Cassio's lines at the start of this scene (60–86) have been compared to a best man's speech at a wedding. He is full of praise for Desdemona, stating that she 'paragons' or surpasses 'description' and 'excels' and exhausts the skill of poets with their 'blazoning pens'. Many critics have wondered if there might be a grain of truth in Iago's later assertions that Cassio is in love with Desdemona.

- Stage directions that suggest voices or cries from [within] indicate calls coming from somewhere offstage.

Segregation:	Shattering	
Tempest:	Storm	
Governor:	The person in charge of Cyprus (prior to this scene, the Governor was Montano but from this scene on it will be Othello)	
Bark:	Ship	
Pilot:	Captain of the ship	

Citadel:	City
Chides:	Criticises
Beguile:	Deceive
Folly:	Stupid or silly behaviour
Profane:	Insulting or worldly (opposite to sacred)
Valiant:	Brave or heroic

Act 2 Scene 1 (Part 1)
A Sea-port in Cyprus: a windstorm batters the quay.

[MONTANO and two Gentlemen enter]

MONTANO	What from the cape can you discern at sea?	
1ST GENTLEMAN	Nothing at all; it is a high-wrought flood.	
	I cannot, 'twixt the heaven and the main,	
	Descry a sail.	
MONTANO	Methinks the wind hath spoke aloud at land;	5
	A fuller blast ne'er shook our battlements:	
	If it hath ruffianed so upon the sea,	
	What ribs of oak, when mountains melt on them,	
	Can hold the mortise? What shall we hear of this?	
2ND GENTLEMAN	A segregation of the Turkish fleet;	10
	For do but stand upon the foaming shore,	
	The chidden billow seems to pelt the clouds;	
	The wind-shaked surge, with high and monstrous mane,	
	Seems to cast water on the burning Bear,	
	And quench the guards o'th'ever-fixèd pole.	15
	I never did like molestation view	
	On the enchafèd flood.	
MONTANO	If that the Turkish fleet	
	Be not ensheltered and embayed, they are drowned;	
	It is impossible they bear it out.	

[3RD GENTLEMAN enters]

3RD GENTLEMAN	News, lads! Our wars are done.	20
	The desperate tempest hath so banged the Turks,	
	That their designment halts. A noble ship of Venice	
	Hath seen a grievous wreck and sufferance	
	On most part of their fleet.	
MONTANO	How? Is this true?	
3RD GENTLEMAN	The ship is here put in,	25
	A Veronesa. Michael Cassio,	
	Lieutenant to the warlike Moor Othello,	
	Is come on shore; the Moor himself at sea,	
	And is in full commission here for Cyprus.	

MONTANO	I am glad on't: 'tis a worthy governor.
3RD GENTLEMAN	But this same Cassio, though he speak of comfort

MONTANO   I am glad on't: 'tis a worthy governor.   30

3RD GENTLEMAN   But this same Cassio, though he speak of comfort
Touching the Turkish loss, yet he looks sadly,
And prays the Moor be safe; for they were parted
With foul and violent tempest.

MONTANO   Pray heavens he be;
For I have served him, and the man commands   35
Like a full soldier. Let's to the seaside, ho!
As well to see the vessel that's come in
As to throw out our eyes for brave Othello,
Even till we make the main and th' aerial blue
An indistinct regard.

3RD GENTLEMAN   Come, let's do so,   40
For every minute is expectancy
Of more arrivance.

[CASSIO enters]

CASSIO   Thanks, you the valiant of this warlike isle,
That so approve the Moor. O, let the heavens
Give him defence against the elements,   45
For I have lost him on a dangerous sea.

MONTANO   Is he well shipped?

CASSIO   His bark is stoutly timbered, his pilot
Of very expert and approved allowance;
Therefore my hopes, not surfeited to death,   50
Stand in bold cure.

VOICES   *[Within]*   A sail! A sail! A sail!

[4TH GENTLEMAN enters]

CASSIO   What noise?

4TH GENTLEMAN   The town is empty; on the brow o' the sea
Stand ranks of people, and they cry 'A sail!'

CASSIO   My hopes do shape him for the Governor.   55

[Guns are heard]

2ND GENTLEMAN   They do discharge their shot of courtesy:
Our friends at least.

CASSIO   I pray you, sir, go forth,
And give us truth who 'tis that's arrived.

2ND GENTLEMAN   I shall.

[2ND GENTLEMAN exits]

MONTANO   But, good Lieutenant, is your General wived?

CASSIO   Most fortunately. He hath achieved a maid   60
That paragons description and wild fame;
One that excels the quirks of blazoning pens,
And in the essential vesture of creation
Does tire the ingener.

[2ND GENTLEMAN re-enters]

	How now? Who has put in?	
2ND GENTLEMAN	'Tis one Iago, ancient to the General.	65
CASSIO	Has had most favourable and happy speed:	
	Tempests themselves, high seas, and howling winds,	
	The guttered rocks and congregated sands,	
	Traitors ensteeped to clog the guiltless keel,	
	As having sense of beauty, do omit	70
	Their mortal natures, letting go safely by	
	The divine Desdemona.	
MONTANO	What is she?	
CASSIO	She that I spake of, our great Captain's captain,	
	Left in the conduct of the bold Iago,	
	Whose footing here anticipates our thoughts	75
	A se'nnight's speed. Great Jove, Othello guard,	
	And swell his sail with thine own powerful breath,	
	That he may bless this bay with his tall ship,	
	Make love's quick pants in Desdemona's arms,	
	Give renewed fire to our extinced spirits,	80
	And bring all Cyprus comfort!	

[DESDEMONA, EMILIA, IAGO, RODERIGO and Attendants enter]

	O, behold,	
	The riches of the ship is come on shore!	
	Ye men of Cyprus, let her have your knees.	
	Hail to thee, lady! And the grace of heaven,	
	Before, behind thee, and on every hand,	85
	Enwheel thee round!	
DESDEMONA	I thank you, valiant Cassio.	
	What tidings can you tell me of my lord?	
CASSIO	He is not yet arrived, nor know I aught	
	But that he's well and will be shortly here.	
DESDEMONA	O, but I fear! – How lost you company?	90
CASSIO	The great contention of the sea and skies	
	Parted our fellowship –	
VOICES	*[Shouting within]* A sail! A sail!	
CASSIO	*[As guns are heard]* But, hark! A sail!	
2ND GENTLEMAN	They give their greeting to the citadel:	
	This likewise is a friend.	
CASSIO	See for the news.	95

[2ND GENTLEMAN exits]

	[To IAGO] Good ancient, you are welcome.	
	[To EMILIA] Welcome, mistress.	
	Let it not gall your patience, good Iago,	

That I extend my manners; 'tis my breeding
That gives me this bold show of courtesy.

[CASSIO kisses EMILIA]

IAGO	Sir, would she give you so much of her lips	100
	As of her tongue she oft bestows on me,	
	You'll have enough.	
DESDEMONA	Alas, she has no speech.	
IAGO	In faith, too much;	
	I find it still, when I have list to sleep.	
	Marry, before your ladyship, I grant,	105
	She puts her tongue a little in her heart,	
	And chides with thinking.	
EMILIA	You have little cause to say so.	
IAGO	Come on, come on: you are pictures out of doors,	
	Bells in your parlours, wild-cats in your kitchens,	110
	Saints in your injuries, devils being offended,	
	Players in your housewifery, and housewives in your beds.	
DESDEMONA	O, fie upon thee, slanderer!	
IAGO	Nay, it is true, or else I am a Turk:	
	You rise to play and go to bed to work.	115
EMILIA	You shall not write my praise.	
IAGO	No, let me not.	
DESDEMONA	What wouldst thou write of me, if thou shouldst praise me?	
IAGO	O gentle lady, do not put me to't,	
	For I am nothing, if not critical.	
DESDEMONA	Come on, assay. There's one gone to the harbour?	120
IAGO	Ay, madam.	
DESDEMONA	I am not merry; but I do beguile	
	The thing I am, by seeming otherwise.	
	Come, how wouldst thou praise me?	
IAGO	I am about it, but indeed my invention	125
	Comes from my pate as birdlime does from frieze;	
	It plucks out brains and all. But my Muse labours,	
	And thus she is delivered:	
	If she be fair and wise, fairness and wit,	
	The one's for use, the other useth it.	130
DESDEMONA	Well praised! How if she be black and witty?	
IAGO	*If she be black, and thereto have a wit,*	
	She'll find a white that shall her blackness fit.	
DESDEMONA	Worse and worse.	
EMILIA	How if fair and foolish?	135
IAGO	*She never yet was foolish that was fair;*	
	For ev'n her folly helped her to an heir.	
DESDEMONA	These are old fond paradoxes to make fools laugh i' the alehouse.	
	What miserable praise hast thou for her that's foul and foolish?	

IAGO	*There's none so foul and foolish thereunto,*	140
	But does foul pranks which fair and wise ones do.	
DESDEMONA	O heavy ignorance! Thou praisest the worst best. But what praise couldst thou bestow on a deserving woman indeed, one that, in the authority of her merit, did justly put on the vouch of very malice itself?	
IAGO	*She that was ever fair and never proud,*	145
	Had tongue at will and yet was never loud,	
	Never lacked gold and yet went never gay,	
	Fled from her wish and yet said, 'Now I may.'	
	She that being angered, her revenge being nigh,	
	Bade her wrong stay and her displeasure fly.	150
	She that in wisdom never was so frail	
	To change the cod's head for the salmon's tail.	
	She that could think and ne'er disclose her mind,	
	See suitors following and not look behind,	
	She was a wight, if ever such wight were —	155
DESDEMONA	To do what?	
IAGO	*To suckle fools and chronicle small beer.*	
DESDEMONA	O most lame and impotent conclusion! — Do not learn of him, Emilia, though he be thy husband — How say you, Cassio? Is he not a most profane and liberal counsellor?	160
CASSIO	He speaks home, madam. You may relish him more in the soldier than in the scholar.	
IAGO	*[Aside]* He takes her by the palm — Ay, well said, whisper! — With as little a web as this will I ensnare as great a fly as Cassio. Ay, smile upon her, do; I will gyve thee in thine own courtship — You say true; 'tis so, indeed — if such tricks as these strip you out of your lieutenantry, it had been better you had not kissed your three fingers so oft, which now again you are most apt to play the sir in. Very good; well kissed! An excellent courtesy! — 'Tis so, indeed — Yet again your fingers to your lips? Would they were clyster-pipes for your sake!	165
		170

[Trumpets sound within]

	The Moor! I know his trumpet.	
CASSIO	'Tis truly so.	
DESDEMONA	Let's meet him and receive him.	
CASSIO	Lo, where he comes!	

[OTHELLO and Attendants enter]

OTHELLO	O my fair warrior!	
DESDEMONA	My dear Othello!	
OTHELLO	It gives me wonder great as my content	
	To see you here before me. O my soul's joy!	175
	If after every tempest come such calms,	
	May the winds blow till they have wakened death!	
	And let the labouring bark climb hills of seas	

Olympus-high and duck again as low
As hell's from heaven! If it were now to die,   180
'Twere now to be most happy, for, I fear,
My soul hath her content so absolute
That not another comfort like to this
Succeeds in unknown fate.

DESDEMONA   The heavens forbid
But that our loves and comforts should increase,   185
Even as our days do grow!

OTHELLO   Amen to that, sweet powers!
I cannot speak enough of this content:
It stops me here; it is too much of joy,
And this, and this – *[Kissing her]* – the greatest discords be
That e'er our hearts shall make!

IAGO   *[Aside]*   O, you are well tuned now!   190
But I'll set down the pegs that make this music,
As honest as I am.

OTHELLO   Come, let us to the castle.
News, friends: our wars are done; the Turks are drowned.
How does my old acquaintance of this isle? –
Honey, you shall be well desired in Cyprus;   195
I have found great love amongst them. O my sweet,
I prattle out of fashion, and I dote
In mine own comforts – I prithee, good Iago,
Go to the bay and disembark my coffers;
Bring thou the master to the citadel;   200
He is a good one, and his worthiness
Does challenge much respect – Come, Desdemona,
Once more, well met at Cyprus.

[OTHELLO, DESDEMONA and Attendants exit]

Text notes

4   **Descry:** Detect.

7–9   **If it hath ruffianed … Can hold the mortise:** A paraphrase of this might read: The sea is so rough that the waves are like mountains, so how will the ships' joints be able to hold together in such a storm ('mortise' = a carpentry joint)?

12   **Chidden billow:** The waves have been rebuked by the land. This is once more emphasising the harshness of the storm.

13–17   **The wind-shaked surge … On the enchafèd flood:** More storm imagery, where the sea is compared with a wild horse and the water thrown about to such an extent that it extinguished the stars. The Gentleman has never experienced such a 'molestation' or disturbance ('burning bear' = a constellation of stars; the 'pole star' = a star important for navigation).

21–22   **The desperate tempest … their designment halts:** The Turks' designs on Cyprus have now been halted by the storm.

29	**In full commission:** In complete command.
39–40	**Even till we make ... An indistinct regard:** Even till we make the blue of the water and sky blend together by looking so intensely.
55	**The Governor:** By this Cassio means the new Governor, Othello.
60–72	**He hath achieved a maid ... The divine Desdemona:** See **Before you read**.
75–76	**Whose footing here ... A se'nnight's speed:** Iago's landing (with Desdemona) is quicker than they expected – possibly a week ('seven nights') early.
76	**Great Jove:** The Roman god Jupiter.
83	**Let her have your knees:** Kneel before Desdemona (as a sign of courtesy).
86	**Enwheel thee round:** Surround or encircle you.
106–07	**She puts her tongue ... chides with thinking:** Iago is joking that, when Emilia is quiet, she 'chides' (criticises) with her thoughts.
109–12	**You are pictures ... and housewives in your beds:** Iago suggests that women (or more specifically wives) are very promiscuous or sexually active. Although this is delivered as a bawdy joke, Iago seems to believe it, to some extent.
113	**Slanderer:** Someone who insults people.
120	**Assay:** Make an attempt.
125–27	**I am about it ... plucks out brains and all:** It was common in Shakespeare's time to coat trees with lime so birds would stick to the branches and they would thus be trapped. 'Frieze' (a coarse, woollen cloth, like hessian) would be difficult to pull off; the image suggests that Iago is trying so hard to come up with a witty reply that it is as if he is pulling his brains out of his head.
127	**My Muse labours:** I am finding it difficult to think of something.
129–30	**If she be fair ... the other useth it:** The joke is that if a woman has beauty and intelligence, beauty is useful and her intelligence lies in her ability to use beauty.
132–33	**If she be black ... that shall her blackness fit:** People look for balance in a partner, so a witty woman with black (or brunette) hair would fit best with her opposite.
138	**Fond paradoxes:** Silly riddles.
140–41	**There's none so foul ... fair and wise ones do:** This paradox presents the view that ugly and stupid women deceive and trick as well as clever, pretty women do.
142–45	**But what praise could thou ... vouch of very malice itself:** Desdemona asks how Iago would praise a woman who really deserves praise, a woman so good that she would not recognise evil. This could be a description of Desdemona herself.
145–55	**She that was ever fair ... if ever such wight were:** Another rhyme subtly charged with sexual imagery.
157	**To suckle fools and chronicle small beer:** Iago completes his rhyme by saying that such a woman would raise foolish children and run up huge bar tabs.
165	**Gyve:** Fetter (put someone in chains); this could also be a play on the word 'give'.
170	**Would they were clyster-pipes for your sake:** Clyster-pipes are tubes for injecting enemas. Obviously, Cassio would not want to kiss something like this. Iago is being quite revolting here, and is hinting at his plan to use Cassio's charm against him.
179	**Olympus-high:** As high as Mount Olympus, which is the home of the gods in Classical mythology.
191–92	**I'll set down the pegs ... honest as I am:** 'Set down' here means to loosen. Loosening the strings of an instrument would cause what should sound sweet to be out of tune.
199	**Disembark my coffers:** Bring my luggage ashore ('coffers' = boxes or chests).

1 What impact does the storm have on the outcome of the naval battle?

2 What is Cassio's attitude towards Desdemona?

3 In his aside (lines 163–70), what does Iago praise about Cassio's behaviour? Why do you think Iago praises these qualities?

4 What literary device does Iago employ in the following statement: 'With as little a web as this will I ensnare as great a fly as Cassio' (lines 163–64)?

5 Copy and complete the following table in your note book to show your understanding of the way Shakespeare uses <u>Othello and Desdemona's language</u> to demonstrate their <u>love for each other</u>.

Language device	Example from lines 174–92
Exaggerated or hyperbolic language	
Poetic or lyrical descriptions	
Completion of each other's lines (of iambic) pentameter	
OTHER	

6 The first part of this scene is full of happy (or comic) elements, but there are also some ominous or foreboding elements. List these in a table, like the one below.

Happy (or comic) elements	Foreboding or potentially negative elements
e.g. Othello and Desdemona's recent marriage	
If the play ended at the conclusion to Act 2 Scene 1, do you think it would be considered a comedy (a happy play) or a tragedy (an unhappy play)? Explain your answer.	

Extend

1 The audience knows that Iago has a plan to make it appear that Cassio is too friendly with Desdemona, and we are reminded of this in his aside (lines 163–70).

a What evidence can you find from Cassio's behaviour that this plan might be successful?

b Other than the aside, does this scene provide any further evidence of tension between Iago and Cassio?

2 Based on his comments in this scene, what do you think is Iago's attitude toward women?

3 In what ways does Iago and Emilia's relationship contrast to Othello and Desdemona's? Create a table to highlight various elements of contrast. Include quotes from the text as evidence.

4 Iago says to Desdemona, 'For I am nothing, if not critical'. In what ways does this seem to be an accurate comment on Iago's character?

5 Iago claims, 'My invention / Comes from my pate as birdlime does from frieze' (lines 125–26). How does this simile have a resonance (or extra meaning) for the audience who know Iago's character better than the characters on stage do? (For further information about these lines see the **Text notes** for lines 125–27.)

6 How does Cassio's use of language provide a contrast to Iago's? Perhaps you might like to create a table to place the various elements of their language alongside each other.

7 In this scene, Desdemona says to Iago, 'I do beguile / The thing I am, by seeming otherwise.' Discuss at least two ways that Desdemona's statement is ironic (Hint: consider her character as well as Iago's).

Discuss

1 Which character are you most sympathetic towards at this stage of the play? Why do you think this is?

2 This scene opens with the stage directions indicating 'A windstorm batters the quay'. If you were directing a production of *Othello*, what theatrical devices would you use to present this violent storm, thus creating a sense of danger, fear and tension? Aspects you might consider: lighting, sound effects, props, voice (volume and pace) and characters' movement and actions.

Press PLAY **Oliver Parker: DVD Chapter 7 (Othello returns from battle)**

1 Parker's film version of *Othello* omits the detail of a raging storm, which the technique box on page 74 claims is an important Shakespearean device for foreshadowing and creating tension. To what extent do you think Parker's version loses some of the tension that is created in this scene?

2 What clever device does Parker use to show Iago spying on Cassio? How is this appropriate? How else might he have done this?

3 How does Parker make use of contrast in the visual and audio elements of the film in order to present Iago's *aside* ('O, you are well-tuned now')? How is this technique appropriate in conveying Iago's character?

A word about pathetic fallacy and foreshadowing

As Act 2 of *Othello* begins, the stage directions indicate that *'a windstorm batters the quay'*. Storms are key theatrical devices in many of Shakespeare's plays, including *The Tempest, Macbeth* and *King Lear*. These storms act as catalysts for change in the central characters, or perhaps as symbols of supernatural intervention in human affairs.

In *Othello*, however, the storm serves two quite different purposes:

1 Pathetic fallacy

When the weather reflects or parallels the atmosphere of a scene or the mood of the characters, this is known in some circles as using pathetic fallacy. For example, Shakespeare's play *Macbeth* opens with thunder and lightning, establishing an atmosphere of chaos and foreboding that is reinforced by the entrance of the Witches.

Q Read lines 1–46 again in Act 2 Scene 1 of *Othello* and jot down various descriptions of the severity of the storm.

Note how the intense natural imagery employed by Shakespeare to describe the storm reflects the intensity experienced by Othello and the Venetians in their battle against the Turks.

2 Foreshadowing

When the creepy music starts in a movie, you know something frightening or terrible is about to happen! It is like the music is sending out a warning or a signal. In a similar way, authors give us hints or warnings about what will happen later in the text, and this is known as **foreshadowing**.

For example, in George Orwell's *Nineteen Eighty-Four*, the appearance of rats in the central character's apartment not only creates a feeling of tension or unease but also hints at events later in the novel when rats are used to torture him. Likewise, in T.S. Eliot's poem *Journey of the Magi*, Eliot describes how the three wise men, on their way to see the newborn Jesus, see 'three trees on the low sky', and this foreshadows Jesus' death on the cross between two criminals.

In Act 2 Scene 1 of *Othello*, Shakespeare uses the storm and Othello's successful battle against the Turks to **foreshadow** a greater conflict that will occur later in the play: a psychological or personal battle within Othello himself.

Q Quote some phrases from lines 43–51 that suggest Othello has successfully navigated the storm and defeated the Turks.

Ironically, although Othello is literally able to navigate 'dangerous seas', he will be unable to navigate the 'foul and violent tempest' within himself, which will destroy him and some of those around him. Watch for Iago's role in Othello's destruction.

Act 2 Scene 1 (Part 2)

Characters	In a nutshell
Iago Roderigo	After everyone else has left, Iago informs Roderigo that Desdemona is in love with Cassio, and insists that she will soon tire of loving Othello. Iago then convinces Roderigo to make Cassio angry, so he will behave rashly and be dismissed from his position. Left alone on stage, Iago reflects on his suspicions that both Othello and Cassio have slept with his wife, Emilia. He outlines his plan to make Othello jealous.

Before you read

- Critics puzzled by Iago's motivations often go to the soliloquy at the end of this scene for answers. Iago speaks of his hatred for Othello and Cassio throughout the play but he gives too many reasons and fails to dwell on any of them for a sufficient length of time to make them convincing. The Romantic poet and critic Samuel Taylor Coleridge found in Iago's speeches 'the motive-hunting of motiveless malignity'. This theory is still the most popular with literary critics today.

- Shakespeare could be in danger of making Roderigo appear too credulous or gullible in this scene. We can observe Shakespeare's craft at work throughout the play in the way that Roderigo initially doubts the things Iago says. The audience is often invited to assume that further persuasion (together with the relaying of the more mundane details of plans) will take place offstage.

Mark:	Pay attention
Prating:	Prattling or talking excessively
Satiety:	Excess
Knave:	A trickster
Eminent:	Important
Lechery:	Lustful behaviour
Pish:	An exclamation expressing contempt or annoyance
Impediment:	Something that hinders progress
Peradventure:	Perhaps

Act 2 Scene 1 (Part 2)
A Sea-port in Cyprus: a windstorm batters the quay.

[Only IAGO and RODERIGO are on stage]

IAGO   Do thou meet me presently at the harbour. Come hither. If thou be'st valiant (as, they say, base men being in love have then a nobility in   205 their natures more than is native to them), list me. The lieutenant tonight watches on the court of guard. First, I must tell thee this: Desdemona is directly in love with him.

RODERIGO With him? Why, 'tis not possible!

IAGO Lay thy finger thus, and let thy soul be instructed. Mark me with what 210
violence she first loved the Moor, but for bragging and telling her
fantastical lies, and will she love him still for prating? Let not thy
discreet heart think it. Her eye must be fed; and what delight shall
she have to look on the devil? When the blood is made dull with the
act of sport, there should be (again to inflame it and to give satiety a 215
fresh appetite) loveliness in favour, sympathy in years, manners and
beauties, all which the Moor is defective in. Now, for want of these
required conveniences, her delicate tenderness will find itself abused,
begin to heave the gorge, disrelish and abhor the Moor; very nature will
instruct her in it and compel her to some second choice. Now, sir, 220
this granted (as it is a most pregnant and unforced position), who
stands so eminent in the degree of this fortune as Cassio does? A
knave very voluble, no further conscionable than in putting on the
mere form of civil and humane seeming, for the better compassing of
his salt and most hidden loose affection? Why, none! Why, none! A 225
slipper and subtle knave, a finder-out of occasions, that has an eye can
stamp and counterfeit advantages, though true advantage never present
itself. A devilish knave! Besides, the knave is handsome, young, and
hath all those requisites in him that folly and green minds look after. A
pestilent complete knave! And the woman hath found him already. 230

RODERIGO I cannot believe that in her: she's full of most blessed condition.

IAGO Blessed fig's-end! The wine she drinks is made of grapes. If she had
been blessed, she would never have loved the Moor. Blessed pudding!
Didst thou not see her paddle with the palm of his hand? Didst not
mark that? 235

RODERIGO Yes, that I did, but that was but courtesy.

IAGO Lechery, by this hand: an index and obscure prologue to the history
of lust and foul thoughts. They met so near with their lips that their
breaths embraced together. Villanous thoughts, Roderigo! When
these mutualities so marshal the way, hard at hand comes the master 240
and main exercise, the incorporate conclusion. Pish! But, sir, be you
ruled by me; I have brought you from Venice. Watch you tonight for
the command; I'll lay't upon you. Cassio knows you not. I'll not be
far from you. Do you find some occasion to anger Cassio, either by
speaking too loud, or tainting his discipline, or from what other 245
course you please, which the time shall more favourably minister.

RODERIGO Well.

IAGO Sir, he is rash and very sudden in choler, and haply may strike at you.
Provoke him, that he may; for even out of that will I cause these of
Cyprus to mutiny, whose qualification shall come into no true taste 250

	again but by the displanting of Cassio. So shall you have a shorter journey to your desires by the means I shall then have to prefer them, and the impediment most profitably removed, without the which there were no expectation of our prosperity.	
RODERIGO	I will do this, if I can bring it to any opportunity.	255
IAGO	I warrant thee. Meet me by and by at the citadel. I must fetch his necessaries ashore. Farewell.	
RODERIGO	Adieu. *[RODERIGO exits]*	
IAGO	That Cassio loves her, I do well believe it;	
	That she loves him, 'tis apt and of great credit.	260
	The Moor, howbeit that I endure him not,	
	Is of a constant, loving, noble nature,	
	And I dare think he'll prove to Desdemona	
	A most dear husband. Now, I do love her too,	
	Not out of absolute lust (though peradventure	265
	I stand accountant for as great a sin),	
	But partly led to diet my revenge,	
	For that I do suspect the lusty Moor	
	Hath leaped into my seat, the thought whereof	
	Doth, like a poisonous mineral, gnaw my inwards;	270
	And nothing can or shall content my soul	
	Till I am evened with him, wife for wife,	
	Or failing so, yet that I put the Moor	
	At least into a jealousy so strong	
	That judgment cannot cure. Which thing to do,	275
	If this poor trash of Venice, whom I trash	
	For his quick hunting, stand the putting on,	
	I'll have our Michael Cassio on the hip,	
	Abuse him to the Moor in the rank garb	
	(For I fear Cassio with my night-cap too),	280
	Make the Moor thank me, love me and reward me	
	For making him egregiously an ass,	
	And practising upon his peace and quiet	
	Even to madness. 'Tis here, but yet confused:	
	Knavery's plain face is never seen till used.	285

[IAGO exits]

Text notes

206   **List me:** Listen to me.

219–20 **Begin to heave the gorge … her to some second choice:** Iago claims that Desdemona will start to find Othello unattractive (to the point of feeling sick) and that this will quickly grow to hatred. Then, Iago claims, she will look for another man.

220–22 Now, sir, this granted … of this fortune as Cassio does: Iago assumes that logically Cassio would be Desdemona's second choice, when she looks elsewhere. The word 'pregnant' carries with it a number of meanings. Here it means obvious, not the modern sense of expecting a child.

222–25 A knave very voluble … and most hidden loose affection: Iago suggests that Cassio would take advantage of the situation because he is morally loose ('voluble' = gullible or easily persuaded; 'conscionable' = conscientious or dedicated; 'salt' relates to being lustful or lecherous).

225–28 A slipper and subtle knave … advantage never present itself: More about Cassio being slippery and immoral and taking advantage of situations.

229 Green: Naive.

232 Fig's end: Rubbish. Like the core of an apple, the end of a fig is thrown away.

233 Pudding: Nonsense.

237 An index and obscure prologue: The 'index' (at the beginning of a book) and 'prologue' (introduction) to further events in a story. It is 'obscure' because it is not the most obvious interpretation of Cassio's actions.

239–41 When these mutualities so marshal … the incorporate conclusion: Iago asserts that this sort of intimacy leads to sex ('mutualities' = intimacies; 'incorporate' = combined into one, probably a biblical allusion relating to husband and wife becoming 'one flesh', as in Genesis 2:24).

248 Very sudden in choler: Suddenly angry ('choler' relates to the ancient Greek belief that bodily fluids affected emotions; someone who was choleric was believed to be controlled by bile, a bitter substance).

276–77 If this poor trash of Venice … stand the putting on: If Roderigo (whom he considers worthless) is up to the challenge of provoking him.

278 On the hip: Disadvantaged: in deer-hunting, the hip was usually the part of the deer that the pursuing hounds first attacked; from this point on the deer's chances of survival were slim.

279 Rank garb: Lustful manner.

280 For I fear Cassio with my night-cap too: Iago fears that Cassio may have also seduced Emilia behind his back; a 'night-cap' was worn to keep someone's head warm in bed at night.

282 Egregiously: Extraordinarily; very badly.

Questions

1 Who does most of talking in the exchange between Iago and Roderigo? What do you think this tells us about the relationship between these two characters?

2 What reasons does Iago give to explain why Desdemona will tire of Othello?

3 What opinion does Iago express of Othello's stories?

4 How does Iago view Cassio's character? What seems to be his motivation for portraying him this way?

5 What does Iago ask Roderigo to do?

6   Find a quote as evidence for each of the following propositions, from Iago's soliloquy at the end of this scene (lines 259–85). In your notes, draw and complete a table like the one below.

Proposition	Quote as evidence
That Othello will probably be a good husband	
That Iago does not really know why he hates Othello	
That Iago suspects Othello has slept with his wife, Emilia	
That Iago finds Desdemona sexually attractive	
That Iago suspects Cassio has slept with Emilia	

Extend

1   How is Shakespeare careful to avoid making Roderigo appear too credulous or gullible? Look carefully at what Roderigo actually says.

2   Why do you think Shakespeare gives us so few details of Iago's plan to make Othello jealous? What might be his dramatic purpose?

Discuss

What is your assessment of Iago's motivation for destroying Othello and Cassio? (See **Before you read** for some ideas.) Can you think of any other reason he might have for hating them?

Thinking about characters' fatal flaws

In Shakespeare's tragedies such as *Othello*, *Macbeth* and *Romeo and Juliet*, one very important idea that he presents to the audience is the notion of a character's **personal weakness** leading to ruin – usually death and destruction. Because the end result is death and destruction, some authors call these personal weaknesses **fatal flaws**. They have also been given the label **base emotions** (the lowest or most negative human qualities) and are the opposite of virtues or positive human qualities such as love, patience, compassion and humility. Examples of base emotions or personal weaknesses in Shakespeare's plays are ambition (in *Macbeth*) and bitterness and impatience (in *Romeo and Juliet*).

The **structure** of Shakespeare's tragedies (the sequence of events and development of ideas) is similar for *Othello*, *Macbeth*, *Hamlet* and *Romeo and Juliet*. Typically, a character's fatal flaws spread to others (throughout Venice and Cyprus in *Othello*) by means of deception. They spread like poison or a disease, often lead to misunderstanding and ultimately result in destruction. The following diagram might make this idea clearer:

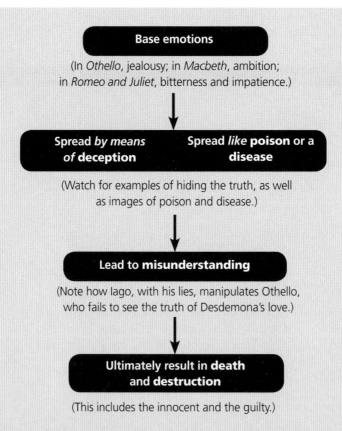

Base emotions

(In *Othello*, jealousy; in *Macbeth*, ambition;
in *Romeo and Juliet*, bitterness and impatience.)

Spread *by means* of deception **Spread *like* poison or a disease**

(Watch for examples of hiding the truth, as well
as images of poison and disease.)

Lead to misunderstanding

(Note how Iago, with his lies, manipulates Othello,
who fails to see the truth of Desdemona's love.)

Ultimately result in death and destruction

(This includes the innocent and the guilty.)

Q 'The thought whereof / Does, like a poisonous mineral, gnaw my inwards' (lines 269–70). Write a paragraph explaining how **jealousy** seems to be spreading from one character to another at this point in the play.

Look for how Shakespeare continues to communicate these ideas in *Othello* beyond Act 2 Scene 1. Watch for characters' **personal weaknesses** (especially jealousy), for further examples of **deception**, references to **disease** and **poison**, instances of **misunderstanding**, and how all of these ultimately result in **tragedy**.

Act 2 Scene 2

Characters In a nutshell

Herald A herald announces a night of festivities to celebrate the recent victory over the Turks and Othello's marriage to Desdemona.

Before you read

- A herald is a messenger or an official delivering proclamations on behalf of a ruler.

Mere:	Nothing more than
Perdition:	Destruction; ruin
Revels:	Celebrations
Nuptial:	Wedding
Offices:	Military storehouses (in this scene)

Act 2 Scene 2   A street.

[A HERALD with a proclamation enters, followed by a crowd of people]

HERALD   *It is Othello's pleasure, our noble and valiant General, that, upon*
certain tidings now arrived, importing the mere perdition of the
Turkish fleet, every man put himself into triumph: some to dance,
some to make bonfires, each man to what sport and revels his
addiction leads him. For, besides these beneficial news, it is the   5
celebration of his nuptial.
So much was his pleasure should be proclaimed. All offices are open,
and there is full liberty of feasting from this present hour of five till
the bell have told eleven. Heaven bless the isle of Cyprus and our
noble General, Othello!   10

[All exit]

Questions

List the positive words that are used to describe Othello in this scene.

Extend

What dramatic purpose might Shakespeare have had in mind for placing such a small scene between the two lengthy scenes in which Iago plots to destroy Othello and Cassio?

Introducing dramatic irony

Imagine your friend is making fun of someone and does not know (but you do!) that your teacher is standing right behind them! How would you feel? Tense? Like diving across in slow motion and shouting, 'Nooooo!'? This is what **dramatic irony** is all about. Sometimes while viewing a play, we are placed in the position of knowing more than the characters on stage. For example, we might know that around the corner is someone with a gun, but the characters are unaware and proceed to walk around the corner. This creates dramatic tension between the characters' limited knowledge and our greater knowledge.

Shakespeare's tragedies such as *Hamlet* and *Othello* contain a great deal of dramatic irony. We (the audience) often know things that the characters don't and this can create a sense of tension, as well as a desire to stop the characters from saying or doing things that might lead to harm.

While dramatic irony can create comedy, it does not tend to work that way in *Othello*. Iago's remarks in the opening scene set up a dramatic tension and irony. The reality of Othello's character in Act 1 Scenes 2 and 3 is quite unlike the character Iago and Roderigo present him as in their speeches. Furthermore, we are aware when Iago is advising Othello in Scene 2 that the advice might not be in Othello's best interests. The next scene is rich in dramatic irony. The audience is aware of Iago's plans, but Cassio and Othello are not. Every significant scene in *Othello* from here on is saturated with dramatic irony, increasing the tension experienced by the audience.

Act 2 Scene 3 (Part 1)

Characters

Iago
Cassio
Othello
Montano
Desdemona
Roderigo
All (look out for this)

In a nutshell

Othello retires to bed with Desdemona, leaving Cassio in command. Iago persuades a reluctant Cassio to drink; the two of them join a larger drinking party, and Cassio becomes increasingly drunk. When Cassio exits, Iago sends Roderigo after Cassio to provoke him. A fight that begins offstage ends up involving Montano, who is seriously wounded by Cassio. The brawl raises Othello, who, despite Iago's disingenuous protests, dismisses Cassio from the post of Lieutenant.

Before you read

- This scene is rich in dramatic irony. Note how manipulative Iago is in talking to and about Cassio. There is little Iago says in this scene that can be taken at face value.

- Two drinking songs are sung in this scene. The first expresses the view that life is short and is to be enjoyed (drinking); Iago uses this song to encourage the men to drink and to place pressure on Cassio. The second concerns King Stephen of England, who was unhappy with his tailor for overcharging him for his pants. The song warns against pride and advises the listeners to be content with their old ('auld') cloaks. This song may reflect Iago's concerns about his low status and his feelings of social inferiority in Cassio's company.

- We already know that Iago resents Cassio for taking the position of Lieutenant ahead of him, and we also know that Iago is jealous of Cassio's charm and charisma (his 'daily beauty'). Bearing this in mind, consider what Iago might be thinking when Cassio asserts that 'the Lieutenant [Cassio] is to be saved before the Ancient [Iago]'.

Discretion: Tact or sound judgement
Ensue: Happen next; occur as a consequence
Wanton: Carefree, with no boundaries
Jove: The Roman god Jupiter
Parley: Talk
Brace: Two
Gallants: Members of the gentry (the upper class)
Infirmity: Weakness
Canakin: A small can

Act 2 Scene 3 (Part 1)   A hall in the castle.

[OTHELLO, DESDEMONA, CASSIO and Attendants enter]

OTHELLO	Good Michael, look you to the guard tonight.
	Let's teach ourselves that honourable stop,
	Not to outsport discretion.
CASSIO	Iago hath direction what to do,
	But, notwithstanding, with my personal eye
	Will I look to't.

OTHELLO   Iago is most honest.
Michael, good night. Tomorrow with your earliest
Let me have speech with you.
[To DESDEMONA]   Come, my dear love.
The purchase made, the fruits are to ensue;
That profit's yet to come 'tween me and you –
Good night.

[OTHELLO, DESDEMONA and Attendants exit]

[IAGO enters]

CASSIO   Welcome, Iago; we must to the watch.
IAGO   Not this hour, Lieutenant; 'tis not yet ten o' the clock. Our General cast us thus early for the love of his Desdemona, who let us not therefore blame: he hath not yet made wanton the night with her, and she is sport for Jove.
CASSIO   She's a most exquisite lady.
IAGO   And, I'll warrant her, full of game.
CASSIO   Indeed, she's a most fresh and delicate creature.
IAGO   What an eye she has! Methinks it sounds a parley of provocation.
CASSIO   An inviting eye, and yet methinks right modest.
IAGO   And when she speaks, is it not an alarum to love?
CASSIO   She is indeed perfection.
IAGO   Well, happiness to their sheets! Come, Lieutenant, I have a stoup of

Line numbers: 5, 10, 15, 20

	wine, and here without are a brace of Cyprus gallants that would fain have a measure to the health of black Othello.	25
CASSIO	Not tonight, good Iago: I have very poor and unhappy brains for drinking; I could well wish courtesy would invent some other custom of entertainment.	
IAGO	O, they are our friends; but one cup; I'll drink for you.	30
CASSIO	I have drunk but one cup tonight, and that was craftily qualified too, and, behold, what innovation it makes here. I am unfortunate in the infirmity, and dare not task my weakness with any more.	
IAGO	What, man! 'Tis a night of revels; the gallants desire it.	
CASSIO	Where are they?	35
IAGO	Here at the door; I pray you, call them in.	
CASSIO	I'll do't, but it dislikes me. *[CASSIO exits]*	
IAGO	If I can fasten but one cup upon him,	
	With that which he hath drunk tonight already,	
	He'll be as full of quarrel and offence	40
	As my young mistress' dog. Now, my sick fool Roderigo,	
	Whom love hath turned almost the wrong side out,	
	To Desdemona hath tonight caroused	
	Potations pottle-deep; and he's to watch.	
	Three lads of Cyprus (noble swelling spirits,	45
	That hold their honours in a wary distance,	
	The very elements of this warlike isle),	
	Have I tonight flustered with flowing cups,	
	And they watch too. Now, 'mongst this flock of drunkards,	
	Am I to put our Cassio in some action	50
	That may offend the isle – But here they come:	
	If consequence do but approve my dream,	
	My boat sails freely, both with wind and stream.	

[CASSIO re-enters, with MONTANO and Gentlemen; servants follow them, carrying wine]

CASSIO	'Fore God, they have given me a rouse already.	
MONTANO	Good faith, a little one; not past a pint, as I am a soldier.	55
IAGO	Some wine, ho!	
	[Sings] And let me the canakin clink, clink;	
	And let me the canakin clink.	
	A soldier's a man,	
	A life's but a span,	60
	Why, then, let a soldier drink.	
	Some wine, boys!	
CASSIO	'Fore God, an excellent song.	
IAGO	I learned it in England, where, indeed, they are most potent in potting; your Dane, your German, and your swag-bellied Hollander – Drink, ho! – are nothing to your English.	65
CASSIO	Is your Englishman so expert in his drinking?	

IAGO	Why, he drinks you with facility, your Dane dead drunk; he sweats not to overthrow your Almain; he gives your Hollander a vomit, ere the next pottle can be filled.	70
CASSIO	To the health of our General!	
MONTANO	I am for it, Lieutenant, and I'll do you justice.	
IAGO	O sweet England!	

> [*Sings*] *King Stephen was a worthy peer,*
>   *His breeches cost him but a crown;*   75
> *He held them sixpence all too dear,*
>   *With that he called the tailor lown.*
> *He was a wight of high renown,*
>   *And thou art but of low degree;*
> *'Tis pride that pulls the country down;*   80
>   *Then take thine auld cloak about thee.*

	Some wine, ho!	
CASSIO	Why, this is a more exquisite song than the other.	
IAGO	Will you hear't again?	
CASSIO	No, for I hold him to be unworthy of his place that does those things. Well, God's above all, and there be souls must be saved, and there be souls must not be saved.	85
IAGO	It's true, good Lieutenant.	
CASSIO	For mine own part – no offence to the General, nor any man of quality – I hope to be saved.	90
IAGO	And so do I too, Lieutenant.	
CASSIO	Ay, but, by your leave, not before me; the Lieutenant is to be saved before the Ancient. Let's have no more of this; let's to our affairs – God forgive us our sins! – Gentlemen, let's look to our business. Do not think, gentlemen, I am drunk. This is my Ancient, this is my right hand, and this is my left. I am not drunk now; I can stand well enough, and speak well enough.	95
ALL	Excellent well.	
CASSIO	Why, very well then; you must not think then that I am drunk.	

[CASSIO exits]

| MONTANO | To the platform, masters; come, let's set the watch. | 100 |

[Several GENTLEMEN exit]

| IAGO | You see this fellow that is gone before? He is a soldier fit to stand by Caesar And give direction. And do but see his vice: 'Tis to his virtue a just equinox, The one as long as the other; 'tis pity of him. I fear the trust Othello puts him in On some odd time of his infirmity Will shake this island. | 105 |
| MONTANO | But is he often thus? | |

IAGO	'Tis evermore the prologue to his sleep;
	He'll watch the horologe a double set,	110
	If drink rock not his cradle.
MONTANO	It were well
	The General were put in mind of it.
	Perhaps he sees it not, or his good nature
	Prizes the virtue that appears in Cassio,
	And looks not on his evils. Is not this true?	115

[RODERIGO enters]

| IAGO | *[Aside to him]* How now, Roderigo! |
| | I pray you, after the Lieutenant; go. |

[RODERIGO exits]

MONTANO	And 'tis great pity that the noble Moor
	Should hazard such a place as his own second
	With one of an ingraft infirmity.	120
	It were an honest action to say
	So to the Moor.
IAGO	Not I, for this fair island.
	I do love Cassio well, and would do much
	To cure him of this evil – But, hark! What noise?

[Cry within: 'Help! help!' CASSIO re-enters, forcing in RODERIGO]

CASSIO	'Zounds, you rogue! You rascal!	125
MONTANO	What's the matter, Lieutenant?
CASSIO	A knave teach me my duty! I'll beat the knave into a twiggen bottle.
RODERIGO	Beat me!
CASSIO	Dost thou prate, rogue?

[CASSIO strikes RODERIGO]

MONTANO	Nay, good Lieutenant; *[MONTANO tries to hold CASSIO back]*	130
	I pray you, sir, hold your hand.
CASSIO	Let me go, sir, or I'll knock you o'er the mazzard.
MONTANO	Come, come; you're drunk.
CASSIO	Drunk!

[MONTANO and CASSIO fight]

| IAGO | *[Aside to RODERIGO]* Away, I say; go out, and cry a mutiny. | 135 |

[RODERIGO exits]

	Nay, good Lieutenant – Alas, gentlemen –
	Help, ho! – Lieutenant! – Sir! – Montano! – Sir! –
	Help, masters! – Here's a goodly watch indeed!

[A bell rings]

Who's that which rings the bell? – *Diablo*, ho! –
The town will rise. God's will, Lieutenant; hold!   140
You will be shamed forever.

[*OTHELLO and Attendants enter*]

| OTHELLO | What is the matter here? |
| MONTANO | 'Zounds, I bleed still; I am hurt to the death. |

[*MONTANO tries to attack CASSIO, but collapses*]

OTHELLO   Hold, for your lives!
IAGO   Hold, ho! Lieutenant! – Sir! – Montano! – Gentlemen!   145
     Have you forgot all sense of place and duty?
     Hold! The General speaks to you! Hold, hold, for shame!
OTHELLO   Why, how now, ho? From whence ariseth this?
     Are we turned Turks, and to ourselves do that
     Which heaven hath forbid the Ottomites?   150
     For Christian shame, put by this barbarous brawl.
     He that stirs next to carve for his own rage
     Holds his soul light; he dies upon his motion.
     Silence that dreadful bell: it frights the isle
     From her propriety. What is the matter, masters?   155
     Honest Iago, that look'st dead with grieving,
     Speak: who began this? On thy love, I charge thee.
IAGO   I do not know; friends all but now, even now,
     In quarter, and in terms like bride and groom
     Devesting them for bed; and then, but now,   160
     As if some planet had unwitted men,
     Swords out, and tilting one at other's breast,
     In opposition bloody. I cannot speak
     Any beginning to this peevish odds,
     And would in action glorious I had lost   165
     Those legs that brought me to a part of it!
OTHELLO   How comes it, Michael, you are thus forgot?
CASSIO   I pray you, pardon me: I cannot speak.
OTHELLO   Worthy Montano, you were wont to be civil;
     The gravity and stillness of your youth   170
     The world hath noted, and your name is great
     In mouths of wisest censure. What's the matter,
     That you unlace your reputation thus
     And spend your rich opinion for the name
     Of a night-brawler? Give me answer to it.   175
MONTANO   Worthy Othello, I am hurt to danger.
     Your officer, Iago, can inform you,
     While I spare speech, which something now offends me,
     Of all that I do know; nor know I aught
     By me that's said or done amiss this night,   180

Unless self-charity be sometimes a vice,
And to defend ourselves it be a sin
When violence assails us.

OTHELLO   Now, by heaven,
My blood begins my safer guides to rule,
And passion, having my best judgment collied,   185
Assays to lead the way. If I once stir,
Or do but lift this arm, the best of you
Shall sink in my rebuke. Give me to know
How this foul rout began, who set it on;
And he that is approved in this offence,   190
Though he had twinned with me, both at a birth,
Shall lose me. What! In a town of war,
Yet wild, the people's hearts brimful of fear,
To manage private and domestic quarrel,
In night, and on the court and guard of safety!   195
'Tis monstrous! Iago, who began't?

MONTANO   If partially affined, or leagued in office,
Thou dost deliver more or less than truth,
Thou art no soldier.

IAGO   Touch me not so near.
I had rather have this tongue cut from my mouth   200
Than it should do offence to Michael Cassio;
Yet, I persuade myself, to speak the truth
Shall nothing wrong him – This it is, General:
Montano and myself being in speech,
There comes a fellow crying out for help,   205
And Cassio following him with determined sword,
To execute upon him. Sir, this gentleman
Steps in to Cassio, and entreats his pause;
Myself the crying fellow did pursue,
Lest by his clamour (as it so fell out)   210
The town might fall in fright; he, swift of foot,
Outran my purpose; and I returned the rather
For that I heard the clink and fall of swords,
And Cassio high in oath; which till tonight
I ne'er might say before. When I came back   215
(For this was brief), I found them close together,
At blow and thrust; even as again they were
When you yourself did part them.
More of this matter cannot I report,
But men are men: the best sometimes forget.   220
Though Cassio did some little wrong to him,
As men in rage strike those that wish them best,
Yet surely Cassio, I believe, received
From him that fled some strange indignity,
Which patience could not pass.

| OTHELLO | I know, Iago, | 225 |

Thy honesty and love doth mince this matter,
Making it light to Cassio – Cassio, I love thee,
But never more be officer of mine –

[DESDEMONA re-enters, followed by her Attendants]

Look, if my gentle love be not raised up! –
I'll make thee an example. 230

| DESDEMONA | What's the matter? |
| OTHELLO | All's well now, sweeting; come away to bed – |

[To MONTANO] Sir, for your hurts, myself will be your surgeon –
Lead him off *[MONTANO is led off]* –
Iago, look with care about the town,
And silence those whom this vile brawl distracted – 235
Come, Desdemona: 'tis the soldiers' life
To have their balmy slumbers waked with strife.

[All but IAGO and CASSIO exit]

Text notes

3   **Not to outsport discretion:** Othello advises Cassio to make sure the celebrations are moderate (that they do not get out of hand).

15–16   **He hath not yet made wanton … sport for Jove:** The marriage has not yet been consummated (Othello and Desdemona have not yet had sex). The Roman god Jove was well known for his sexual 'conquests', thus this reference follows Iago's language paralleling military with sexual conquest.

18   **I'll warrant her, full of game:** Iago is being bawdy or rude here, speculating about Desdemona's sexual responsiveness.

20   **Sounds a parley of provocation:** Sounds a trumpet; Iago is suggesting Desdemona has a roaming eye (that she is a flirt).

21   **An inviting eye, and yet methinks right modest:** Cassio contradicts Iago while being conciliatory. He admits that Desdemona does have beautiful eyes but protests she doesn't use them to flirt.

31–32   **That was craftily qualified … innovation it makes here:** The drink Cassio has previously drunk was very strong and he is feeling the effects of it already.

43–44   **Caroused potations pottle-deep:** They have partied hard and have drunk to excess ('pottle' = a drinking vessel that contains two quarts of liquid, equivalent to 2.4 litres).

45–47   **Noble swelling spirits … this warlike isle:** Iago got three particularly high-spirited or big-headed men drunk, men who are typical of the war-like island of Cyprus.

52–53   **If consequence do … with wind and stream:** A rough paraphrase might read: if things fall out in accordance to my plan, I will sail freely downstream with the wind.

60   **Span:** A short time (a span is the measurement from the tip of the thumb to the tip of the little finger when the hand is fully extended).

64   **Most potent in potting:** Powerful drinkers.

68   **He drinks you with facility:** He out-drinks you.

69 **Almain:** German.

77 **Lown:** A lout or thug.

78 **Wight:** Man (this archaic word often implied strength and courage in battle).

89 **Any man of quality:** Any man of high rank or position. This remark is likely to annoy Iago, who is of a lower rank than Cassio.

102 **Caesar:** Julius Caesar, a great Roman political and military leader.

103–5 **And do but see … 'tis pity of him:** Iago points out that it is a shame that Cassio has the 'vice' of drunkenness, conceding that it balances against or cancels out his good qualities.

106–8 **I fear the trust Othello … shake this Island:** Iago fears that the trust Othello places in the alcoholic Cassio could put Cyprus in danger (especially in this time of war).

109–11 **'Tis evermore … rock not his cradle:** Iago claims that Cassio often drinks to excess before he goes to bed; otherwise he cannot sleep at all ('horologe' = clock; 'a double set' = goes round twice, i.e. 24 hours).

120 **Ingraft infirmity:** Deep-rooted condition or weakness.

127 **Twiggen bottle:** A bottle encased with wicker-work; a very strange threat, perhaps emphasising Cassio's drunkenness.

129 **Prate:** Prattle or talk.

132 **Mazzard:** A colloquial (conversational) term for someone's head.

135 **Mutiny:** A rebellion against proper or legal authority.

139 **Diablo:** Italian for Devil.

155 **Propriety:** Normal peaceful state.

160 **Devesting them:** Undressing themselves.

161 **As if some planet had unwitted men:** Many in Shakespeare's time believed that the movement of the planets had an effect on human actions on the earth.

163–66 **I cannot speak … to a part of it:** Iago says that he doesn't know how the brawl began, and adds, in fake exasperation, that he wishes he had lost his legs in battle so he would not have been able to get to this terrible brawl.

169–72 **Worthy Montano, you … wisest censure:** Othello points out that Montano was considered by the wisest critics a man of restraint, of good reputation.

183 **Assails:** Attacks.

184–85 **My blood begins my safer … best judgement collied:** Othello claims the rage in his blood is no longer held in check by reason and calmer judgment ('assays' = attempts; 'collied' = blackened).

189 **Rout:** Uproar.

197 **If partially affined, or leagued in office:** Montano implores or begs Iago not to take sides simply because Cassio is his superior in the army.

Questions

1 Find an example of dramatic irony in the opening ten lines of this scene.

2 Explain one of the metaphors Iago uses in lines 13–26.

3 Iago and Cassio have a conversation about Desdemona early in this scene. What are some of the differences in the way they each discuss her? What does this tell us about the characters of Iago and Cassio?

4   What is Cassio's initial reaction when he is invited to drink?

5   How does Iago persuade Cassio to have a drink? That is, what tactics does he employ?

6   What does Iago say to Montano about Cassio's drinking? How is this an example of dramatic irony?

7   What steps does Iago take to ensure the fight causes maximum disturbance? Why would he want to do this?

8   Whom does Cassio injure? Why is this particularly shameful?

9   How does Iago give the impression of being a loyal friend to Cassio, when Othello is questioning him?

10   Othello says to Iago, 'Thy love and honesty doth mince this matter / Making it light to Cassio'. Here, the word mince means to cut into smaller pieces (thus minimise or reduce the importance of something). How are these lines another example of dramatic irony?

11   What action does Othello take against Cassio?

Extend

1   Find some evidence from the beginning of this scene that Othello and Desdemona have yet to consummate their marriage (i.e. sleep with each other).

2   Why do you think Shakespeare has a Venetian saying that the English are expert drinkers?

3   What cause for offence do you think Iago would find in Cassio's drunken remarks?

4   Copy and complete the following table in your notes to show your understanding of the dramatic and language devices Shakespeare uses to demonstrate Cassio's drunkenness (see especially lines 85–144).

Device	Example showing Cassio's drunkenness
Repetition of words and phrases	
Stage directions	
Shouting of insults	
Irrational or nonsensical sentences	
Mispronunciation of words	

5   Why do you think Iago uses the simile 'in terms like bride and groom / Devesting them for bed' to describe the mood before the brawl? (Hint: 'devesting' means undressing.) Why is this particularly ironic?

6   How do Othello's final lines to Cassio show that Othello balances friendship and duty with great competence?

Discuss If you were given the role as director of this scene, how might you present Cassio's drunken state? Consider such devices as his voice (pace, volume) as well as his actions and movement.

Annotating a soliloquy: Iago's 'Divinity of hell' speech

Reproduced here is Iago's famous 'Divinity of hell' soliloquy from Act 2 Scene 3, lines 298–324. It has been annotated, which means notes have been added that explain various aspects of Shakespeare's language and ideas. Carefully read the soliloquy and the annotations, then read the scene as a whole. The **Text notes** for this soliloquy appear on the next page.

Repetition of words and phrases is a key device used here to reveal something of Iago's character: note that the words 'villain' and 'honest' have been repeated throughout the passage.

Note the frequent use of antithesis (contrast of opposites) in Iago's speech: free/enfettered, make/unmake, love/lust, virtue/pitch.

Shakespeare deliberately creates *irony in the contrast* between black-skinned Othello's honesty and white Iago's villainous heart of 'blackest sins'.

Shakespeare uses particularly biblical language to emphasise the contrast between Othello (baptism, redeemed, love) and Iago (villain, devil, divinity of hell, sin).

And what's he then that says I *play* the villain?
When this advice is free I give and honest,
Probal to thinking and indeed the course   300
To win the Moor again? For 'tis most easy
The inclining Desdemona to *subdue*
In any honest suit: she's framed as fruitful
As the free elements. And then for her
To win the Moor, were't to renounce his baptism,
All seals and symbols of redeemèd sin,
His soul is so enfettered to her love,
That she may make, unmake, do what she list,
Even as her appetite shall play the god
With his weak function. How am I then a villain   310
To counsel Cassio to this parallel course,
Directly to his good? **Divinity of hell!**
When devils will the *blackest sins* put on,
They do suggest at first with heavenly *shows*,
As I do now. For whiles this honest fool
Plies Desdemona to repair his fortunes
And she for him pleads strongly to the Moor,
I'll pour this pestilence into his ear,
That she repeals him for her body's lust,
And by how much she strives to do him good,   320
She shall undo her credit with the Moor.
So will I turn her virtue into pitch,
And out of her own goodness make the net
That shall enmesh them all.

Dramatic irony is evident in Iago's constant use of the word 'honest', as he admits here that his honesty is merely a 'play' or 'show', that he plans to manipulate the other characters.

Alliteration of the f and s sounds creates a harsh quality to Iago's language, and contributes to the malicious tone of his soliloquy.

Note the **abundant use of words**, phrases and images **relating to the DEVIL** in this soliloquy: blackest sins, devils, divinity of hell!

An important image that appears throughout the play is that of poison. It is here that we see the source of the poison or disease that infects the other characters: Iago.

300	**Probal to thinking:** Likely, probable.
301–3	**For 'tis most easy ... honest suit:** Desdemona will be sympathetic to any honest request.
305–6	**Were't to renounce ... symbols of redeemèd sin:** All the symbols of the Christian faith, which point to Christ's forgiveness of sin.
307–10	**His soul is so enfettered ... With his weak function:** Othello is so taken with or affected by Desdemona that she can do (or suggest) what she likes, given Othello's weak control over his lust.
316	**Plies:** Petitions or pleads with someone.

Act 2 Scene 3 (Part 2)

Characters

Iago
Cassio
Roderigo

In a nutshell

Beginning to sober up, Cassio complains to Iago of his shame. Iago advises him to obtain Desdemona's support in order to be reinstated to his position. When Cassio leaves, Iago gloats at his triumph and unfolds his plan to make Othello jealous. When Roderigo enters, complaining about his situation, Iago quickly convinces him that their mutual aims were achieved. After dismissing Roderigo, Iago unfolds further practical details of his plan.

Before you read

- The soliloquy towards the end of this scene is one of Iago's most famous speeches in the play. In this soliloquy, he boasts that his arguments are based on the 'divinity' or theology of 'hell' (for more on this, read the box entitled **Iago and the Devil** on page 98). This speech is also a great example of how Shakespeare uses antithesis. The words: 'hell', 'sins' and 'devils' are set against the phrase 'heavenly shows', and the word 'villain' is set against 'honest'.

Bestial:	Animal-like, as opposed to human
Imperious:	Kingly; powerful
Indiscreet:	Lacking tact or discretion
Swagger:	Walk arrogantly or proudly
Wherefore:	Why
Hydra:	A monster with many heads
Beseech:	Beg, request
Divinity:	Theology (refers to God)
Cashiered:	Dismissed or sacked

Act 2 Scene 3 (Part 2)   A hall in the castle.

IAGO	What, are you hurt, Lieutenant?	
CASSIO	Ay, past all surgery.	
IAGO	Marry, heaven forbid!	240
CASSIO	Reputation, reputation, reputation! O, I have lost my reputation! I have lost the immortal part of myself, and what remains is bestial. My reputation, Iago! My reputation!	
IAGO	As I am an honest man, I thought you had received some bodily wound; there is more sense in that than in reputation. Reputation is an idle and most false imposition, oft got without merit, and lost without deserving. You have lost no reputation at all, unless you repute yourself such a loser. What, man? There are ways to recover the General again; you are but now cast in his mood, a punishment more in policy than in malice, even so as one would beat his offenceless dog to affright an imperious lion. Sue to him again, and he's yours.	
CASSIO	I will rather sue to be despised than to deceive so good a commander with so slight, so drunken, and so indiscreet an officer. Drunk? And speak parrot? And squabble? Swagger? Swear? And discourse fustian with one's own shadow? O thou invisible spirit of wine, if thou hast no name to be known by, let us call thee devil!	255
IAGO	What was he that you followed with your sword? What had he done to you?	
CASSIO	I know not.	
IAGO	Is't possible?	260
CASSIO	I remember a mass of things, but nothing distinctly: a quarrel, but nothing wherefore. O God, that men should put an enemy in their mouths to steal away their brains! That we should, with joy, pleasance, revel and applause, transform ourselves into beasts!	
IAGO	Why, but you are now well enough. How came you thus recovered?	265
CASSIO	It hath pleased the devil drunkenness to give place to the devil wrath; one unperfectness shows me another, to make me frankly despise myself.	
IAGO	Come, you are too severe a moraler. As the time, the place and the condition of this country stands, I could heartily wish this had not befallen; but, since it is as it is, mend it for your own good.	270
CASSIO	I will ask him for my place again; he shall tell me I am a drunkard. Had I as many mouths as Hydra, such an answer would stop them all. To be now a sensible man, by and by a fool, and presently a beast! O strange! Every inordinate cup is unblessed and the ingredient is a devil.	275
IAGO	Come, come; good wine is a good familiar creature, if it be well used: exclaim no more against it. And, good Lieutenant, I think you think I love you.	
CASSIO	I have well approved it, sir. I, drunk!	280

IAGO	You or any man living may be drunk at some time, man. I'll tell you what you shall do. Our General's wife is now the general; I may say so in this respect, for that he hath devoted and given up himself to the contemplation, mark, and denotement of her parts and graces. Confess yourself freely to her; importune her help to put you in your place again. She is of so free, so kind, so apt, so blessed a disposition, she holds it a vice in her goodness not to do more than she is requested. This broken joint between you and her husband entreat her to splinter, and (my fortunes against any lay worth naming) this crack of your love shall grow stronger than it was before.	
		290
CASSIO	You advise me well.	
IAGO	I protest, in the sincerity of love and honest kindness.	
CASSIO	I think it freely, and betimes in the morning I will beseech the virtuous Desdemona to undertake for me. I am desperate of my fortunes if they check me here.	
		295
IAGO	You are in the right. Good night, Lieutenant; I must to the watch.	
CASSIO:	Good night, honest Iago.	

[*CASSIO exits*]

IAGO	And what's he then that says I play the villain?	
	When this advice is free I give and honest,	
	Probal to thinking and indeed the course	300
	To win the Moor again? For 'tis most easy	
	The inclining Desdemona to subdue	
	In any honest suit: she's framed as fruitful	
	As the free elements. And then for her	
	To win the Moor, were't to renounce his baptism,	305
	All seals and symbols of redeemèd sin,	
	His soul is so enfettered to her love,	
	That she may make, unmake, do what she list,	
	Even as her appetite shall play the god	
	With his weak function. How am I then a villain	310
	To counsel Cassio to this parallel course,	
	Directly to his good? Divinity of hell!	
	When devils will the blackest sins put on,	
	They do suggest at first with heavenly shows,	
	As I do now. For whiles this honest fool	315
	Plies Desdemona to repair his fortunes	
	And she for him pleads strongly to the Moor,	
	I'll pour this pestilence into his ear,	
	That she repeals him for her body's lust,	
	And by how much she strives to do him good,	320
	She shall undo her credit with the Moor.	
	So will I turn her virtue into pitch,	
	And out of her own goodness make the net	
	That shall enmesh them all.	

[RODERIGO re-enters]

How now, Roderigo!

RODERIGO   I do follow here in the chase, not like a hound that hunts, but one   325
that fills up the cry. My money is almost spent; I have been tonight
exceedingly well cudgelled, and I think the issue will be, I shall have
so much experience for my pains, and so, with no money at all and
a little more wit, return again to Venice.

IAGO   How poor are they that have not patience.   330
What wound did ever heal but by degrees?
Thou know'st we work by wit, and not by witchcraft,
And wit depends on dilatory time.
Does't not go well? Cassio hath beaten thee.
And thou, by that small hurt, hast cashiered Cassio.   335
Though other things grow fair against the sun,
Yet fruits that blossom first will first be ripe.
Content thyself awhile. By the mass, 'tis morning!
Pleasure and action make the hours seem short.
Retire thee; go where thou art billeted.   340
Away, I say; thou shalt know more hereafter.
Nay, get thee gone.

[RODERIGO exits]

Two things are to be done:

My wife must move for Cassio to her mistress
(I'll set her on);
Myself the while to draw the Moor apart,   345
And bring him jump when he may Cassio find
Soliciting his wife. Ay, that's the way!
Dull not device by coldness and delay.

[Exit]

Text notes

246   **Imposition:** Burden.

249–50   **A punishment more in policy … affright an imperious lion:** Iago insists that Cassio has
to take this sort of action as an example of punishing his minor wrong ('offenceless dog') to
prevent major wrongs ('imperious lion').

254–55   **And discourse fustian with one's own shadow:** And speak nonsense to yourself
('fustian' = nonsense).

269   **Moraler:** Moraliser or self-critic.

275   **Every inordinate cup:** Every extra drink.

283–84   **He hath devoted and given up … her parts and graces:** He has given up everything
(most importantly his command) to Desdemona.

285   **Importune her help:** Strongly request or beg her help.

287–90 **This broken joint ... grow stronger than it was before:** Iago uses a metaphor from carpentry, to say that Desdemona will repair Cassio and Othello's friendship and make it stronger than it was before.

295   **Check:** Stop.

298–324 See **Annotating a soliloquy**, page 92.

327   **Cudgelled:** Beaten.

333   **Dilatory:** Sluggish.

338   **By the mass:** A mild oath in Renaissance England ('mass' = Communion ceremony).

343   **My wife must move for Cassio to her mistress:** Iago wants his wife, Emilia, to ask Desdemona to plead for Cassio's reinstatement ('move' = plead).

346–47 **And bring him ... Soliciting his wife:** Iago looks to bring Othello in at the exact moment Cassio is asking favours from Desdemona.

Questions

1   What literary devices does Cassio employ to convey his disgust at his own behaviour? In a table like the one below, list the devices and give one or two examples of each.

Literary device	One or two examples

2   Summarise what Iago says about reputation in this scene.

3   What advice does Iago give to Cassio on how to recover his position?

4   Cassio's final words in this scene are 'Good night, honest Iago'. Explain what dramatic device Shakespeare uses here.

5   What plan does Iago outline in this scene?

6   What reasons does Iago have for thinking that his plan should succeed?

7   With what supernatural power does Iago align himself, in this scene, to accomplish his plan?

8   What is Roderigo's complaint at the end of scene? How does Iago respond to this?

Extend

1   Why do you think Shakespeare chooses to have Roderigo return at the end of this scene?

2   The final two lines of Act 2 are in the form of a rhyming couplet. Do you think this an effective end to this scene? Why or why not?

Discuss

1 Do you think Roderigo's character is too gullible to be believed? Consider some arguments for and against.

2 If you were given the role of director of this scene, how would you have Iago deliver his famous 'Divinity of hell' soliloquy? In small groups, discuss as many aspects as possible: facial expression, voice, actions, blocking (positioning on the stage as well as character movement), lighting and music. Report your group's findings to the rest of the class and take note of the variety of interpretations that are presented. See page 92, **Annotating a soliloquy**, for possible ideas.

Press PLAY **Oliver Parker: DVD Chapter 10 ('Divinity of hell')**

1 During this scene, how does Parker show Iago's manipulation of Cassio and Roderigo? Discuss aspects such as Iago's voice and the camera work, as well as Iago's actions and facial expressions.

2 Draw up and complete a table like the one below to show your understanding of Parker's interpretation of Iago's 'Divinity of hell' soliloquy.

Cinematic / dramatic device	Use of this device to present Iago's character and ideas	How else might Parker have used this device?
Voice (e.g. whisper, pause)		
Camera work		
Symbolic props (fire/log/charcoal)		
Iago's actions		
OTHER?		

3 What might Parker have been suggesting about Iago's character by having him put his hand up to the camera at the end of this scene? Is it effective? How might he have presented this attribute of Iago's character differently?

Divinity of hell!
Iago and the Devil

When the English poet John Milton wrote his epic poem *Paradise Lost* in the 1660s, he looked to *Othello* for inspiration. The subject of the poem primarily concerns Satan's rebellion against God, and what better model to use for the character of Satan than Iago, the Ensign at war with his General?

It would be difficult to miss the numerous references in the play that align Iago with Satan. Iago invokes 'hell' and the Devil or devils (demons) throughout the play. In his soliloquy in Act 2, Scene 3, Iago claims to employ 'divinity of hell', that is, the theology (or thinking) of hell. In the final scene of the play, when the horrible truth is revealed, Othello states: 'I look down at his feet, but that's a fable' – what he is looking for is the cloven hooves that would prove Iago a demon.

There are other references to 'divinity of hell' that a modern audience might miss. Shakespeare's audience would have instantly recognised that Iago's phrase 'I am not what I am' is set against Saint Paul's statement in his first letter to the Corinthians: 'By the grace of God, I am what I am'. Towards the end of Act 1, Iago asserts:

> *But we have reason to cool our raging motions, our carnal stings, our*
> *unbitted lusts, whereof I take this that you call love to be a sect or scion.*

Shakespeare's English audience was predominantly Christian, and they would have recognised this as sound psychology: man has lusts and sinful desires remaining from the Fall in the Garden of Eden, and has been given reason to keep these baser desires in check. But, as critic Peter Saccio points out, Iago omits the part of this teaching, which was well-known to Shakespeare's audience: the power of God's grace to redeem and restore humanity. In effect, Iago denies the operation of any greater spiritual power.

Many critics have noted that Iago embodies similar qualities to the Devil in the Medieval Mystery plays and the character of Vice in Morality plays. Vice was thought to be a messenger of the Devil sent to tempt Everyman (a character representing the common man) to do evil. Like Iago, Vice would stage-manage his victim's downfall, while posing as their friend and commenting on the action throughout the play, as Iago does in his soliloquies and asides. Also like Iago, Vice lacked a clear motive but seemed to thoroughly enjoy his work; he even invited the audience to share in his triumphs. His aim was to reduce the characters on stage from a state of grace to utter ruin.

Saint Augustine presented sin as a parody or perversion of God's good gifts. Lust he considered a perversion of love, and wastefulness a distortion of generosity. This serves as a useful framework for understanding Iago's character. Iago dismisses love as 'a sect' of lust, and transforms the idea of Othello's love into something bestial: 'making the beast with two backs'. He is guided by his own self-interest, and despises people who do not keep their 'hearts attending on themselves'.

Iago sees human beings merely as calculating animals and leaves no place for the higher motives of generosity and self-sacrifice. It is Iago's inability to recognise these qualities in others that leads to his undoing.

Characters

Cassio
Emilia
Clown
1ST Musician
Iago

In a nutshell

Cassio enters with a party of musicians to wake Othello but, before they have played for long, a clown advises them to stop. Cassio talks with Iago and Emilia, sharing his anxiety and his desire to reclaim his position through Desdemona's support. Emilia assures Cassio that Desdemona is talking to Othello on his behalf, and Cassio requests to speak to Desdemona in private.

Before you read

- It was a courtly custom in Shakespeare's England for newly married couples to be woken with music, organised by friends or relatives. In this case, Cassio orders a group of musicians to play in order to wake Othello. Unfortunately for Cassio, Othello seems in no mood for music.

- This scene, or at least the clowning part of it, is cut from most contemporary productions of *Othello*.

Marry:	An exclamation of surprise or frustration; a mild oath referring to the Virgin Mary
Prithee:	A polite introduction to a request (abbreviated form of 'I pray thee')
Quillets:	Quibbles or hair-splitting distinctions
Entreats:	Strongly requests or begs
Suit:	A petition or request to someone in authority
Procure:	Obtain (something)

Enter Clown
Shakespeare's clowns

While the audience might find some of Iago's lines darkly amusing, *Othello* contains less humour than most of Shakespeare's plays. Nevertheless, there are two brief episodes of clowning. Clowns would not necessarily be dressed differently to the other characters on stage, but these characters might take a few more liberties with the script, and add some physical comedy.

The principal comic actor was among the stars of any company and very popular with the audience. In the early years of Shakespeare's company (The Lord Chamberlain's Men), William Kemp was the main comic actor but he left the company in 1599. The following year, he famously Morris-danced almost 150 km from London to Norwich in response to a bet, and later wrote about the experience in the book, *Kemp's Nine Daies Wonder*. By the 1590s, Kemp's more physical style of comedy had become unfashionable in the theatres and audiences were ready for a new kind of comic actor.

William Kemp was replaced by Robert Armin, who probably played the part of the clown in *Othello*. While Kemp was renowned for dancing and physical comedy, Armin had a famous singing voice, which suited the later comic roles Shakespeare wrote, such as Feste in *Twelfth Night*.

Act 3 Scene 1   Before the castle.

[CASSIO and some Musicians enter]

| CASSIO | Masters, play here; I will content your pains. |
| | Something that's brief, and bid 'Good morrow, General'. |

[Music plays and CLOWN enters]

CLOWN	Why masters, have your instruments been in Naples, that they speak I' the nose thus?	
1ST MUSICIAN	How, sir? How?	5
CLOWN	Are these, I pray you, wind instruments?	
1ST MUSICIAN	Ay, marry, are they, sir.	
CLOWN	O, thereby hangs a tail.	
1ST MUSICIAN	Whereby hangs a tale, sir?	
CLOWN	Marry, sir, by many a wind instrument that I know. But, masters, Here's money for you; and the General so likes your music, that he desires you, for love's sake, to make no more noise with it.	10
1ST MUSICIAN	Well, sir, we will not.	
CLOWN	If you have any music that may not be heard, to't again; but, as they say, to hear music the General does not greatly care.	15
1ST MUSICIAN	We have none such, sir.	
CLOWN	Then put up your pipes in your bag, for I'll away. Go; vanish into air; away!	

[Musicians exit]

CASSIO	Dost thou hear, my honest friend?	
CLOWN	No, I hear not your honest friend; I hear you.	20
CASSIO	Prithee, keep up thy quillets. There's a poor piece of gold for thee. If the gentlewoman that attends the General's wife be stirring, tell her there's one Cassio entreats her a little favour of speech. Wilt thou do this?	
CLOWN	She is stirring, sir. If she will stir hither, I shall seem to notify unto her.	25
CASSIO	Do, good my friend.	

[Clown exits; IAGO enters]

In happy time, Iago.

IAGO	You have not been abed, then?	
CASSIO	Why, no; the day had broke	
	Before we parted. I have made bold, Iago,	
	To send in to your wife. My suit to her	30
	Is that she will to virtuous Desdemona	
	Procure me some access.	
IAGO	I'll send her to you presently,	
	And I'll devise a mean to draw the Moor	
	Out of the way, that your converse and business	35
	May be more free.	
CASSIO	I humbly thank you for't.	

[IAGO exits]

I never knew

A Florentine more kind and honest.

[EMILIA enters]

EMILIA	Good morrow, good Lieutenant. I am sorry	
	For your displeasure, but all will sure be well.	40
	The General and his wife are talking of it,	
	And she speaks for you stoutly. The Moor replies	
	That he you hurt is of great fame in Cyprus,	
	And great affinity, and that in wholesome wisdom	
	He might not but refuse you; but he protests he loves you	45
	And needs no other suitor but his likings	
	To take the safest occasion by the front	
	To bring you in again.	
CASSIO	Yet, I beseech you,	
	If you think fit, or that it may be done,	
	Give me advantage of some brief discourse	50
	With Desdemona alone.	
EMILIA	Pray you, come in.	
	I will bestow you where you shall have time	
	To speak your bosom freely.	
CASSIO	I am much bound to you.	

[Exit]

Text notes

1	**I will content your pains:** I will pay you for your trouble.
3–9	**Why masters, have your instruments … hangs a tale, sir:** An obscure sexual pun relating to venereal disease, which was called the Neapolitan disease.
35	**Converse:** Conversation (used here as a noun).
44	**Great affinity:** Well-connected, knowing many important people.
50	**Discourse:** Conversation.
54	**I am much bound to you:** Something like, 'I am much indebted to you' or 'I owe you a great deal'.

Questions

Iago's plan is to make it appear that Desedmona and Cassio are having an affair. List and explain the decisions that the characters make in this scene and how these will suit Iago's purposes.

Extend

What do you think is Shakespeare's dramatic purpose for including some comedy at the beginning of the scene? In your answer, consider what comes before and after this scene.

A word about puns

A pun is a play on words. It might play on the fact that a word has a double meaning ('lie' as in lying down, or 'lie' as in not telling the truth), or it could play on the fact that two words sound similar to each other, such as 'tale' and 'tail', which is a pun used in Act 3 Scene 1.

In some of Shakespeare's other plays, such as *Much Ado about Nothing* and *The Taming of the Shrew*, the characters engage in deliberate punning or plays on words, adding to the comical aspects of these plays. Apart from some minor witticisms by Iago in Act 1, and the Clown's dialogue in Act 3 (which is full of jokes and sexual innuendoes), *Othello* is a painfully tragic play, so punning is rarely used for comic effect.

In the previous scene (lines 1–25) and then again in Scene 4 (lines 1–16), the Clown makes numerous puns, relieving some of the tension that has been building:
- Scene 1, lines 3–5: a double entendre (deliberate or intended double meaning) on the word 'instruments'
- Scene 1, lines 8–9: using the homophones (words that sound the same but have different meanings) 'tail' and 'tale' to confuse the 1st Musician
- Scene 4, lines 15–16: another obscure, vulgar pun on 'man's wit' and a more obvious reference to 'doing it'.

Besides the Clown's crude puns, he also uses simpler plays on words.

Q Explain the Clown's pun that is used in Act 3 Scene 1, lines 19–20.

Q In Act 3 Scene 1, line 25, what are two possible understandings of the words 'stirring' and 'stir'?

Q Explain the various ways that the Clown plays on the word 'lie' or 'lies' in Act 3 Scene 4, lines 1–9.

Act 3 Scene 2

Characters
Othello
Iago
Gentleman

In a nutshell
Othello gives Iago some letters, instructing him to post them back to Venice by sea. Othello and a group of gentlemen then leave to review the island's defences.

Pilot: Captain

Works: Fortification or defences

Act 3 Scene 2   A room in the castle.

[OTHELLO, IAGO and Gentlemen enter]

OTHELLO	These letters give, Iago, to the pilot,	
	And by him do my duties to the Senate.	
	That done, I will be walking on the works;	
	Repair there to me.	
IAGO	Well, my good lord; I'll do't.	5
OTHELLO	This fortification, gentlemen, shall we see't?	
GENTLEMAN	We'll wait upon your lordship.	

[All exit]

Questions

How does Shakespeare present Othello as an efficient and effective leader in this brief scene?

... the man commands like a full soldier
A soldier's life

Othello is set in a period we now know as the Renaissance. It was a time of increasing conflict in Europe that gave rise to a new type of soldier. Whereas medieval armies were generally made up of part-timers, the new breed of soldier was typically professional.

European armies of this period increasingly relied on mercenaries: men who fought under contract for foreign states. In serving Venice, both Othello, from northern Africa, and Cassio, from the neighbouring Italian city-state of Florence, are mercenaries. Many men enjoyed the freedom of this adventurous lifestyle and thought of themselves as a class apart

Portrait of a Condottiero (1622) by the Italian painter Artemisia Gentileschi

from ordinary society. The paintings of that period depict the soldiers' masculine and rebellious (unconventional) qualities, emphasising their flamboyant dress and hairstyles, bulging codpieces and sexually aggressive strut.

As a foreign general, Othello is what was known as a condottiero (con-dot-ee-AIR-o). Many Italian city-states employed condottieri, especially at times of political instability, mainly because they posed a lesser threat to the established local government than a native general. Some condottieri achieved great fame fighting for their adopted countries, and some, such as Gattamelata, were even honoured with statues.

The Renaissance was also a time when warfare was becoming more scientific. Although Iago resents Othello's promotion of the 'bookish theoric' to the position of Lieutenant, Cassio's temperament and education would make him a more likely choice than Iago. Knowledge of military theory and mathematics was considered increasingly important during the Renaissance. A Lieutenant was also expected to resolve disputes, which further explains Cassio's shame at the end of Act 2. Military codes of conduct at the time imposed harsh penalties for drunkenness on duty, and brawling on campaign could even be punishable by death. Othello's judgement on Cassio, in fact, appears rather lenient in the light of history.

It was unusual for women to go on campaign in the Renaissance. English regulations prohibited the presence of any women in the camp and this extended to soldiers' wives. This situation explains Cassio's concern at being seen with Bianca in public. When Cassio appeals to Desdemona to recover his position, at Iago's suggestion, he ignores the military protocol and this has grave consequences for the central characters.

Detail of the statue of Gattamelata by the sculptor and painter Donatello (c. 1386–1466), in the Italian city of Padua

Act 3 Scene 3 (Part 1)

Characters

Iago
Othello
Desdemona
Cassio
Emilia

In a nutshell

Desdemona assures Cassio that she will do all she can to help him reclaim his position. When Othello and Iago enter, Cassio leaves, being too ashamed to stay. Desdemona raises the issue of Cassio's reinstatement but Othello appears unwilling to discuss the matter. After she leaves, Iago suggests that he has some great secret, relating to Cassio and Desdemona, but that he is reluctant to share it. After warning Othello against jealousy, Iago finally reveals his suspicion that Cassio and Desdemona are having an affair, giving circumstantial evidence in support of his claim. Iago then urges Othello to delay reinstating Cassio in order to observe the extent to which Desdemona appeals on Cassio's behalf.

Before you read

- Note the subtlety with which Iago raises the issue of Desdemona's infidelity. He has already engineered a situation in which Othello glimpses Cassio sneaking away from a secretive meeting with Desdemona. Then Iago asks questions about Desdemona and Cassio's history and relationship, suggesting that he has a dark thought that he is unwilling to share. After refusing to reveal his thought, he then talks of the importance of 'good name in man or woman', before warning Othello to beware of jealousy. All this occurs before he specifically warns Othello to observe his wife's behaviour more closely. Iago masterfully withholds information, hints at things and speaks indirectly in general terms, leaving Othello's imagination to fill in the gaps.

- It is highly ironic that, in his conversation with Othello, Iago says: 'Men should be what they seem'. Take note of Iago's masterful use of deception in this scene.

- Notice how details that could be cited to prove Desdemona's love (the boundaries she has crossed and what she has given up to marry Othello) are here cited as proof that she is 'unnatural' and 'deceptive'.

Bounteous:	Generous
Shrift:	Confession
Discretion:	Sound judgement or good sense
Suitor:	Someone making a request
Languishes:	Wastes time or suffers
Hence:	From here
Prithee:	Used to introduce a request (short for 'I pray thee')
Sooth:	True; truly
Boon:	A request or petition
Aught:	Anything

Act 3 Scene 3 (Part 1)   The garden of the castle.

[DESDEMONA, CASSIO and EMILIA enter]

DESDEMONA	Be thou assured, good Cassio, I will do
	All my abilities in thy behalf.
EMILIA	Good madam, do. I warrant it grieves my husband,
	As if the case were his.
DESDEMONA	O, that's an honest fellow. Do not doubt, Cassio,

5

But I will have my lord and you again
As friendly as you were.

CASSIO   Bounteous madam,
Whatever shall become of Michael Cassio,
He's never any thing but your true servant.

DESDEMONA   I know't; I thank you. You do love my lord;   10
You have known him long, and be you well assured
He shall in strangeness stand no further off
Than in a politic distance.

CASSIO   Ay, but, lady,
That policy may either last so long,
Or feed upon such nice and waterish diet,   15
Or breed itself so out of circumstance,
That, I being absent and my place supplied,
My General will forget my love and service.

DESDEMONA   Do not doubt that; before Emilia here
I give thee warrant of thy place. Assure thee,   20
If I do vow a friendship, I'll perform it
To the last article. My lord shall never rest;
I'll watch him tame and talk him out of patience;
His bed shall seem a school, his board a shrift;
I'll intermingle everything he does   25
With Cassio's suit. Therefore be merry, Cassio,
For thy solicitor shall rather die
Than give thy cause away.

EMILIA   Madam, here comes my lord.

CASSIO   Madam, I'll take my leave.   30

DESDEMONA   Why, stay, and hear me speak.

CASSIO   Madam, not now: I am very ill at ease,
Unfit for mine own purposes.

DESDEMONA   Well, do your discretion.

[CASSIO exits; OTHELLO and IAGO enter]

IAGO   Ha! I like not that.   35

OTHELLO   What dost thou say?

IAGO   Nothing, my lord; or if – I know not what.

OTHELLO   Was not that Cassio parted from my wife?

IAGO	Cassio, my lord? No, sure, I cannot think it,	
	That he would steal away so guilty-like,	40
	Seeing you coming.	
OTHELLO	I do believe 'twas he.	
DESDEMONA	How now, my lord!	
	I have been talking with a suitor here,	
	A man that languishes in your displeasure.	
OTHELLO	Who is't you mean?	45
DESDEMONA	Why, your Lieutenant, Cassio. Good my lord,	
	If I have any grace or power to move you,	
	His present reconciliation take,	
	For if he be not one that truly loves you,	
	That errs in ignorance and not in cunning,	50
	I have no judgement in an honest face.	
	I prithee, call him back.	
OTHELLO	Went he hence now?	
DESDEMONA	Yes, faith; so humbled	
	That he hath left part of his grief with me,	
	To suffer with him. Good love, call him back.	55
OTHELLO	Not now, sweet Desdemona; some other time.	
DESDEMONA	But shall't be shortly?	
OTHELLO	The sooner, sweet, for you.	
DESDEMONA	Shall't be tonight at supper?	
OTHELLO	No, not tonight.	
DESDEMONA	Tomorrow dinner, then?	
OTHELLO	I shall not dine at home;	
	I meet the captains at the citadel.	60
DESDEMONA	Why then, tomorrow night, on Tuesday morn,	
	On Tuesday noon or night, on Wednesday morn.	
	I prithee, name the time, but let it not	
	Exceed three days. In faith, he's penitent,	
	And yet his trespass, in our common reason	65
	(Save that, they say, the wars must make examples	
	Out of their best) is not almost a fault	
	To incur a private check. When shall he come?	
	Tell me, Othello: I wonder in my soul,	
	What you would ask me, that I should deny,	70
	Or stand so mammering on. What? Michael Cassio,	
	That came a-wooing with you, and so many a time,	
	When I have spoke of you dispraisingly,	
	Hath ta'en your part; to have so much to do	
	To bring him in? By'r Lady, I could do much –	75
OTHELLO	Prithee, no more. Let him come when he will;	
	I will deny thee nothing.	

DESDEMONA	Why, this is not a boon;
	'Tis as I should entreat you wear your gloves,
	Or feed on nourishing dishes, or keep you warm,
	Or sue to you to do a peculiar profit 80
	To your own person. Nay, when I have a suit
	Wherein I mean to touch your love indeed,
	It shall be full of poise and difficult weight
	And fearful to be granted.
OTHELLO	I will deny thee nothing;
	Whereon, I do beseech thee, grant me this: 85
	To leave me but a little to myself.
DESDEMONA	Shall I deny you? No; farewell, my lord.
OTHELLO	Farewell, my Desdemona; I'll come to thee straight.
DESDEMONA	Emilia, come – Be as your fancies teach you;
	Whate'er you be, I am obedient. 90

[DESDEMONA and EMILIA exit]

OTHELLO	Excellent wretch! Perdition catch my soul,
	But I do love thee! And when I love thee not,
	Chaos is come again.
IAGO	My noble lord –
OTHELLO	What dost thou say, Iago?
IAGO	Did Michael Cassio, when you wooed my lady, 95
	Know of your love?
OTHELLO	He did, from first to last. Why dost thou ask?
IAGO	But for a satisfaction of my thought;
	No further harm.
OTHELLO	Why of thy thought, Iago?
IAGO	I did not think he had been acquainted with her. 100
OTHELLO	O, yes, and went between us very oft.
IAGO	Indeed!
OTHELLO	Indeed? Ay, indeed! Discern'st thou aught in that?
	Is he not honest?
IAGO	Honest, my lord? 105
OTHELLO	Honest? Ay, honest!
IAGO	My lord, for aught I know.
OTHELLO	What dost thou think?
IAGO	Think, my lord?
OTHELLO	'Think, my lord?' By heaven, he echoes me,
	As if there were some monster in his thought 110
	Too hideous to be shown. Thou dost mean something;
	I heard thee say even now, thou likedst not that,
	When Cassio left my wife. What didst not like?
	And when I told thee he was of my counsel
	In my whole course of wooing, thou criedst, 'Indeed!' 115

	And didst contract and purse thy brow together,	
	As if thou then hadst shut up in thy brain	
	Some horrible conceit. If thou dost love me,	
	Show me thy thought.	
IAGO	My lord, you know I love you.	120
OTHELLO	I think thou dost;	
	And, for I know thou'rt full of love and honesty,	
	And weigh'st thy words before thou givest them breath,	
	Therefore these stops of thine fright me the more;	
	For such things in a false disloyal knave	
	Are tricks of custom, but in a man that's just	125
	They are close delations, working from the heart	
	That passion cannot rule.	
IAGO	For Michael Cassio,	
	I dare be sworn I think that he is honest.	
OTHELLO	I think so too.	
IAGO	Men should be what they seem,	
	Or those that be not, would they might seem none!	130
OTHELLO	Certain, men should be what they seem.	
IAGO	Why, then, I think Cassio's an honest man.	
OTHELLO	Nay, yet there's more in this:	
	I prithee, speak to me as to thy thinkings,	
	As thou dost ruminate, and give thy worst of thoughts	135
	The worst of words.	
IAGO	Good my lord, pardon me:	
	Though I am bound to every act of duty,	
	I am not bound to that all slaves are free to.	
	Utter my thoughts? Why, say they are vile and false,	
	As where's that palace whereinto foul things	140
	Sometimes intrude not? Who has a breast so pure,	
	But some uncleanly apprehensions	
	Keep leets and law-days and in session sit	
	With meditations lawful?	
OTHELLO	Thou dost conspire against thy friend, Iago,	145
	If thou but think'st him wronged and mak'st his ear	
	A stranger to thy thoughts.	
IAGO	I do beseech you,	
	Though I perchance am vicious in my guess	
	(As I confess it is my nature's plague	
	To spy into abuses, and oft my jealousy	150
	Shapes faults that are not), that your wisdom yet,	
	From one that so imperfectly conceits,	
	Would take no notice, nor build yourself a trouble	
	Out of his scattering and unsure observance.	
	It were not for your quiet nor your good,	155

	Nor for my manhood, honesty, or wisdom,	
	To let you know my thoughts.	
OTHELLO	What dost thou mean?	
IAGO	Good name in man and woman, dear my lord,	
	Is the immediate jewel of their souls;	
	Who steals my purse steals trash; 'tis something, nothing;	160
	'Twas mine, 'tis his, and has been slave to thousands;	
	But he that filches from me my good name	
	Robs me of that which not enriches him	
	And makes me poor indeed.	
OTHELLO	By heaven, I'll know thy thoughts.	165
IAGO	You cannot, if my heart were in your hand,	
	Nor shall not, whilst 'tis in my custody.	
OTHELLO	Ha!	
IAGO	O, beware, my lord, of jealousy!	
	It is the green-eyed monster which doth mock	
	The meat it feeds on. That cuckold lives in bliss	170
	Who, certain of his fate, loves not his wronger;	
	But, O, what damnèd minutes tells he o'er	
	Who dotes, yet doubts, suspects, yet strongly loves!	
OTHELLO	O misery!	
IAGO	Poor and content is rich and rich enough,	175
	But riches fineless is as poor as winter	
	To him that ever fears he shall be poor.	
	Good God, the souls of all my tribe defend	
	From jealousy!	
OTHELLO	Why, why is this?	
	Think'st thou I'd make a life of jealousy,	180
	To follow still the changes of the moon	
	With fresh suspicions? No; to be once in doubt	
	Is once to be resolved. Exchange me for a goat,	
	When I shall turn the business of my soul	
	To such exsufflicate and blown surmises,	185
	Matching thy inference. 'Tis not to make me jealous	
	To say my wife is fair, feeds well, loves company,	
	Is free of speech, sings, plays and dances well;	
	Where virtue is, these are more virtuous.	
	Nor from mine own weak merits will I draw	190
	The smallest fear or doubt of her revolt,	
	For she had eyes, and chose me. No, Iago,	
	I'll see before I doubt; when I doubt, prove;	
	And on the proof, there is no more but this:	
	Away at once with love or jealousy!	195
IAGO	I am glad of this, for now I shall have reason	
	To show the love and duty that I bear you	

	With franker spirit; therefore, as I am bound,	
	Receive it from me. I speak not yet of proof.	
	Look to your wife; observe her well with Cassio;	200
	Wear your eyes thus, not jealous nor secure.	
	I would not have your free and noble nature,	
	Out of self-bounty, be abused. Look to't:	
	I know our country disposition well;	
	In Venice they do let heaven see the pranks	205
	They dare not show their husbands; their best conscience	
	Is not to leave't undone, but keep't unknown.	
OTHELLO	Dost thou say so?	
IAGO	She did deceive her father, marrying you;	
	And when she seemed to shake and fear your looks,	210
	She loved them most.	
OTHELLO	And so she did.	
IAGO	Why, go to then;	
	She that, so young, could give out such a seeming	
	To seal her father's eyes up close as oak	
	He thought 'twas witchcraft – But I am much to blame.	
	I humbly do beseech you of your pardon	215
	For too much loving you.	
OTHELLO	I am bound to thee for ever.	
IAGO	I see this hath a little dashed your spirits.	
OTHELLO	Not a jot, not a jot.	
IAGO	I' faith, I fear it has.	
	I hope you will consider what is spoke	220
	Comes from my love. But I do see you're moved;	
	I am to pray you not to strain my speech	
	To grosser issues nor to larger reach	
	Than to suspicion.	
OTHELLO	I will not.	
IAGO	Should you do so, my lord,	225
	My speech should fall into such vile success	
	As my thoughts aim not at. Cassio's my worthy friend –	
	My lord, I see you're moved.	
OTHELLO	No, not much moved;	
	I do not think but Desdemona's honest.	
IAGO	Long live she so! And long live you to think so!	230
OTHELLO	And yet, how nature erring from itself –	
IAGO	Ay, there's the point! As to be bold with you,	
	Not to affect many proposèd matches	
	Of her own clime, complexion, and degree,	
	Whereto we see in all things nature tends –	235
	Foh! One may smell in such a will most rank,	
	Foul disproportion thoughts unnatural.	

But pardon me; I do not in position
Distinctly speak of her; though I may fear
Her will, recoiling to her better judgement,   240
May fall to match you with her country forms
And happily repent.

OTHELLO   Farewell, farewell.
If more thou dost perceive, let me know more;
Set on thy wife to observe. Leave me, Iago.

IAGO   *[Going]* My lord, I take my leave.   245

OTHELLO   Why did I marry? This honest creature doubtless
Sees and knows more, much more, than he unfolds.

IAGO   *[Returning]* My lord, I would I might entreat your honour
To scan this thing no further; leave it to time:
Although 'tis fit that Cassio have his place,   250
For sure, he fills it up with great ability,
Yet, if you please to hold him off awhile,
You shall by that perceive him and his means.
Note, if your lady strain his entertainment
With any strong or vehement importunity,   255
Much will be seen in that. In the mean time,
Let me be thought too busy in my fears,
As worthy cause I have to fear I am,
And hold her free, I do beseech your honour.

OTHELLO   Fear not my government.   260

IAGO   I once more take my leave.

[IAGO exits]

Text notes

14–18   **That policy may either … forget my love and service:** Cassio is concerned that
Othello's strategy ('policy') of remaining aloof or appearing detached (stand-offish) will last
so long that their friendship will weaken to the point that it cannot be sustained. Here 'nice'
and 'waterish' mean something like fussy and diluted, perhaps in the same way that adding
water to soup makes it lose its strength or flavour.

27   **Solicitor:** An advocate or go-between. Desdemona will plead on Cassio's behalf.

64–68   **In faith, he's penitent … incur a private check:** Desdemona insists that Cassio is truly
sorry, arguing that if it were not a time of war, it would hardly rate as a private matter
worth worrying about, let alone be deserving of a public reprimand ('check').

71   **Or stand so mammering on:** Stammering or hesitating, stopping and starting in his
conversation.

75   **By'r Lady:** A mild oath, swearing by the Virgin Mary, or 'By Our Lady'.

89–90   **Be as your fancies … I am obedient:** 'Fancies' = desires or perhaps imaginations.
Desdemona leaves Othello to his thoughts, and promises her obedience.

91–92   **Excellent wretch … But I do love thee:** Here, 'wretch' could be interpreted as romantic
teasing, almost a tender term of endearment. 'Perdition, catch my soul' is a mild oath,
similar to 'I'll be damned' or 'Damn it!'

118 **Conceit:** Thought, idea or imagination.

125–27 **But in a man that's ... passion cannot rule:** Your pauses, coming from someone so honest and trustworthy, are like accusations ('delations'), or perhaps like a writer who deliberately holds back the details of a story, causing impatience ('passion') in a reader.

135 **Ruminate:** Ponder or thoughtfully consider, like a cow chewing its cud.

139–41 **Why, say they are vile ... intrude not:** Iago claims that his thoughts (which he is pretending that he does not want to share) might be dirty, in the same way that even a royal palace can contain dirt.

141–44 **Who has a breast so pure ... meditations lawful:** 'Leets' are courts for private matters, thus Iago suggests that even the purest person's heart (which would be as honest as a court session) contains impure thoughts or 'unclean apprehensions'.

148 **Perchance:** Perhaps or possibly.

152 **Imperfectly conceits:** Wrongly judges.

162 **Filches:** Steals.

170 **Cuckold:** A man whose wife has been unfaithful.

173 **Dotes:** Loves obsessively; becomes infatuated with someone, thus clouding a person's judgement and causing foolish behaviour.

175–77 **Poor and content is rich ... fears he shall be poor:** Iago ironically argues that to be poor and content is to be truly rich, but to have infinite wealth ('riches fineless') is as poor or lifeless as winter to the person who is worried about losing his money.

181–83 **To follow still the changes ... once to be resolved:** Othello does not want to be continually ('still') jealous or suspicious, month after month ('changes of the moon'), as once doubt begins, it will once and for all control his thoughts and actions, or what he 'resolves' to do.

183–86 **Exchange me for a goat ... Matching thy inference:** Othello claims he might as well be traded in for a goat if he starts living according to inflated ('exsufflicate') and exaggerated ('blown') thoughts.

198 **Franker spirit:** An honest and open attitude.

204 **I know our country disposition well:** I know how we think and act in our country (Venice).

219 **Not a jot:** A 'jot' is another name for the smallest letter of the Greek alphabet, iota (i); thus 'not a jot' carries with it the idea of not even the smallest amount or degree.

233–35 **Not to affect ... all things nature tends:** Iago observes that people naturally tend to marry those of their own country ('clime'), colour ('complexion') and social class ('degree').

239–42 **Though I may fear ... And happily repent:** Iago suggests to Othello that Desdemona's sexual desire ('will') might lead her astray from rational thought ('better judgement'), and now she wishes she had married someone from her own race instead of Othello.

254–56 **Note, if your lady strain ... will be seen in that:** Take note of Desdemona, to see if she pleads a little too passionately for Cassio's case; this will reveal a great deal about Desdemona's feelings for Cassio.

Questions

1   How might Desdemona's claim in lines 22–26 ('My Lord shall never rest', etc.) make the audience uneasy? Of what dramatic device is this an example?

2   Cassio is particularly polite and charming when talking to Desdemona. Write down some words that exhibit these aspects of his character?

3   How does Iago use Cassio's embarrassment to his advantage?

4   Do you think Desdemona says too much about Cassio (or labours the point) in this scene? What seems to be Shakespeare's dramatic purpose here?

5   Identify the speakers of the following statements from this scene. How do they have a greater resonance (or further meaning) when read in the context of the rest of the play?

Statement	Speaker	Importance in the context of the rest of the play?
Whate'er you be, I am obedient (line 90).		
And when I love thee not, / Chaos is come again (lines 92–93).		

6   What reasons does Othello have to think Iago is caring and concerned? Use evidence from their dialogue.

7   What general details does Iago use to furnish his argument for Desdemona's infidelity?

8   Why does Iago advise Othello not to reinstate Cassio immediately?

9   What is Iago's strategy in saying that Cassio 'fills' his position 'up with great ability' (line 253)? What dramatic device is Shakespeare employing here?

Extend

1   Desdemona reassures Cassio: 'I give thee warrant of thy place' (line 20).

   a   To what extent is she promising something beyond her authority?

   b   Do you think this statement supports Iago's claim that 'our General's wife is now the General'?

2   Iago claims that a 'good name in man and woman … is the immediate jewel of their souls'. Is this contradicting what he said to Cassio in his speech on 'reputation' (Act 2 Scene 3, lines 241–51)? Explain the irony of what Iago says here.

3   Write a short paragraph, analysing how Iago is guarded or tactically cautious in raising the possibility of Desdemona's infidelity (unfaithfulness) with Othello. Identify and explain at least three tactics he employs.

4   When Othello states that he believes Desdemona to be honest, Iago replies (line 230), 'Long live she so! And long live you to think so!' How might this answer cause Othello to become suspicious?

5   Why do you think Iago says, 'But pardon me; I do not in position / Distinctly speak of her' (lines 238–39)? Give two possible explanations.

Discuss **1** Many critics have suggested that Othello is too easily persuaded in this exchange. What is your opinion? Raise and consider evidence both for and against this view.

2 If you were directing this scene, what would you have Othello <u>do</u> whilst listening to Iago's manipulative suggestions? Consider his facial expressions, posture, positioning, movement, and so on.

Press PLAY **Oliver Parker: DVD Chapter 11 ('Beware the green-eyed monster')**

Copy and complete the following table to show your understanding of specific cinematic and dramatic devices that Parker uses to present Iago 'pouring the pestilence of jealousy' into Othello's ear.

Cinematic / dramatic device	How is this device used to show Iago 'pouring … jealousy' into Othello's ear?	How else might Parker have portrayed this?
Iago's whispered voice		
Projections of Othello's imagination		
Intense music		
Extreme close-ups		
Blurry focus		

A word about hyperbole (hy-*per*-bo-lee)

Hyperbole involves using a deliberately exaggerated statement to emphasise a point. It is a figure of speech that your parents have used on you <u>billions</u> of times and is not to be taken literally. Imagine something dreadful happens, so you scream, 'It's the end of the world!' It is not *literally* the end of the world but we know what you mean: you are deliberately exaggerating to let us know you are upset.

In the following scene, Iago works Othello up into a wild fit of jealousy, causing him to imagine that his 'fair Desdemona', whom he has only recently married, is having an affair with Cassio. Shakespeare shows the extent of Othello's jealous rage in the exaggerated language he uses. For instance, he explodes in numerous emotional outbursts: 'Death and damnation! O!' and 'I'll tear her all to pieces' are a couple of simple examples from this scene.

Q In your note book, copy the following excerpt from Act 3 Scene 3 (lines 372–77):

> OTHELLO If thou dost slander her and torture me,
> Never pray more; abandon all remorse;
> On horror's head horrors accumulate;
> Do deeds to make heaven weep, all earth amazed,
> For nothing canst thou to damnation add
> Greater than that.

  a Underline examples of hyperbole that Othello uses in these lines.

  b What does Othello mean when he says, 'all earth amazed, / For nothing canst thou to damnation add / Greater than that'?

Q One particular use of hyperbole by Othello occurs later in the scene (line 446):
'O, that the slave had forty thousand lives'.

  a Which part of this quote is deliberately exaggerated?

  b What point is Othello emphasising about Desdemona in using this hyperbole?

Act 3 Scene 3 (Part 2)

Characters

Othello
Iago
Emilia
Desdemona

In a nutshell

Left alone, Othello reflects on his situation. He begins thinking that, if Desdemona's unfaithfulness is proven, he will leave her, but his thoughts quickly turn to hatred. When Desdemona enters to accompany him to dinner, he tells her he has a headache. Desdemona uses her handkerchief as a pressure-bandage for Othello but he lets it drop to the ground as the couple exit. Emilia picks up the handkerchief, which Iago immediately takes from her. When Emilia exits, Iago concocts a plan to plant the handkerchief in Cassio's lodgings. Othello enters, clearly disturbed, and after making it clear he had rather not known about Desdemona's unfaithfulness, grabs Iago and challenges him to prove Desdemona's infidelity. Iago invents a story of hearing Cassio talking in his sleep about his affair with Desdemona and of having seen Cassio with Desdemona's handkerchief. These stories enrage Othello and the scene ends with Iago and Othello swearing revenge and with Othello making Iago his new Lieutenant.

Before you read

- A cuckold is a man whose wife has committed adultery (cheated on him). Being a cuckold (noun) or being cuckolded (verb) was the fear of every man in Shakespeare's day. In popular culture, cuckolds were portrayed with horns growing from their forehead, which could be seen by everyone except the cuckold. Many critics have speculated that Shakespeare is making a dark little joke when Othello complains about a headache. Could this be the cuckold's horns beginning to grow? Certainly when Othello talks about the 'forked plague' he is referring to the cuckold's horns.

- Although the handkerchief is definitely lost in this scene, the original texts offer no stage directions in this regard. Since then, various editions have added a stage direction that apportions blame to either Desdemona (e.g. 'She lets it drop') or Othello (e.g. 'It drops'). Performances of the play have offered a number of different interpretations of this important detail. Whichever interpretation you choose, Desdemona loses the handkerchief in an act of kindness, trying to relieve Othello's headache. This brings a poignancy to Iago's claim that out of Desdemona's 'goodness' he will 'make the net that shall enmesh them all'.

- Many critics have pointed out that the revenge-pact, which ends this scene with Iago and Othello kneeling down and making vows, is a parody of a wedding ceremony.

Chide:	Criticise
Negligence:	Neglect or carelessness
Filch:	Steal
Import:	Of importance
Trifle:	Unimportant thing
Avaunt:	Be gone
Remorse:	Strong feelings of regret and repentance
Imputation:	Reputation, prestige
Lewd:	Rude
Minx:	A bold, flirtatious girl

Act 3 Scene 3 (Part 2)   The garden of the castle.

OTHELLO	This fellow's of exceeding honesty,	
	And knows all qualities with a learnèd spirit	
	Of human dealings. If I do prove her haggard,	
	Though that her jesses were my dear heartstrings,	265
	I'd whistle her off and let her down the wind,	
	To pray at fortune. Haply, for I am black,	
	And have not those soft parts of conversation	
	That chamberers have, or for I am declined	
	Into the vale of years – yet that's not much –	270
	She's gone. I am abused, and my relief	
	Must be to loathe her. O curse of marriage,	
	That we can call these delicate creatures ours,	
	And not their appetites! I had rather be a toad,	

	And live upon the vapour of a dungeon,	275
	Than keep a corner in the thing I love	
	For others' uses. Yet, 'tis the plague of great ones:	
	Prerogatived are they less than the base;	
	'Tis destiny unshunnable, like death.	
	Even then this forkèd plague is fated to us	280
	When we do quicken.	

[DESDEMONA and EMILIA re-enter]

	Look where she comes!	
	If she be false, O, then heaven mocks itself!	
	I'll not believe't.	
DESDEMONA	How now, my dear Othello!	
	Your dinner, and the generous islanders	
	By you invited, do attend your presence.	285
OTHELLO	I am to blame.	
DESDEMONA	Why do you speak so faintly?	
	Are you not well?	
OTHELLO	I have a pain upon my forehead here.	
DESDEMONA	'Faith, that's with watching; 'twill away again.	
	Let me but bind it hard, within this hour	290
	It will be well.	
OTHELLO	Your napkin is too little.	

[He removes her handkerchief from his head, and it drops unnoticed to the ground]

| | Let it alone. Come, I'll go in with you. | |
| DESDEMONA | I am very sorry that you are not well. | |

[OTHELLO and DESDEMONA exit]

EMILIA	I am glad I have found this napkin:	
	This was her first remembrance from the Moor.	295
	My wayward husband hath a hundred times	
	Wooed me to steal it; but she so loves the token,	
	For he conjured her she should ever keep it,	
	That she reserves it evermore about her	
	To kiss and talk to. I'll have the work ta'en out,	300
	And give't Iago: what he will do with it	
	Heaven knows, not I;	
	I nothing but to please his fantasy.	

[IAGO re-enters]

IAGO	How now! What do you here alone?	
EMILIA	Do not you chide; I have a thing for you.	305
IAGO	A thing for me? It is a common thing –	
EMILIA	Ha!	
IAGO	To have a foolish wife.	
EMILIA	O, is that all? What will you give me now	

	For that same handkerchief?	
IAGO	What handkerchief?	310
EMILIA	What handkerchief?	
	Why, that the Moor first gave to Desdemona,	
	That which so often you did bid me steal.	
IAGO	Hast stol'n it from her?	
EMILIA	No, 'faith; she let it drop by negligence,	315
	And, to the advantage, I, being here, took't up.	
	Look, here it is.	
IAGO	A good wench; give it me.	
EMILIA	What will you do with't, that you have been so earnest	
	To have me filch it?	
IAGO	[Snatches it] Why, what's that to you?	
EMILIA	If it be not for some purpose of import,	320
	Give't me again. Poor lady, she'll run mad	
	When she shall lack it.	
IAGO	Be not acknown on't; I have use for it.	
	Go, leave me.	

[EMILIA exits]

	I will in Cassio's lodging lose this napkin,	325
	And let him find it. Trifles light as air	
	Are to the jealous confirmations strong	
	As proofs of holy writ. This may do something.	
	The Moor already changes with my poison;	
	Dangerous conceits are, in their natures, poisons,	330
	Which at the first are scarce found to distaste,	
	But with a little act upon the blood	
	Burn like the mines of Sulphur. I did say so.	
	Look, where he comes!	

[OTHELLO re-enters]

	Not poppy, nor mandragora,	
	Nor all the drowsy syrups of the world,	335
	Shall ever medicine thee to that sweet sleep	
	Which thou owedst yesterday.	
OTHELLO	Ha! Ha! False to me?	
IAGO	Why, how now, General? No more of that.	
OTHELLO	Avaunt! Be gone! Thou hast set me on the rack.	
	I swear 'tis better to be much abused	340
	Than but to know't a little.	
IAGO	How now, my lord?	
OTHELLO	What sense had I of her stol'n hours of lust?	
	I saw't not, thought it not, it harmed not me;	
	I slept the next night well, fed well, was free and merry;	
	I found not Cassio's kisses on her lips.	345

	He that is robbed, not wanting what is stol'n,	
	Let him not know't, and he's not robbed at all.	
IAGO	I am sorry to hear this.	
OTHELLO	I had been happy, if the General camp,	
	Pioners and all, had tasted her sweet body,	350
	So I had nothing known. O, now, for ever	
	Farewell the tranquil mind! Farewell content!	
	Farewell the plumèd troop, and the big wars,	
	That make ambition virtue! O, farewell!	
	Farewell the neighing steed, and the shrill trump,	355
	The spirit-stirring drum, the ear-piercing fife,	
	The royal banner, and all quality,	
	Pride, pomp and circumstance of glorious war!	
	And, O you mortal engines, whose rude throats	
	The immortal Jove's dread clamours counterfeit,	360
	Farewell! Othello's occupation's gone!	
IAGO	Is't possible, my lord?	
OTHELLO	*[Grabs IAGO by the throat]* Villain, be sure thou prove my love a whore!	
	Be sure of it; give me the ocular proof,	
	Or by the worth of man's eternal soul,	365
	Thou hadst been better have been born a dog	
	Than answer my waked wrath!	
IAGO	Is't come to this?	
OTHELLO	Make me to see't; or, at the least, so prove it,	
	That the probation bear no hinge nor loop	
	To hang a doubt on; or woe upon thy life!	370
IAGO	My noble lord –	
OTHELLO	If thou dost slander her and torture me,	
	Never pray more; abandon all remorse;	
	On horror's head horrors accumulate;	
	Do deeds to make heaven weep, all earth amazed,	375
	For nothing canst thou to damnation add	
	Greater than that.	
IAGO	O grace! O heaven forgive me!	
	Are you a man? Have you a soul or sense?	
	God be wi' you; take mine office. O wretched fool,	
	That livest to make thine honesty a vice!	380
	O monstrous world! Take note, take note, O world,	
	To be direct and honest is not safe.	
	I thank you for this profit, and from hence	
	I'll love no friend, sith love breeds such offence.	
OTHELLO	Nay, stay; thou shouldst be honest.	385
IAGO	I should be wise, for honesty's a fool	
	And loses that it works for.	
OTHELLO	By the world,	

	I think my wife be honest and think she is not;	
	I think that thou art just and think thou art not.	
	I'll have some proof. Her name, that was as fresh	390
	As Dian's visage, is now begrimed and black	
	As mine own face. If there be cords, or knives,	
	Poison, or fire, or suffocating streams,	
	I'll not endure it. Would I were satisfied!	
IAGO	I see, sir, you are eaten up with passion;	395
	I do repent me that I put it to you.	
	You would be satisfied?	
OTHELLO	Would? Nay, I will.	
IAGO	And may, but how? How satisfied, my lord?	
	Would you, the supervisor, grossly gape on?	
	Behold her topped?	
OTHELLO	Death and damnation! O!	400
IAGO	It were a tedious difficulty, I think,	
	To bring them to that prospect. Damn them then,	
	If ever mortal eyes do see them bolster	
	More than their own! What then? How then?	
	What shall I say? Where's satisfaction?	405
	It is impossible you should see this,	
	Were they as prime as goats, as hot as monkeys,	
	As salt as wolves in pride, and fools as gross	
	As ignorance made drunk. But yet, I say,	
	If imputation and strong circumstances,	410
	Which lead directly to the door of truth,	
	Will give you satisfaction, you may have't.	
OTHELLO	Give me a living reason she's disloyal.	
IAGO	I do not like the office;	
	But, sith I am entered in this cause so far,	415
	Pricked to't by foolish honesty and love,	
	I will go on. I lay with Cassio lately,	
	And, being troubled with a raging tooth,	
	I could not sleep.	
	There are a kind of men so loose of soul,	420
	That in their sleeps will mutter their affairs:	
	One of this kind is Cassio.	
	In sleep I heard him say, 'Sweet Desdemona,	
	Let us be wary, let us hide our loves.'	
	And then, sir, would he gripe and wring my hand,	425
	Cry, 'O sweet creature!' and then kiss me hard,	
	As if he plucked up kisses by the roots	
	That grew upon my lips; then laid his leg	
	Over my thigh, and sighed, and kissed; and then	
	Cried, 'Cursèd fate that gave thee to the Moor!'	430

OTHELLO	O monstrous! Monstrous!	
IAGO	Nay, this was but his dream.	
OTHELLO	But this denoted a foregone conclusion:	
	'Tis a shrewd doubt, though it be but a dream.	
IAGO	And this may help to thicken other proofs	
	That do demonstrate thinly.	
OTHELLO	I'll tear her all to pieces.	435
IAGO	Nay, but be wise: yet we see nothing done;	
	She may be honest yet. Tell me but this,	
	Have you not sometimes seen a handkerchief	
	Spotted with strawberries in your wife's hand?	
OTHELLO	I gave her such a one; 'twas my first gift.	440
IAGO	I know not that; but such a handkerchief –	
	I am sure it was your wife's – did I today	
	See Cassio wipe his beard with.	
OTHELLO	If it be that –	
IAGO	If it be that, or any that was hers,	
	It speaks against her with the other proofs.	445
OTHELLO	O, that the slave had forty thousand lives!	
	One is too poor, too weak for my revenge.	
	Now do I see 'tis true. Look here, Iago:	
	All my fond love thus do I blow to heaven.	
	'Tis gone.	450
	Arise, black vengeance, from thy hollow hell!	
	Yield up, O love, thy crown and hearted throne	
	To tyrannous hate! Swell, bosom, with thy fraught,	
	For 'tis of aspics' tongues!	
IAGO	Yet be content.	
OTHELLO	O, blood! Blood! Blood!	455
IAGO	Patience, I say; your mind perhaps may change.	
OTHELLO	Never, Iago. Like to the Pontic Sea,	
	Whose icy current and compulsive course	
	Ne'er feels retiring ebb, but keeps due on	
	To the Propontic and the Hellespont,	460
	Even so my bloody thoughts, with violent pace,	
	Shall ne'er look back, ne'er ebb to humble love,	
	Till that a capable and wide revenge	
	Swallow them up!	

[OTHELLO kneels]

	Now, by yond marble heaven,	
	In the due reverence of a sacred vow,	465
	I here engage my words.	
IAGO	Do not rise yet.	

[IAGO kneels next to OTHELLO]

Witness, you ever-burning lights above,
You elements that clip us round about,
Witness that here Iago doth give up
The execution of his wit, hands, heart,   470
To wronged Othello's service! Let him command,
And to obey shall be in me remorse,
What bloody business ever.

[They rise]

OTHELLO   I greet thy love,
Not with vain thanks, but with acceptance bounteous,
And will upon the instant put thee to't: 475
Within these three days let me hear thee say
That Cassio's not alive.

IAGO   My friend is dead; 'tis done at your request;
But let her live.

OTHELLO   Damn her, lewd minx! O, damn her!
Come, go with me apart; I will withdraw,   480
To furnish me with some swift means of death
For the fair devil. Now art thou my Lieutenant.

IAGO   I am your own for ever.

[Both exit]

Text notes

264–67 If I do prove her haggard … To pray at fortune: Using an extended metaphor (conceit),
Othello compares Desdemona with a wild ('haggard') hawk. 'Jesses' are leather and silk
straps that bind a hawk's legs to a leash. Comparing himself with a hawk trainer or falconer,
Othello claims that if Desdemona is unfaithful, he will order her away (like a falconer's
'whistle') downwind. 'Prey' is a pun on the word 'pray' (beg) and the predatory nature of
the hawk.

268–69 And have not those … That chamberers have: Othello claims he lacks the refined
manners of Venice's courtly gentlemen ('chamberers'), merely because he is black.

277–81 Yet 'tis the plague … we do quicken: The assumption is made here by Othello that the
upper classes are destined to be less privileged ('prerogatived') than the lower or 'base'
classes, because upper-class wives tend to be more unfaithful. The 'forkèd plague' relates to
the Jacobean practice of depicting a cuckold with horns (see **Before you read**, page 117).

300 I'll have the work ta'en out: Copy the pattern of the embroidery.

328 Proofs of holy writ: Evidence as strong and trustworthy as the sacred Scriptures.

330 Conceits: Thoughts or ideas.

333 Burn like the mines of Sulphur: Iago compares Othello's jealous thoughts with sulphur
mines, possibly suggesting that they are painful or torturous like the fires of hell.

334–37 Not poppy, nor mandragora … thou owedst yesterday: No medicinal herbs or sleeping
potion ('drowsy syrup') will be able to help Othello enjoy ('owe') sleep again.

350 Pioners: Labourers or construction workers.

355–60 **Farewell the neighing steed … Jove's dead clamours counterfeit:** Othello bids farewell to numerous things associated with war, such as his war horse ('neighing steed'), bugle ('shrill trump'), flute ('fife'), and killing machines ('mortal engines', such as cannon) that imitate Jove's thunder – Jove or Jupiter was also the god of thunder in Roman mythology.

364 **Ocular proof:** Visual proof. Othello wants to see the proof of Desdemona's faithfulness with his own eyes. (See the section 'Desdemona's handkerchief' in the box **Props as symbols in Othello** on page 179 for a more detailed explanation of this concept.)

369–70 **That the probation bear no hinge nor loop / To hang a doubt on:** Othello threatens Iago with death if Iago does not find a watertight scheme as proof or 'probation' of Desdemona's unfaithfulness ('hinge' and 'loop' relate to the term loophole).

390–92 **Her name, that was as fresh … mine own face:** In Roman mythology, Diana was the goddess associated with both the moon and chastity. Desdemona's unfaithfulness, according to Othello, has changed her name or reputation from being as white (hence pure) as the face of the full moon to being stained with dirt ('begrimed'), as black as Othello's own face.

392 **Cords:** Rope, with which to kill Desdemona.

400 **Topped:** 'Tupped' in Act 1 Scene 1 (line 89). Iago uses this word regularly in a vulgar, sexual sense.

432–33 **But this denoted … though it be but a dream:** 'Foregone conclusion' in Shakespeare's time meant something different to what it means today (inevitable), and carried with it the idea of something that had already taken place. Othello continues to doubt his wife's faithfulness and views Cassio's dream as further proof of his suspicion. It is believed that the phrase 'foregone conclusion' was invented by Shakespeare.

453–54 **Swell, bosom … 'tis of aspics' tongues:** Othello's heart ('bosom') is swelling with the load or freight ('fraught') of jealousy that Iago has delivered, like the poison of a snake ('aspic').

457–64 **Like to the Pontic Sea … Swallow them up!** Just as the Black Sea ('Pontic Sea') inevitably flows with strong, unstoppable currents into the Mediterranean through the Dardanelles ('Hellespont'), Othello's violent thoughts will flow into acts of revenge.

464 **By yond marble heaven:** While kneeling (see stage direction), Othello makes a vow 'by yond marble heaven'. Marble is a hard stone, one that would endure, like heaven, virtually forever.

Questions

1 Find and explain an example of dramatic irony near the beginning of Scene 3 (Part 2).

2 Read Othello's speech, beginning 'This fellow's of exceeding honesty' (see lines 262–81). What does Othello resolve to do regarding Desdemona if it is proved that she is unfaithful?

3 What comparison does Othello use to express his disgust at being cheated on by Desdemona?

4 In line 279, Othello compares the thought of being cuckolded (see **Before you read** on page 117) to death. What does this comparison tell us about Othello's character?

5 What item does Desdemona lose while trying to care for Othello?

6 What does Iago plan to do with the item mentioned in Question 5?

7 What does Othello mean when he says: 'He that is robbed, not wanting what is stol'n / Let him not know't, and he's not robbed at all' (lines 346–47)? Hint: 'wanting' means 'lacking' in this context.

8   Create and complete a table like the one below to demonstrate your understanding of the devices Shakespeare uses in lines 400–82 to show Othello's disgust and anger.

Language device	Example from lines 400–82
e.g. Short sentences	'Monstrous!' (line 431) – find another example.

9   How does Iago successfully prevent Othello from seeking advice from other people? What tactic or tactics does he employ?

10   Iago provides Othello with two further 'proofs' of Desdemona's unfaithfulness at the end of this scene. What are they?

11   What do Iago and Othello resolve to do at the end of this scene?

12   How does Othello reward Iago for his perceived loyalty at the end of this scene?

13   This scene moves at an incredible pace. What might Shakespeare be suggesting about the nature of jealousy through the pace of this scene?

Extend

1   When Emilia picks up Desdemona's handkerchief and resolves to give it to Iago, she says, 'I nothing but to please his fantasy' (line 303). What does this tell us about the couple's relationship?

2   What can we, the audience, tell about Iago and Emilia's relationship from their dialogue? List at least three points and support them with evidence.

3   What does Iago mean by the following lines: 'Trifles light as air / Are to the jealous confirmations strong / As proofs of holy writ (lines 326–28)?

4   Why does Iago use 'goats' and 'monkeys' in his descriptions of Cassio and Desdemona? What is he insinuating about Desdemona and Cassio? How does he want Othello to react?

5   When Iago tells Othello about the handkerchief, why do you think he includes the detail of Cassio wiping his beard with it (line 443)?

6   It has been said that Iago and Othello's revenge-pact is a grotesque parody of a wedding ceremony. List all the similarities you can find between their pact and a wedding ceremony. Do you think this interpretation enriches your reading of this scene in any way?

Discuss

1   How easy would it be for Othello to discover the truth? How might he do this and why do you think he does not ask more questions of people other than Iago?

2   In what different ways could the dialogue between Iago and Othello be performed?

...again at Iago's speech, lines 414–30: Note the three lines of ...mplete iambic pentameter (lines 414, 419 and 422) in this speech. ...hat dramatic purpose might be fulfilled here? Note that Iago is concocting a story *ad lib* – that is, he is improvising at this stage. What actions, gestures, etc. could he be employing during these pauses?

Press PLAY Oliver Parker: DVD Chapters 12 to 17 (jealousy and revenge)

1   How does Parker show various transformations in Othello's character, as his poisonous jealousy is aroused by Iago's machinations? Besides the actual language Othello uses (which shifts in tone and focus), consider the cinematic and dramatic devices that Parker employs, such as camera work, violent actions, interaction between characters, music and setting to name a few.

2   Parker chooses to rearrange the narrative flow, moving the action from Act 3 Scene 3 (Part 2) to later in the film. Do you find this effective?

3   Some critics say lines 464–83 are a parody of a wedding ceremony, but Parker creates a rather different tone (see Chapter 17 of the DVD). What sort of tone does he create? What cinematic and dramatic devices does he use to create such a tone? Discuss in particular the music, setting and characters' voices.

4   If you were given the role of directing lines 464–83, what might you have done differently? Discuss specific film techniques in your response, especially camera work, music and editing.

More about imagery

In our introduction to imagery (see page 33), we saw how authors create pictures in our minds simply by their choice of words. Now, in Act 3 Scenes 3 and 4, we see that the villainous Iago has been busy manufacturing his own pictures in Othello's mind, deliberately orchestrating the downward spiral of his mental state and behaviour. Othello's deterioration is effectively signalled by Shakespeare's employment of a number of powerful images and combinations of images (known as image clusters).

1 Animal images

Reinforcing the 'monstrous' nature of Iago's manipulative scheming and Othello's personal decline, Act 3 Scene 3 contains numerous references to animals: a hawk (lines 264–67), a toad (line 274), a dog (line 366), goats, monkeys and wolves (lines 406–9), snakes (line 454), and a minx (line 479).

Q In Act 1, only Iago spoke using animal imagery; now in Act 3, so does Othello. What do you think this might suggest about Othello's character at this point in the play?

2 Images associated with poison or disease

Expanding on the idea raised on page 79 (**Thinking about characters' fatal flaws**), the base emotion of jealousy that originated from Iago is now spreading like poison, and even the plague, throughout Cyprus, infecting various characters. Take note of how the words 'jealous' and 'jealousy' are repeated throughout Scenes 3 and 4. Also note which characters are jealous.

Q Read Act 3 Scene 3, lines 277–81, 329–37, 454, and Scene 4, lines 151–55. How does Shakespeare portray jealousy as a poison or disease in these lines?

3 The irony of seeing, yet not seeing

Pivotal to the conflict or tension within the play is Othello's demand for visible or 'ocular proof' of Desdemona's unfaithfulness (Act 3 Scene 3, lines 363–64). This idea will be explored in greater detail in Act 5 (see **Props as symbols in *Othello***, on page 179). For now, notice in Act 3 that Othello is desperate to 'see' what he has already imagined: Desdemona's infidelity. Frequent repetition of words associated with sight (e.g. 'see' and 'eye') is a salient feature of Othello's language in these scenes.

Q Despite the irony of Othello's obsession with 'seeing' what is not there, what is it about Iago that he ironically **cannot** see?

This aspect of irony is further reinforced throughout the play by the antithesis between the words 'honest' (or 'truth') and 'lies', each of which is often repeated in Act 3.

4 Images associated with violence

Foreshadowing the violent and tragic conclusion to the play, Othello's jealousy leads to both physical and verbal violence in Act 3.

Q How is Othello's physical violence in Scene 3, line 363 evidence of his character's transformation since we first saw him in Act 1?

Q List some of the violent images that dominate Othello's language in Act 3 (e.g. lines 392–93, 400, 435, 451–55, 479–82).

Q One particular picture of violence forms another image cluster in Scene 3, lines 457–64. How does Shakespeare compare Othello's violent thoughts with the Pontic Sea in these lines?

Like an animal possessed, Othello's poisonous jealousy blinds him to the truth and propels him on a violent path to 'black vengeance'. Whereas in Act 2 Othello was able to conquer the 'monstrous mane' of the 'desperate tempest' and defeat the Turks, he is now unable to quell the storm of his own 'bloody thoughts'. Consequently, Othello is set on a 'compulsive course' of 'tyrannous hate' towards Desdemona, ready to 'tear her all to pieces'.

Act 3 Scene 4

Characters

Othello
Desdemona
Cassio
Emilia
Bianca
Clown

In a nutshell

While looking for Cassio's lodgings, Desdemona has a brief conversation with a clown. Othello enters and demands to see the handkerchief, which he thinks Desdemona has 'lost'. As Othello becomes increasingly enraged, Desdemona pleads for Cassio to be reinstated. After Othello storms off, Iago enters with Cassio and emphasises the urgency of his suit to reclaim his position. Desdemona answers that she cannot persuade Othello at the present time, and explains that he is not himself. After Desdemona and Emilia leave, Bianca enters and complains to Cassio that she has not seen him for a week. Cassio assures her that he will see her soon, and gives her the handkerchief (which Iago planted in his lodgings) for her to make a copy of the needlework.

Before you read

- The clown Desdemona meets is simply a comic character and probably wouldn't be dressed as a clown. Shakespeare's company always had at least one comic actor to play these sorts of parts.

- This scene is rich in dramatic irony. The audience winces as Desdemona, under Othello's interrogation, says 'I pray, talk me of Cassio' and 'you'll never meet a more sufficient man'. There is similar ironic discomfort when Cassio enters and begs Desdemona to plead for him to Othello.

- Bianca is an important minor character. She is a courtesan or prostitute, a fact that explains Cassio's unease at being seen with her in front of Othello.

- For more information on clowns, see the box entitled **Shakespeare's clowns** on page 100.

Sirrah:	Similar to 'Sir' but used to address social inferiors
Humours:	Moods
Dissemble:	Deceive
Frank:	Generous; honest and up-front
Amiable:	Loving and tender
Perdition:	Destruction
Hallowed:	Regarded as holy
Veritable:	Rightly named
Beshrew:	Curse

Act 3 Scene 4   Before the castle.

[DESDEMONA, EMILIA and CLOWN enter]

DESDEMONA	Do you know, sirrah, where Lieutenant Cassio lies?	
CLOWN	I dare not say he lies anywhere.	
DESDEMONA	Why, man?	
CLOWN	He's a soldier, and for one to say a soldier lies, is stabbing.	
DESDEMONA	Go to; where lodges he?	5
CLOWN	To tell you where he lodges, is to tell you where I lie.	
DESDEMONA	Can any thing be made of this?	
CLOWN	I know not where he lodges, and for me to devise a lodging and say he lies here or he lies there, were to lie in mine own throat.	
DESDEMONA	Can you inquire him out, and be edified by report?	10
CLOWN	I will catechise the world for him; that is, make questions, and by them answer.	
DESDEMONA	Seek him; bid him come hither. Tell him I have moved my lord on his behalf, and hope all will be well.	
CLOWN	To do this is within the compass of man's wit, and therefore I will attempt the doing it.	15

[CLOWN exits]

DESDEMONA	Where should I lose that handkerchief, Emilia?	
EMILIA	I know not, madam.	
DESDEMONA	Believe me, I had rather have lost my purse	
	Full of crusadoes; and, but my noble Moor	20
	Is true of mind and made of no such baseness	
	As jealous creatures are, it were enough	
	To put him to ill thinking.	
EMILIA	Is he not jealous?	
DESDEMONA	Who, he? I think the sun where he was born	
	Drew all such humours from him.	
EMILIA	Look, where he comes.	25

[OTHELLO enters]

DESDEMONA	I will not leave him now till Cassio	
	Be called to him – How is't with you, my lord?	
OTHELLO	Well, my good lady. *[Aside]* O, hardness to dissemble! –	
	How do you, Desdemona?	
DESDEMONA	Well, my good lord.	
OTHELLO	Give me your hand. This hand is moist, my lady.	30
DESDEMONA	It yet hath felt no age nor known no sorrow.	
OTHELLO	This argues fruitfulness and liberal heart.	
	Hot, hot, and moist: this hand of yours requires	
	A sequester from liberty, fasting and prayer,	
	Much castigation, exercise devout;	35

	For here's a young and sweating devil here, That commonly rebels. 'Tis a good hand, A frank one.	
DESDEMONA	You may, indeed, say so; For 'twas that hand that gave away my heart.	
OTHELLO	A liberal hand: the hearts of old gave hands, But our new heraldry is hands, not hearts.	40
DESDEMONA	I cannot speak of this. Come now, your promise.	
OTHELLO	What promise, chuck?	
DESDEMONA	I have sent to bid Cassio come speak with you.	
OTHELLO	I have a salt and sorry rheum offends me; Lend me thy handkerchief.	45
DESDEMONA	Here, my lord.	
OTHELLO	That which I gave you.	
DESDEMONA	I have it not about me.	
OTHELLO	Not?	
DESDEMONA	No, indeed, my lord.	
OTHELLO	That is a fault.	
	That handkerchief Did an Egyptian to my mother give. She was a charmer, and could almost read The thoughts of people. She told her, while she kept it, 'Twould make her amiable and subdue my father Entirely to her love, but if she lost it Or made gift of it, my father's eye Should hold her loathèd and his spirits should hunt After new fancies. She, dying, gave it me, And bid me, when my fate would have me wive, To give it her. I did so; and (take heed on't) Make it a darling like your precious eye. To lose't or give't away were such perdition As nothing else could match.	50 55 60
DESDEMONA	Is't possible?	
OTHELLO	'Tis true; there's magic in the web of it: A sibyl, that had numbered in the world The sun to course two hundred compasses, In her prophetic fury sewed the work; The worms were hallowed that did breed the silk, And it was dyed in mummy which the skilful Conserved of maidens' hearts.	 65
DESDEMONA	Indeed! Is't true?	
OTHELLO	Most veritable; therefore, look to't well.	70
DESDEMONA	Then would to God that I had never seen't!	
OTHELLO	Ha! Wherefore?	
DESDEMONA	Why do you speak so startingly and rash?	

OTHELLO	Is't lost? Is't gone? Speak: is it out o' th' way?	
DESDEMONA	Heaven bless us!	75
OTHELLO	Say you?	
DESDEMONA	It is not lost; but what if it were?	
OTHELLO	How?	
DESDEMONA	I say, it is not lost.	
OTHELLO	Fetch't; let me see't!	
DESDEMONA	Why, so I can, sir, but I will not now.	
	This is a trick to put me from my suit.	80
	Pray you, let Cassio be received again.	
OTHELLO	Fetch me the handkerchief; my mind misgives –	
DESDEMONA	Come, come!	
	You'll never meet a more sufficient man –	
OTHELLO	The handkerchief!	
DESDEMONA	I pray, talk me of Cassio –	85
OTHELLO	The handkerchief!	
DESDEMONA	A man that all his time	
	Hath founded his good fortunes on your love,	
	Shared dangers with you –	
OTHELLO	The handkerchief!	
DESDEMONA	In sooth, you are to blame –	
OTHELLO	Away!	90

[OTHELLO exits]

EMILIA	Is not this man jealous?	
DESDEMONA	I ne'er saw this before.	
	Sure, there's some wonder in this handkerchief;	
	I am most unhappy in the loss of it.	
EMILIA	'Tis not a year or two shows us a man:	95
	They are all but stomachs, and we all but food;	
	They eat us hungerly, and when they are full,	
	They belch us. Look you, Cassio and my husband!	

[CASSIO and IAGO enter]

IAGO	There is no other way: 'tis she must do't,	
	And, lo, the happiness! Go, and importune her.	100
DESDEMONA	How now, good Cassio! What's the news with you?	
CASSIO	Madam, my former suit. I do beseech you	
	That by your virtuous means I may again	
	Exist, and be a member of his love	
	Whom I with all the office of my heart	105
	Entirely honour. I would not be delayed.	
	If my offence be of such mortal kind	
	That nor my service past, nor present sorrows,	
	Nor purposed merit in futurity,	
	Can ransom me into his love again,	110

	But to know so must be my benefit;	
	So shall I clothe me in a forced content,	
	And shut myself up in some other course,	
	To fortune's alms.	
DESDEMONA	Alas, thrice-gentle Cassio!	
	My advocation is not now in tune.	115
	My lord is not my lord, nor should I know him,	
	Were he in favour as in humour altered.	
	So help me every spirit sanctified,	
	As I have spoken for you all my best	
	And stood within the blank of his displeasure	120
	For my free speech! You must awhile be patient;	
	What I can do I will, and more I will	
	Than for myself I dare. Let that suffice you.	
IAGO	Is my lord angry?	
EMILIA	He went hence but now,	
	And certainly in strange unquietness.	125
IAGO	Can he be angry? I have seen the cannon,	
	When it hath blown his ranks into the air,	
	And, like the devil, from his very arm	
	Puffed his own brother – and can he be angry?	
	Something of moment then. I will go meet him;	130
	There's matter in't indeed, if he be angry.	
DESDEMONA	I prithee, do so. *[IAGO exits]* Something, sure, of state	
	(Either from Venice, or some unhatched practice	
	Made demonstrable here in Cyprus to him)	
	Hath puddled his clear spirit; and in such cases	135
	Men's natures wrangle with inferior things,	
	Though great ones are their object. 'Tis even so.	
	For let our finger ache, and it indues	
	Our other healthful members even to that sense	
	Of pain. Nay, we must think men are not gods,	140
	Nor of them look for such observances	
	As fit the bridal. Beshrew me much, Emilia:	
	I was, unhandsome warrior as I am,	
	Arraigning his unkindness with my soul;	
	But now I find I had suborned the witness,	145
	And he's indicted falsely.	
EMILIA	Pray heaven it be	
	State-matters, as you think, and no conception,	
	No, nor no jealous toy concerning you.	
DESDEMONA	Alas the day! I never gave him cause.	150
EMILIA	But jealous souls will not be answered so:	
	They are not ever jealous for the cause,	

	But jealous for they are jealous. 'Tis a monster	
	Begot upon itself, born on itself.	
DESDEMONA	Heaven keep that monster from Othello's mind!	155
EMILIA	Lady, amen.	
DESDEMONA	I will go seek him. Cassio, walk hereabout:	
	If I do find him fit, I'll move your suit	
	And seek to effect it to my uttermost.	
CASSIO	I humbly thank your ladyship.	160

[DESDEMONA and EMILIA exit; BIANCA enters]

BIANCA	Save you, friend Cassio!	
CASSIO	What make you from home?	
	How is it with you, my most fair Bianca?	
	I' faith, sweet love, I was coming to your house.	
BIANCA	And I was going to your lodging, Cassio.	
	What, keep a week away? Seven days and nights?	165
	Eight score eight hours? And lovers' absent hours,	
	More tedious than the dial eight score times?	
	O weary reckoning!	
CASSIO	Pardon me, Bianca:	
	I have this while with leaden thoughts been pressed;	
	But I shall, in a more continuate time,	170
	Strike off this score of absence. Sweet Bianca,	

[Giving her DESDEMONA's handkerchief]

	Take me this work out.	
BIANCA	O Cassio! Whence came this?	
	This is some token from a newer friend;	
	To the felt absence now I feel a cause.	
	Is't come to this? Well, well.	
CASSIO	Go to, woman!	175
	Throw your vile guesses in the devil's teeth,	
	From whence you have them. You are jealous now	
	That this is from some mistress, some remembrance.	
	No, in good troth, Bianca.	
BIANCA	Why, whose is it?	
CASSIO	I know not, sweet; I found it in my chamber.	180
	I like the work well; ere it be demanded	
	(As like enough it will), I'd have it copied.	
	Take it, and do't, and leave me for this time.	
BIANCA	Leave you! Wherefore?	
CASSIO	I do attend here on the General,	185
	And think it no addition, nor my wish,	
	To have him see me womaned.	
BIANCA	Why, I pray you?	
CASSIO	Not that I love you not.	

BIANCA	But that you do not love me.
	I pray you, bring me on the way a little, 190
	And say if I shall see you soon at night.
CASSIO	'Tis but a little way that I can bring you,
	For I attend here; but I'll see you soon.
BIANCA	'Tis very good; I must be circumstanced.

[BIANCA and CASSIO exit]

Text notes

10   **Be edified by report:** 'Edify' is a biblical word (e.g. Romans 14:19) meaning to strengthen or build someone up; here it implies that the Clown will be instructed ('edified') by what he finds out.

11   **Catechise the world for him:** The Clown follows on from Desdemona's biblical usage of 'edify', by claiming to 'catechise' the world. A catechism is a way of teaching doctrine by repeating a series of questions and answers.

15   **Within the compass of man's wit:** Human intelligence ('wit') falls within the bounds ('compass') of possibility. The Clown also creates a vague sexual pun, especially on the meaning of 'doing it'.

20   **Crusadoes:** Portugese gold coins with a crucifix or cross (*crux*) on them.

24–25   **I think the sun where … humours from him:** Desdemona refers to the intense African sun, which she claims figuratively has 'drawn' all jealousy from Othello's mind. In Jacobean times, 'humours' were bodily fluids that were believed to control someone's personality or temperament.

32–37   **This argues fruitfulness … That commonly rebels:** Othello claims that Desdemona's hand, being hot and sweaty, proves she is characterised by lustful appetite ('fruitfulness') and sexual desire ('liberal heart'). Therefore, he recommends she purify herself like a nun, by being separated ('sequestered'), with fasting and praying, self-punishment ('castigation') and religious discipline ('exercise devout').

41   **But our new heraldry is hands, not hearts:** A paraphrase might read: In the past, women made promises or vows with their hands (e.g. they gave their hand in marriage), but today's easy women give away their symbols of courtship ('heraldry') without their hearts.

43   **Chuck:** A term of endearment, similar to 'dear' or 'darling'.

45   **I have a salt and sorry rheum offends me:** A runny nose and sore eyes (like a head cold), or perhaps referring to Desdemona's supposed lustful character ('salt'), which 'offends' Othello.

64–69   **A sibyl, that had numbered … of maidens' hearts:** A 'sibyl' was a prophetess in ancient times. Othello reports that a 200-year-old Egyptian prophetess embroidered the handkerchief, which was made from the silk of holy silkworms and the preserved hearts of virgins or 'maidens' (the words 'mummy' and 'conserve' refer here to a substance like a jelly or jam).

99–100   **There is no other way … Go, and importune her:** Iago sees no other solution but that Desdemona must beg Othello to help Cassio, and is amazed at his supposed luck ('happiness') that Desdemona just happens to be there with Cassio.

107–11   **If my offence … so must be my benefit:** Cassio declares that if his offence is so fatal or hopeless ('mortal'), that neither his past military service nor present sorrow nor future actions can buy back ('ransom') Othello's love, then just knowing this will help him move on.

112–14   **So shall I clothe … To fortune's alms:** Cassio will force himself to be happy being rejected by Othello, and will lock himself in ('shut' himself up) in another career or destiny ('fortune'). Here, 'alms' are good deeds.

115   **My advocation is not now in tune:** Shakespeare's music imagery here has Desdemona suggesting that she is so out of tune with Othello that her powers of pleading ('advocation') would be useless.

118   **Sanctified:** Set apart to God; made holy.

123   **Suffice:** Satisfy.

129   **Puffed his own brother:** Iago recalls seeing Othello's brother obliterated ('puffed', as in disappearing in a puff of smoke) by cannon fire. Given that Othello was sold into slavery as a child, Iago is probably referring to a fellow soldier here, a brother-in-arms, rather than a literal blood relation.

131   **There's matter in't indeed, if he be angry:** Othello, unfazed by the death of someone close to him (see note for line 129), must have had something serious to contend with to make him angry like this.

136–37   **Men's natures wrangle ... are their object:** Desdemona argues that men naturally wrestle or argue ('wrangle') over minor issues, while ignoring the more important or 'great' matters.

138–42   **For let our finger ... As fit the bridal:** A paraphrase might be: A sore finger will cause ('endure') someone's other fingers to hurt in sympathy. Men aren't perfect and I cannot really expect him to be in control of himself all the time. Note that 'bridal' is perhaps a play on words here: referring to herself as a bride who is being ignored by a battle-stressed husband, or possibly the bridle that controls a horse.

144–46   **Arraigning his unkindness ... he's indicted falsely:** The imagery used by Desdemona here relates to legal matters: she claims she has unjustly taken Othello to court ('arraigned' him) and accused him of judging her; now she feels she has metaphorically bribed ('suborned') an imaginary witness to lie. This is a complicated conceit: merely note how Desdemona is willing to blame herself rather than see any fault in Othello's character.

166–67   **Eight score eight hours ... eight score times:** A 'score' is 20, thus 'eight score eight hours' is 168 hours or one week. Bianca is tired of watching the 'dial' of the clock, waiting for Cassio to return.

194   **I must be circumstanced:** Bianca reluctantly submits herself to circumstances, accepting things the way they are.

Questions

1   Why do you think Shakespeare places the comic aspects at the beginning of this scene directly after the revenge-pact of the previous scene?

2   Why is the handkerchief Desdemona has lost so important to Othello?

3   Quote a phrase from Desdemona's dialogue and explain how it would further enrage Othello or cause him to become more suspicious. Of what dramatic device is this an example?

4   What do you think Desdemona means by stating to Cassio: 'My lord is not my lord'?

5   What does Desdemona think is a possible cause of Othello's recent behaviour?

6   How does Bianca interpret Cassio's possession of the handkerchief? What common theme of the play does her conversation with Cassio reinforce?

Extend

1   The start of this scene involves punning on the word 'lie'. Why is the subject of this punning particularly appropriate?

2   Why would the audience feel a sense of foreboding at Desdemona's assertion 'I will not leave him now till Cassio / Be called to him' (lines 26–27)?

3   Beginning with Desdemona's 'Indeed! Is't true!' (see lines 69–90), Shakespeare employs a fast-paced dialogue, with single phrases being exchanged. This technique, which is called **stichomythia** (*stik-oh-mith-ya),* was developed in ancient Greek drama. What do you think Shakespeare is emphasising by employing this device?

4   Read lines 95–98 and answer the following questions:

   a   What is Emilia's view of men in general?

   b   What literary device does she employ to explain her views?

   c   Why do you think Emilia uses inclusive language ('we' and 'us') in this speech?

   d   What might it suggest about Emilia and Desdemona's relationship?

   e   Might it also suggest Emilia's thoughts on Othello's treatment of Desdemona?

5   Why do you think Shakespeare has Cassio arriving to talk to Desdemona of his 'suit' after Othello and Desdemona's argument?

6   Explain (or paraphrase) what you understand to be Emilia's view of jealousy, using evidence from this scene.

Discuss

1   Desdemona is obviously unaware of what Iago has been saying. Do you think, however, her pleading for Cassio's reinstatement in this scene is foolish or naïve in any way? Consider arguments for and against this view.

2   If you were to direct a production of this scene, how would you direct actors to play the parts of Othello and Desdemona in lines 73–90, when Othello demands to see Desdemona's handkerchief? Discuss aspects such as voice, lighting and blocking (movement and positioning on the stage).

Press
PLAY   ## Oliver Parker: DVD Chapter 14 ('The handkerchief!')

1   Othello shows a degree of aloofness, coldness or detachment towards Desdemona in this scene. What cinematic and dramatic devices does Parker use to show this aspect of Othello's behaviour? Are these devices effective? How else might he have directed this scene to achieve the same aim?

2   Tension builds in this scene when Othello demands to see Desdemona's handkerchief. How does Parker show this growing tension? Discuss aspects such as the characters' use of voice, body language, positioning and movement. How does Parker's presentation of this scene differ from your ideas in the second **Discussion** question above?

Act 4

Characters

Iago
Othello
Cassio
Bianca

In a nutshell

During their discussion of Desdemona's infidelity, Iago claims to Othello that Cassio has confessed to having an affair with her. This causes Othello to suffer an epileptic fit. Upon entering, Cassio offers assistance but Iago insists that the convulsion must take its course. After Cassio exits, Othello recovers and Iago advises him to hide himself so that he can overhear Iago's conversation with Cassio. Because Othello is some distance away, Iago is able to manipulate the situation so that Othello interprets their conversation about Bianca as concerning Desdemona. Bianca enters in a jealous rage, refusing to make a copy of the handkerchief Cassio gave her. She storms off and Cassio chases after her, to calm her down.

Before you read

- This scene presents some staging difficulties for directors. They must place Othello in hiding, in a way that the audience is convinced he can only hear the louder parts of the conversation that they are hearing between Iago and Cassio. Othello also has a few asides in this scene. These comments are for the benefit of the audience, and the other characters on stage cannot hear them.

- As mentioned earlier, Bianca is a prostitute, probably exclusively Cassio's mistress for the time he is on the island of Cyprus. Many derogatory or unflattering terms are used to describe her in this scene, including 'strumpet', 'fitchew' and 'a perfumed one'. It is interesting that Shakespeare uses a villainous character such as Iago to remind us that Bianca sells her body simply to buy herself 'bread and clothes'. This is typical of the sympathy Shakespeare shows for the poor in many of his plays, and is also characteristic of the way in which Shakespeare's analysis of society is never simplistic.

Abroad:	About the place, freely at large
Belie:	Deceive
Fulsome:	Distasteful or repulsive; lustful
Pish:	An expression of annoyance or contempt

Credulous: Gullible

Chaste: Sexually pure

Reproach: A criticism or insult

Forbear: Avoid or stop

Importune: Beg someone insistently

Prithee: Used to introduce a request (short for 'I pray thee')

Act 4 Scene 1 (Part 1)   Cyprus, before the castle.

[OTHELLO and IAGO enter]

IAGO	Will you think so?
OTHELLO	Think so, Iago!
IAGO	What,
	To kiss in private?
OTHELLO	An unauthorised kiss.
IAGO	Or to be naked with her friend in bed
	An hour or more, not meaning any harm?
OTHELLO	Naked in bed, Iago, and not mean harm! 5
	It is hypocrisy against the devil.
	They that mean virtuously, and yet do so,
	The devil their virtue tempts, and they tempt heaven.
IAGO	So they do nothing: 'tis a venial slip;
	But if I give my wife a handkerchief – 10
OTHELLO	What then?
IAGO	Why, then, 'tis hers, my lord; and, being hers,
	She may, I think, bestow't on any man.
OTHELLO	She is protectress of her honour too.
	May she give that? 15
IAGO	Her honour is an essence that's not seen;
	They have it very oft that have it not.
	But, for the handkerchief –
OTHELLO	By heaven, I would most gladly have forgot it.
	Thou said'st – O, it comes o'er my memory, 20
	As doth the raven o'er the infected house,
	Boding to all! – He had my handkerchief.
IAGO	Ay, what of that?
OTHELLO	That's not so good now.
IAGO	What
	If I had said I had seen him do you wrong?
	Or heard him say – as knaves be such abroad, 25
	Who having, by their own importunate suit,
	Or voluntary dotage of some mistress,
	Convinced or supplied them, cannot choose
	But they must blab –

OTHELLO	Hath he said anything?
IAGO	He hath, my lord; but be you well assured, 30
	No more than he'll unswear.
OTHELLO	What hath he said?
IAGO	'Faith, that he did ... I know not what he did.
OTHELLO	What? What?
IAGO	Lie ...
OTHELLO	With her?
IAGO	With her, on her; what you will.
OTHELLO	Lie with her? Lie on her? We say, 'Lie on her' when they belie her. Lie 35
	with her! 'Zounds! That's fulsome – Handkerchief! – Confessions –
	Handkerchief! – To confess, and be hanged for his labour: first, to be
	hanged, and then to confess! I tremble at it. Nature would not invest
	herself in such shadowing passion without some instruction. It is not words
	that shake me thus. Pish! Noses, ears, and lips – Is't possible? – Confess – 40
	Handkerchief! – O devil! –

[OTHELLO falls in a trance]

IAGO	Work on,
	My medicine, work! Thus credulous fools are caught,
	And many worthy and chaste dames even thus,
	All guiltless, meet reproach –

[CASSIO enters]

	What, ho! My lord! 45
	My lord, I say! Othello! – How now, Cassio!
CASSIO	What's the matter?
IAGO	My lord is fallen into an epilepsy.
	This is his second fit; he had one yesterday.
CASSIO	Rub him about the temples.
IAGO	No, forbear: 50
	The lethargy must have his quiet course;
	If not, he foams at mouth and by and by
	Breaks out to savage madness. Look he stirs.
	Do you withdraw yourself a little while;
	He will recover straight. When he is gone, 55
	I would on great occasion speak with you.

[CASSIO exits]

	How is it, General? Have you not hurt your head?
OTHELLO	Dost thou mock me?
IAGO	I mock you? No, by heaven.
	Would you would bear your fortune like a man!
OTHELLO	A hornèd man's a monster and a beast. 60
IAGO	There's many a beast then in a populous city,
	And many a civil monster.

| OTHELLO | Did he confess it? |
| IAGO | Good sir, be a man; |

Think every bearded fellow that's but yoked
May draw with you. There's millions now alive | 65
That nightly lie in those unproper beds
Which they dare swear peculiar; your case is better.
O, 'tis the spite of hell, the fiend's arch-mock,
To lip a wanton in a secure couch,
And to suppose her chaste! No, let me know; | 70
And knowing what I am, I know what she shall be.

| OTHELLO | O, thou art wise; 'tis certain. |
| IAGO | Stand you awhile apart; |

Confine yourself but in a patient list.
Whilst you were here o'erwhelmèd with your grief
(A passion most unsuiting such a man), | 75
Cassio came hither. I shifted him away,
And laid good 'scuse upon your ecstasy,
Bade him anon return and here speak with me,
The which he promised. Do but encave yourself,
And mark the fleers, the gibes, and notable scorns, | 80
That dwell in every region of his face;
For I will make him tell the tale anew,
Where, how, how oft, how long ago, and when
He hath, and is again to cope your wife.
I say, but mark his gesture. Marry, patience; | 85
Or I shall say you are all in all in spleen,
And nothing of a man.

| OTHELLO | Dost thou hear, Iago? |

I will be found most cunning in my patience;
But – dost thou hear? – most bloody.

| IAGO | That's not amiss; |

But yet keep time in all. Will you withdraw? | 90

[OTHELLO hides]

Now will I question Cassio of Bianca,
A housewife that by selling her desires
Buys herself bread and clothes; it is a creature
That dotes on Cassio; as 'tis the strumpet's plague
To beguile many and be beguiled by one; | 95
He, when he hears of her, cannot refrain
From the excess of laughter. Here he comes.

[CASSIO re-enters]

As he shall smile, Othello shall go mad,
And his unbookish jealousy must construe
Poor Cassio's smiles, gestures and light behaviour, | 100

	Quite in the wrong. How do you now, Lieutenant?	
CASSIO	The worser that you give me the addition	
	Whose want even kills me.	
IAGO	Ply Desdemona well, and you are sure on't.	
	[Speaking lower] Now, if this suit lay in Bianca's power,	105
	How quickly should you speed!	
CASSIO	Alas, poor caitiff!	
OTHELLO	Look, how he laughs already!	
IAGO	I never knew woman love man so.	
CASSIO	Alas, poor rogue! I think, i' faith, she loves me.	
OTHELLO	Now he denies it faintly, and laughs it out.	110
IAGO	Do you hear, Cassio?	
OTHELLO	Now he importunes him	
	To tell it o'er. Go to; well said, well said.	
IAGO	She gives it out that you shall marry her.	
	Do you intend it?	
CASSIO	Ha, ha, ha!	115
OTHELLO	Do you triumph, Roman? Do you triumph?	
CASSIO	I marry her! What? A customer! Prithee, bear some charity to my	
	wit; do not think it so unwholesome. Ha, ha, ha!	
OTHELLO	So, so, so, so: they laugh that win.	
IAGO	'Faith, the cry goes that you shall marry her.	120
CASSIO	Prithee, say true.	
IAGO	I am a very villain else.	
OTHELLO	Have you scored me? Well.	
CASSIO	This is the monkey's own giving out: she is persuaded I will marry	
	her, out of her own love and flattery, not out of my promise.	125
OTHELLO	Iago beckons me; now he begins the story.	
CASSIO	She was here even now; she haunts me in every place. I was the other	
	day talking on the sea-bank with certain Venetians, and thither comes	
	the bauble, and, by this hand, she falls me thus about my neck –	
OTHELLO	Crying, 'O dear Cassio!' as it were; his gesture imports it.	130
CASSIO	So hangs, and lolls, and weeps upon me; so shakes, and pulls me. Ha,	
	ha, ha!	
OTHELLO	Now he tells how she plucked him to my chamber. O, I see that nose	
	of yours, but not that dog I shall throw it to.	
CASSIO	Well, I must leave her company.	135
IAGO	Before me! Look, where she comes.	
CASSIO	'Tis such another fitchew! Marry, a perfumed one.	

[BIANCA enters]

	What do you mean by this haunting of me?	
BIANCA	Let the devil and his dam haunt you! What did you mean by that	
	same handkerchief you gave me even now? I was a fine fool to	140
	take it. I must take out the work? A likely piece of work, that you	

	should find it in your chamber, and not know who left it there! This is some minx's token, and I must take out the work? There; give it your hobby-horse! Wheresoever you had it, I'll take out no work on't.	145
CASSIO	How now, my sweet Bianca? How now? How now?	
OTHELLO	By heaven, that should be my handkerchief!	
BIANCA	An you'll come to supper tonight, you may; an you will not, come when you are next prepared for.	

[BIANCA exits]

IAGO	After her, after her!	150
CASSIO	'Faith, I must; she'll rail in the street else.	
IAGO	Will you sup there?	
CASSIO	'Faith, I intend so.	
IAGO	Well, I may chance to see you, for I would very fain speak with you.	
CASSIO	Prithee, come; will you?	155
IAGO	Go to; say no more.	

[CASSIO exits]

Text notes

9   **Venial slip:** A 'venial sin' is a minor sin, so a 'slip' suggests something more trivial.

14   **Honour:** Good name or reputation.

16–17   **Her honour is an essence … oft that have it not:** Iago points out that people often seem honourable when in reality they are not.

20–22   **O, it comes o'er my … Boding to all:** Othello describes this thought as foreboding. The raven was associated with death, thus a raven flying over a house that was subject to illness or 'infection' was considered a particularly bad sign.

25–29   **As knaves be such abroad … they must blab:** A paraphrase might read: As men sometimes talk or boast about their flirting with or pursuit of some woman (a 'knave' is a troublemaker).

60   **A hornèd man's a monster and a beast:** This is another reference to the cuckold's horns. The betrayed husband was said to grow horns that could be seen by everyone but him and, in this way, he was a beast.

61–62   **There's many a beast … a civil monster:** Iago answers Othello by claiming there are beasts (cuckolds) living in every city by Othello's definition.

64–67   **Think every bearded fellow … draw with you:** Iago alludes to the cuckold's horns, in telling Othello to think of every man that's married as 'yoked' or drawing a plough like an ox in the same way that Othello does. This plays on the idea that both oxen (who draw ploughs) and cuckolds have horns.

65–67   **There's millions now alive … your case is better:** Iago insists that millions of men are cheated on and do not know it, but that Othello's situation is better because he knows his wife has been unfaithful.

68–69   **O, 'tis the spite of hell … in a secure couch:** A paraphrase might read: The devil mocks men who kiss ('lip') a faithless woman ('wanton') in a bed that is free from suspicion.

72–73   **Stand you awhile apart … in a patient list:** Iago instructs Othello to stand out of the way and listen within the bounds of patience ('list' = a boundary or a barrier), or to hide behind a barrier in order to overhear his conversation with Cassio.

80 **And mark the fleers, the gibes:** Pay attention to the mocks ('fleers') or jeers ('gibes').

86 **You are all in all in spleen:** In a passionate fit. Jacobeans believed that passion, particularly bitterness, resided in the spleen.

95 **To beguile many and be beguiled by one:** Iago claims that many men are tricked or infatuated by a particular prostitute but that prostitute, in turn, is infatuated by a single customer: in this case, Cassio.

102–3 **The worser that you … want even kills me:** When Iago enquires how Cassio is, he addresses him as Lieutenant (line 101). Cassio replies that he is worse for the 'addition' Iago has given him by calling him Lieutenant, the title that he now lacks or 'want[s]'. He claims that the lack of the title is killing him.

106 **Caitiff:** Wretched creature.

129 **Bauble:** Toy or plaything.

137 **Fitchew:** A polecat, which is an animal noted for being extremely sexually active or promiscuous.

144 **Hobby-horse:** Prostitute (in this case another mistress).

148 **An you'll come to supper … you are next prepared for:** Basically, come tonight if you want; if not, come the next time you feel like it (here, 'an' = if).

Questions

1 Why do you think Iago uses the phrase 'not meaning any harm' (line 4)? What might his strategy be in making this sort of comment?

2 How does Iago take control of the situation when Cassio enters?

3 Summarise what Cassio says about Bianca in this scene. Whom does Othello think he is discussing? How is this an example of dramatic irony?

4 Why does Cassio find the idea that he will marry Bianca amusing?

5 Quote and explain two phrases from Cassio's speech that Othello would find particularly offensive. How is Othello's interpretation of these lines an example of dramatic irony?

6 Read line 119 in context. What do you think this quote suggests about Othello at this point in the play?

7 Why might Othello find it particularly infuriating that Cassio has given his handkerchief to Bianca?

8 Why would Iago be keen for Cassio to follow quickly after Bianca?

9 How do you think Othello in this scene presents a contrast to the Othello of Act 1? Write a short paragraph and provide examples from both scenes.

Extend &

1 Why do you think Iago uses the phrase 'I know not what he did' (line 32)? Explain his strategy in making this sort of comment.

2 Why do you think Iago describes Othello's epileptic fit as 'a passion most unsuiting such a man' (line 75), as well as stating 'Or I shall think you are all in spleen / And nothing of a man' (lines 86–87)? What is his purpose or strategy in using these phrases?

3   How does Cassio's instruction to 'rub [Othello] about the temples' (line 50), suggest his former closeness to Othello?

4   Quote an example (a phrase or a line) of a racist assumption that Iago makes in this scene.

5   When Iago advises Othello to hide, he uses phrases such as 'confine yourself' and 'encave yourself'. What do you think Shakespeare is suggesting about Othello's situation through these terms?

6   How does Othello's submission to Iago's command to hide himself away contrast to his behaviour in Act 1 Scene 2?

7   How is Cassio's language when he is talking about (and to) Bianca different from the language he uses to address Desdemona? Perhaps you might like to construct a table to illustrate your understanding of this concept.

8   In this scene, Shakespeare makes constant reference to the antithesis between man and beast, using a great deal of animal imagery to do so. How does this language device highlight the deterioration of Othello's character?

9   Using the information in the box entitled **Thinking about characters' fatal flaws** (page 79), explain how jealousy is spreading by means of deception and is leading to misunderstanding in this scene.

Discuss   How fortunate do you think Iago is that everything works to support his purposes in this scene? Is Iago taking too many risks, in your opinion?

Press
PLAY   **Oliver Parker: DVD Chapters 15–16 (Iago manipulates Othello)**

1   How do the setting and the way Iago 'encaves' (cramps or restricts) Othello emphasise aspects of Othello's psychological state?

2   How do you think the diegetic sound of water dripping might complement what is happening to Othello?

3   When Iago causes Othello to have an epileptic fit, what cinematic and dramatic devices (camera work, lighting, editing, props, blocking, etc.) does Parker use to show the following?

    a   Othello's pain and confusion?

    b   Iago's manipulation of, and lack of compassion for, Othello?

4   How does Parker make it obvious to the audience that Othello misunderstands what Iago and Cassio are discussing? Discuss specific techniques such as lighting, sound and camera work in your response.

The deterioration of Othello's language

Shakespeare is a master craftsman when it comes to using language for dramatic effect. Of particular note in *Othello* is the skilful way Shakespeare signals Othello's personal deterioration by a corresponding deterioration in his language. (In the table below, 1.2.25 refers to Act 1 Scene 1, line 25.)

Characteristics of Othello's language reflecting his moral decline	
Acts 1 & 2	Acts 3 & 4
Poetic declarations of love for Desdemona (1.2.25; 1.3.91, 125–69, 295–97; 2.1.173–189; 2.3.8–10) and peace towards others (1.2.6, 59, 81–3; 1.3.80 and following lines).	Venomous pronouncements of hatred towards Desdemona (3.3.363, 435, 479–82; 4.2.71–92), with numerous images associated with violence, animals and disease (see **Imagery**, p. 127; 4.1.21, 60, 94, 134, 186–89).
Completion of each other's lines of iambic pentameter emphasises Othello's bond with Desdemona (2.1.173–86).	Interruption of Desdemona's speech emphasises Othello's revulsion of her (3.4.82–90).
Extended lyrical descriptions (1.3.125–69; 2.1.173–89).	Short, abrupt sentences, with numerous exclamation marks (a brief perusal of Acts 3 and 4 will confirm this point).
Gentle, moderate pace emphasising Othello's tenderness and dignified composure (1.3.125–69; 2.1.173–89).	Fast, 'violent pace' created by rapid exchange of dialogue (known as **stichomythia**) and partial lines (see throughout 4.1 and 3.4.71–81).
Poetic use of hyperbole (2.1.174–79).	Frustrated and violent use of hyperbole (see p. 116).
Lyrical repetition of phrases (1.3.159–160).	Violent, tortured repetition (3.3.431, 455, 479; 3.4.85–90; 4.1.35–41, 178–79).
Eloquent phrasing in speeches, reflecting his calm nobility (1.3.125–169; 2.1.173–89).	Fragmented sentences (often in prose); unfinished babblings and cries, bordering on animalistic grunts (called 'savage madness' by Iago in 4.1.53). See especially 4.1.31–41, where we see that Othello's personal or moral decline is doubly reinforced: firstly by his linguistic deterioration, and secondly by his physical disintegration (epileptic fit).

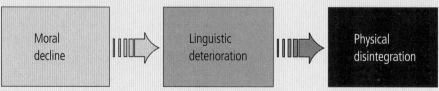

It is interesting, and certainly ironic, to observe that in Act 5, while Othello's actions decline to the point of murderous violence, his language returns, to a significant extent, to its former dignified composure and poetic richness.

Act 4 Scene 1 (Part 2)

Characters

Othello
Iago
Lodovico
Desdemona

In a nutshell

Iago persuades the furious Othello to strangle Desdemona in their marriage bed, and Iago vows to kill Cassio. Lodovico arrives with letters recalling Othello to Venice and declaring Cassio as his replacement in Cyprus. When Desdemona expresses happiness at this, Othello strikes her, shocking Lodovico. Left alone with Iago, Lodovico expresses his concern about Othello's fitness to govern, and Iago suggests that Lodovico has not seen the worst of Othello's behaviour.

Before you read

- Notice how Othello interprets Desdemona's every word as some sort of proof of her infidelity. He even uses her obedience in turning back, when he orders her to do so, as an illustration of her deceptive nature, her ability to 'turn' or deceive.

- Note, again, how rich this scene is in dramatic irony. Knowledge of the previous scene affects how we interpret almost every line, increasing the dramatic tension.

Iniquity: Wrong-doing
Expostulate: Argue at length or plead
Lest: In case
Breach: A break or disruption in relations
Beseech: Beg; forcefully request (entreat)
Avaunt: Be gone
Censure: Blame or judgement

Act 4 Scene 1 (Part 2)   Cyprus, before the castle.

OTHELLO	*[Advancing out of hiding]* How shall I murder him, Iago?	
IAGO	Did you perceive how he laughed at his vice?	
OTHELLO	O Iago!	
IAGO	And did you see the handkerchief?	160
OTHELLO	Was that mine?	
IAGO	Yours, by this hand; and to see how he prizes the foolish woman, your wife! She gave it him, and he hath given it his whore.	
OTHELLO	I would have him nine years a-killing. A fine woman! A fair woman! A sweet woman!	165

IAGO	Nay, you must forget that.
OTHELLO	Ay, let her rot, and perish, and be damned tonight, for she shall not live! No, my heart is turned to stone: I strike it, and it hurts my hand. O, the world hath not a sweeter creature; she might lie by an emperor's side and command his tasks. 170
IAGO	Nay, that's not your way.
OTHELLO	Hang her! I do but say what she is: so delicate with her needle; an admirable musician (O! She will sing the savageness out of a bear); of so high and plenteous wit and invention –
IAGO	She's the worse for all this. 175
OTHELLO	O, a thousand thousand times; and then, of so gentle a condition!
IAGO	Ay, too gentle.
OTHELLO	Nay, that's certain. But yet the pity of it, Iago! O Iago, the pity of it, Iago!
IAGO	If you are so fond over her iniquity, give her patent to offend; for, 180 if it touch not you, it comes near nobody.
OTHELLO	I will chop her into messes. Cuckold me!
IAGO	O, 'tis foul in her.
OTHELLO	With mine officer!
IAGO	That's fouler. 185
OTHELLO	Get me some poison, Iago; this night, I'll not expostulate with her, lest her body and beauty unprovide my mind again. This night, Iago.
IAGO	Do it not with poison; strangle her in her bed, even the bed she hath contaminated.
OTHELLO	Good, good. The justice of it pleases. Very good. 190
IAGO	And for Cassio, let me be his undertaker; you shall hear more by midnight.
OTHELLO	Excellent good!

[A trumpet sounds within]

| | What trumpet is that same? |
| IAGO | I warrant, something from Venice: 'Tis Lodovico 195 Come from the Duke; and, see, your wife is with him. |

[LODOVICO, DESDEMONA and Attendants enter]

LODOVICO	God save you, worthy General!
OTHELLO	With all my heart, sir.
LODOVICO	The Duke and senators of Venice greet you.

[LODOVICO gives him a letter]

| OTHELLO | I kiss the instrument of their pleasures. |

[Opens the letter, and reads]

| DESDEMONA | And what's the news, good cousin Lodovico? 200 |
| IAGO | I am very glad to see you, signior. Welcome to Cyprus. |

LODOVICO	I thank you. How does Lieutenant Cassio?
IAGO	Lives, sir.
DESDEMONA	Cousin, there's fallen between him and my lord 205
	An unkind breach; but you shall make all well.
OTHELLO	Are you sure of that?
DESDEMONA	My lord?
OTHELLO	*[Reads] This fail you not to do, as you will* –
LODOVICO	He did not call: he's busy in the paper. 210
	Is there division 'twixt my lord and Cassio?
DESDEMONA	A most unhappy one; I would do much
	To atone them, for the love I bear to Cassio.
OTHELLO	Fire and brimstone!
DESDEMONA	My lord?
OTHELLO	Are you wise?
DESDEMONA	What, is he angry? 215
LODOVICO	Maybe the letter moved him;
	For, as I think, they do command him home,
	Deputing Cassio in his government.
DESDEMONA	Trust me, I am glad on't.
OTHELLO	Indeed!
DESDEMONA	My lord?
OTHELLO	I am glad to see you mad.
DESDEMONA	Why, sweet Othello –
OTHELLO	Devil! *[OTHELLO strikes her]* 220
DESDEMONA	I have not deserved this.
LODOVICO	My lord, this would not be believed in Venice,
	Though I should swear I saw't. 'Tis very much.
	Make her amends: she weeps.
OTHELLO	O devil, devil!
	If that the earth could teem with woman's tears, 225
	Each drop she falls would prove a crocodile.
	Out of my sight!
DESDEMONA	I will not stay to offend you.

[DESDEMONA turns to go]

LODOVICO	Truly, an obedient lady;
	I do beseech your lordship, call her back.
OTHELLO	Mistress!
DESDEMONA	My lord?
OTHELLO	What would you with her, sir? 230
LODOVICO	Who, I, my lord?
OTHELLO	Ay, you did wish that I would make her turn.
	Sir, she can turn, and turn, and yet go on,
	And turn again; and she can weep, sir, weep;
	And she's obedient, as you say, obedient, 235

Very obedient – Proceed you in your tears –
Concerning this, sir – O well-painted passion! –
I am commanded home – Get you away;
I'll send for you anon – Sir, I obey the mandate,
And will return to Venice – Hence, avaunt!   240

[DESDEMONA exits]

Cassio shall have my place. And, sir, tonight,
I do entreat that we may sup together;
You are welcome, sir, to Cyprus – Goats and monkeys!

[OTHELLO exits]

LODOVICO	Is this the noble Moor whom our full senate
	Call all in all sufficient? Is this the nature 245
	Whom passion could not shake? Whose solid virtue
	The shot of accident, nor dart of chance,
	Could neither graze nor pierce?
IAGO	He is much changed.
LODOVICO	Are his wits safe? Is he not light of brain?
IAGO	He's that he is: I may not breathe my censure 250
	What he might be; if what he might he is not,
	I would to heaven he were!
LODOVICO	What? Strike his wife?
IAGO	'Faith, that was not so well, yet would I knew
	That stroke would prove the worst!
LODOVICO	Is it his use?
	Or did the letters work upon his blood, 255
	And new-create this fault?
IAGO	Alas, alas!
	It is not honesty in me to speak
	What I have seen and known. You shall observe him,
	And his own courses will denote him so
	That I may save my speech. Do but go after, 260
	And mark how he continues.
LODOVICO	I'm sorry that I am deceived in him.

[Both exit]

Text notes

176   **So gentle a condition:** Well-bred and gentle.

177   **Ay, too gentle:** Iago suggests that Desdemona is 'too gentle' or ineffective in resisting
       Cassio's advances.

180   **Give her patent to offend:** Give her permission to go and commit adultery. A 'patent',
       in this case, is a legal right to do something. In Jacobean England, adultery was against
       the law.

225–26 **If the earth could teem … would prove a crocodile:** It was thought that crocodiles shed tears to deceive potential prey. Othello uses this striking image to emphasise Desdemona's deception.

250–52 **He's that he is … to heaven he were:** Iago hints that Lodovico's fears might be well-founded; his remarks, though, are difficult to interpret: ambiguous and cryptic enough for him not to be accused of being disloyal to his General ('censure' = criticism).

Questions

1 Towards whom is Othello's anger initially directed?

2 Quote a line or sentence that conveys Othello's continuing admiration for Desdemona.

3 Quote a phrase that suggests Iago is much bolder with Othello in this scene than he was when he first raised the possibility of Desdemona's infidelity.

4 What do you think Othello means by the sentence: 'No, my heart is turned to stone: I strike it, and it hurts my hand' (line 168)?

5 How does Shakespeare use various features of Othello's language to demonstrate his protagonist's suffering and confusion? You might like to construct a table to show your understanding of this notion.

6 Othello's language in talking to Lodovico is very polite and consistent with his way of speaking in Act 1. Quote an example (a sentence, line or phrase) of polite and dignified language from Othello's speech in this scene.

7 What aspects of Othello's words and actions in this scene do you think could make the audience particularly sympathetic toward him?

8 In response to Lodovico's question, Iago says of Cassio that he 'lives' (line 204). Explain the irony of Iago's response.

9 Desdemona states: 'I would do much / To atone them, for the love I bear to Cassio' (lines 212–13). Why does Othello react rashly at this comment? What dramatic device is Shakespeare employing here?

10 Why do you think Desdemona does not stand up for herself more forcefully in this scene?

11 What does Iago suggest to Lodovico about Othello's striking Desdemona? How is this particularly unfair and even ironic?

Extend

1 Othello's language at this point in the play resembles Iago's. Quote some examples from this scene and explain what it might indicate about Othello's character.

2 How does Iago turn Othello's praise of Desdemona to his own advantage? Explain one example.

3 Why do you think Iago would prefer to have Othello 'strangle' Desdemona than 'poison' her? Suggest at least two reasons.

4 What do you think Othello's final words in this scene ('Goats and monkeys!') suggest? How does this imagery echo phrases from earlier in the play?

5   What does Lodovico mean by the comment: 'I'm sorry that I am deceived in him'? How is this comment ironic?

6   Read lines 164–82. Construct and complete a table like the one below to demonstrate your understanding of Shakespeare's use of antithesis (clash of opposites) in these lines.

Evidence that Othello still loves Desdemona	Evidence that Othello hates Desdemona	What does this clash of opposites suggest about Othello at this point in the play? *Write one paragraph …*

7   There is evidence here of violence in Othello's language. But how is his use of <u>physical</u> violence in this scene evidence of a change in his character in comparison to the earliest scenes of the play (see Act 4 Scene1 lines 244–62)?

Discuss

1   To what extent does Othello's vengeful language in this scene (e.g. line 182: 'I will chop her into messes') cause you to lose sympathy for him?

2   If you were given the role of directing this scene, how would you have Othello demonstrate his internal conflict between loving and hating Desdemona? In your response, consider dramatic devices such as the actor's voice, body language, position and movement on the stage, as well as theatrical components such as music and lighting.

Truly, an obedient lady
Women, marriage and society

Women had few rights in Jacobean England and Renaissance Venice. In Shakespeare's time, education was becoming more widespread and accessible to the middle classes but few women were able to receive an education. It was mostly girls from upper-class families who received any formal education, often through hired tutors or through being placed with another upper-class family. Even so, no matter how intelligent a girl was, she could never expect to go to university. The education girls received was generally less rigorous than boys' tuition, and often involved additional skills considered more appropriate to the female domain, including sewing and singing: there is evidence in the play of Desdemona being able to do both of these things. It is a measure of Desdemona's confidence that she stands before the educated men of the Senate and calmly states her case.

Desdemona marries for love at a time when arranged marriages, especially among the upper classes, were still common. In Jacobean England, a girl needed her father's consent to marry, and the marriage was seen as a transfer of property. For this reason, it had become customary for the father to 'give away' the bride at the altar: the father was officially giving away, or transferring, his property to another man. This explains why Iago cries, 'Thieves, thieves, thieves!' to Brabantio in the opening of the play. In not requesting Brabantio's consent to marry, Othello has stolen Desdemona, Brabantio's property. This concept is continued throughout the play with Desdemona being compared to material objects such as a 'jewel' and a treasure ship ('carack'); at one point she is even described as a 'prize'. Furthermore, Iago employs the language of conquest and invasion to vilify Othello's marriage to Desdemona, and in so doing presents Othello as a foreign power invading territory (or claiming property) that does not belong him.

The man was recognised as the head of the household, not to be contradicted, and women were expected to be obedient to their husbands. This convention was reinforced by the teachings of the Church and the laws of the State. While Lodovico is shocked at Othello's violent treatment of Desdemona in Act 4 Scene 1, he still commends her obedience. In the final act of *Othello,* even the fiery Emilia acknowledges that it is right that she obey her husband when he orders her home, but her choice to disobey him only serves to highlight the lies that have led to Desdemona's murder.

Sexual hypocrisy, both in Renaissance Venice and Jacobean England, was widespread. While a woman's virginity and fidelity within marriage were highly valued and guarded, men generally enjoyed more freedom. Jacobeans associated sexual desire with men, and expected wives to be passive sexual partners. Both Desdemona and Emilia subvert (or contradict) this convention. In Act 1, Desdemona insists before the Senate that she not be denied her marriage rites, and obtains permission to accompany Othello to Cyprus. Similarly, in Act 4, Emilia speaks out against straying husbands and maintains that women have similar desires to men.

The theatre in England provided a platform for writers to challenge conventional expectations and these and many other prejudices.

Act 4 Scene 2 (Part 1)

Characters
Othello
Desdemona
Emilia
Iago

In a nutshell
Othello questions Emilia about what she has observed of Desdemona and Cassio's behaviour, before commanding her to summon Desdemona. Without disclosing particular details, Othello then accuses Desdemona of infidelity, leaving her upset and confused. After Othello storms off, Emilia fetches Iago, who pretends to offer comfort. Emilia raises the possibility of some immoral person telling lies to Othello about Desdemona but Iago quickly dismisses this, after which Desdemona reasserts her unswerving love for Othello.

Before you read

- Convinced of Desdemona's infidelity, Othello uses terms relating to prostitution in his conversations with Emilia and Desdemona. He treats Emilia as the madam of a brothel (a 'bawd') and addresses Desdemona as a 'whore' and a 'strumpet' (prostitute), and even refers to her customers ('procreants'). Venice was famous for its courtesans or prostitutes and this could be playing on Othello's mind.

Dispatch:	Deal with something quickly
Affliction:	Suffering
Cistern:	An underground reservoir
Meet:	Fitting or appropriate
Chide / chid:	Tell off or criticise someone
Discourse:	Conversation
Humour:	Mood
Warrant:	Permit (noun); guarantee or merit (verb)

Act 4 Scene 2 (Part 1)   A room in the castle.

[OTHELLO and EMILIA enter]

OTHELLO	You have seen nothing then?	
EMILIA	Nor ever heard, nor ever did suspect.	
OTHELLO	Yes, you have seen Cassio and she together.	
EMILIA	But then I saw no harm, and then I heard	
	Each syllable that breath made up between them.	5
OTHELLO	What, did they never whisper?	
EMILIA	Never, my lord.	

OTHELLO	Nor send you out o' the way?	
EMILIA	Never.	
OTHELLO	To fetch her fan, her gloves, her mask, nor nothing?	
EMILIA	Never, my lord.	
OTHELLO	That's strange.	10
EMILIA	I durst, my lord, to wager she is honest,	
	Lay down my soul at stake; if you think other,	
	Remove your thought: it doth abuse your bosom.	
	If any wretch have put this in your head,	
	Let heaven requite it with the serpent's curse!	15
	For, if she be not honest, chaste, and true,	
	There's no man happy; the purest of their wives	
	Is foul as slander.	
OTHELLO	Bid her come hither: go.	

[EMILIA exits]

	She says enough, yet she's a simple bawd	
	That cannot say as much. This is a subtle whore,	20
	A closet lock and key of villanous secrets,	
	And yet she'll kneel and pray; I have seen her do't.	

[DESDEMONA enters with EMILIA]

DESDEMONA	My lord, what is your will?	
OTHELLO	Pray, chuck, come hither.	
DESDEMONA	What is your pleasure?	
OTHELLO	Let me see your eyes;	
	Look in my face.	
DESDEMONA	What horrible fancy's this?	25
OTHELLO	*[To EMILIA]* Some of your function, mistress;	
	Leave procreants alone and shut the door;	
	Cough, or cry 'hem' if anybody come.	
	Your mystery, your mystery. Nay, dispatch!	

[EMILIA exits]

DESDEMONA	Upon my knees, what doth your speech import?	30
	I understand a fury in your words,	
	But not the words.	
OTHELLO	Why, what art thou?	
DESDEMONA	Your wife, my lord; your true	
	And loyal wife.	
OTHELLO	Come, swear it; damn thyself,	
	Lest, being like one of heaven, the devils themselves	35
	Should fear to seize thee. Therefore, be double damned:	
	Swear thou art honest.	
DESDEMONA	Heaven doth truly know it.	
OTHELLO	Heaven truly knows that thou art false as hell.	

DESDEMONA	To whom, my lord? With whom? How am I false?	
OTHELLO	O Desdemona! Away! Away! Away!	40
DESDEMONA	Alas the heavy day! Why do you weep?	

DESDEMONA
To whom, my lord? With whom? How am I false?

OTHELLO
O Desdemona! Away! Away! Away!   40

DESDEMONA
Alas the heavy day! Why do you weep?
Am I the motive of these tears, my lord?
If haply you my father do suspect
An instrument of this your calling back,
Lay not your blame on me. If you have lost him,   45
Why, I have lost him too.

OTHELLO
                                  Had it pleased heaven
To try me with affliction; had they rained
All kinds of sores and shames on my bare head,
Steeped me in poverty to the very lips,
Given to captivity me and my utmost hopes,   50
I should have found in some place of my soul
A drop of patience. But, alas, to make me
A fixèd figure for the time of scorn
To point his slow unmoving finger at!
Yet could I bear that too; well, very well.   55
But there, where I have garnered up my heart,
Where either I must live, or bear no life,
The fountain from the which my current runs,
Or else dries up; to be discarded thence!
Or keep it as a cistern for foul toads   60
To knot and gender in! – Turn thy complexion there,
Patience, thou young and rose-lipped cherubin;
Ay, there, look grim as hell!

DESDEMONA
I hope my noble lord esteems me honest.

OTHELLO
O, ay; as summer flies are in the shambles,   65
That quicken even with blowing. O thou weed,
Who art so lovely fair and smell'st so sweet
That the sense aches at thee,
Would thou hadst ne'er been born!

DESDEMONA
Alas, what ignorant sin have I committed?   70

OTHELLO
Was this fair paper, this most goodly book,
Made to write 'whore' upon? What committed?
Committed? O thou public commoner!
I should make very forges of my cheeks,
That would to cinders burn up modesty,   75
Did I but speak thy deeds. What committed?
Heaven stops the nose at it and the moon winks;
The bawdy wind that kisses all it meets
Is hushed within the hollow mine of earth,
And will not hear it. What committed!   80
Impudent strumpet!

DESDEMONA
                              By heaven, you do me wrong.

OTHELLO	Are you not a strumpet?
DESDEMONA	No, as I am a Christian.
	If to preserve this vessel for my lord
	From any other foul unlawful touch
	Be not to be a strumpet, I am none. 85
OTHELLO	What, not a whore?
DESDEMONA	No, as I shall be saved.
OTHELLO	Is't possible?
DESDEMONA	O, heaven forgive us!
OTHELLO	I cry you mercy, then:
	I took you for that cunning whore of Venice
	That married with Othello – *[Raising his voice]* You, mistress, 90
	That have the office opposite to Saint Peter,
	And keep the gate of hell!

[EMILIA re-enters]

                      You, you; ay, you!
We have done our course; there's money for your pains.
I pray you, turn the key and keep our counsel.

[OTHELLO exits]

EMILIA	Alas, what does this gentleman conceive? 95
	How do you, madam? How do you, my good lady?
DESDEMONA	'Faith, half asleep.
EMILIA	Good madam, what's the matter with my lord?
DESDEMONA	With who?
EMILIA	Why, with my lord, madam. 100
DESDEMONA	Who is thy lord?
EMILIA	He that is yours, sweet lady.
DESDEMONA	I have none. Do not talk to me, Emilia:
	I cannot weep, nor answers have I none,
	But what should go by water. Prithee, tonight
	Lay on my bed my wedding sheets. Remember, 105
	And call thy husband hither.
EMILIA	Here's a change indeed!

[EMILIA exits]

DESDEMONA	'Tis meet I should be used so, very meet.
	How have I been behaved, that he might stick
	The small'st opinion on my least misuse?

[EMILIA re-enters with IAGO]

IAGO	What is your pleasure, madam? How is't with you? 110
DESDEMONA	I cannot tell. Those that do teach young babes
	Do it with gentle means and easy tasks.
	He might have chid me so; for, in good faith,
	I am a child to chiding.

IAGO	What's the matter, lady?	
EMILIA	Alas, Iago, my lord hath so bewhored her,	115
	Thrown such despite and heavy terms upon her,	
	As true hearts cannot bear.	
DESDEMONA	Am I that name, Iago?	
IAGO	What name, fair lady?	
DESDEMONA	Such as she says my lord did say I was.	
EMILIA	He called her 'whore'. A beggar in his drink	120
	Could not have laid such terms upon his callet.	
IAGO	Why did he so?	
DESDEMONA	I do not know; I am sure I am none such.	
IAGO	Do not weep; do not weep. Alas the day!	
EMILIA	Hath she forsook so many noble matches,	125
	Her father and her country and her friends,	
	To be called 'whore'? Would it not make one weep?	
DESDEMONA	It is my wretchèd fortune.	
IAGO	Beshrew him for't!	
	How comes this trick upon him?	
DESDEMONA	Nay, heaven doth know.	
EMILIA	I will be hanged, if some eternal villain,	130
	Some busy and insinuating rogue,	
	Some cogging, cozening slave, to get some office,	
	Have not devised this slander. I'll be hanged else.	
IAGO	Fie, there is no such man; it is impossible.	
DESDEMONA	If any such there be, heaven pardon him!	135
EMILIA	A halter pardon him! And hell gnaw his bones!	
	Why should he call her whore? Who keeps her company?	
	What place? What time? What form? What likelihood?	
	The Moor's abused by some most villanous knave,	
	Some base notorious knave, some scurvy fellow.	140
	O heaven, that such companions thou'ldst unfold,	
	And put in every honest hand a whip	
	To lash the rascals naked through the world	
	Even from the east to the west!	
IAGO	Speak within door.	
EMILIA	O, fie upon them! Some such squire he was	145
	That turned your wit the seamy side without,	
	And made you to suspect me with the Moor.	
IAGO	You are a fool; go to.	
DESDEMONA	Alas, Iago,	
	What shall I do to win my lord again?	
	Good friend, go to him; for, by this light of heaven,	150
	I know not how I lost him. Here I kneel:	
	If e'er my will did trespass 'gainst his love,	
	Either in discourse of thought or actual deed,	

	Or that mine eyes, mine ears, or any sense	
	Delighted them in any other form;	155
	Or that I do not yet, and ever did,	
	And ever will (though he do shake me off	
	To beggarly divorcement) love him dearly.	
	Comfort forswear me! Unkindness may do much,	
	And his unkindness may defeat my life,	160
	But never taint my love. I cannot say 'whore';	
	It does abhor me now I speak the word.	
	To do the act that might the addition earn	
	Not the world's mass of vanity could make me.	
IAGO	I pray you, be content: 'tis but his humour;	165
	The business of the state does him offence,	
	And he does chide with you.	
DESDEMONA	If 'twere no other —	
IAGO	'Tis but so, I warrant.	

[Trumpets sound within]

	Hark, how these instruments summon to supper!	
	The messengers of Venice stay the meat.	170
	Go in, and weep not; all things shall be well.	

[DESDEMONA and EMILIA exit]

Text notes

26–29 **Some of your function … your mystery:** Othello casts Emilia in the role of the madam of a brothel and suggests that she should shut the door to keep other customers out, instructing her to warn them if someone is approaching. 'Mystery' here means occupation (a madam of a brothel).

43–46 **If haply you my father … I have lost him too:** Desdemona suspects that Othello's annoyance might be because of the letter from Venice calling him back, and asks Othello not to blame her ('haply' = by chance).

53 **A fixèd figure:** Something on show, like a statue.

53–54 **For the time of scorn … moving finger at:** The slow finger refers to the hand of the clock. Othello is thinking of his reputation and imagining himself the joke (or scorn) of the time.

56–61 **But there, where I have … knot and gender in:** Othello states that he has invested everything in his marriage to Desdemona, comparing their love to a fountain from which life either flows or dries up. He speculates on the possibility of being discarded or maintaining the supposed current situation where he is being cheated on. He uses the grotesque image of mating toads to illustrate the latter possibility.

73 **O thou public commoner:** You prostitute!

74–76 **I should make very forges … but speak thy deeds:** Othello claims he would burn his own cheeks and all modesty would be burnt to ash, if he had to describe Desdemona's sins.

77–80 **Heaven stops the nose … will not hear it:** Othello says that heaven holds its nose at the smell of Desdemona's sin. The moon, which is associated with the goddess of chastity, also refuses to see it. Even the wind, sluttish because it touches everything, hides in the bowels of the earth rather than hear of her sin.

83	**Vessel:** Body.
90–92	**You, mistress ... keep the gate of hell:** Saint Peter was said to keep the gate of heaven. Here, as Othello is portraying Emilia as the keeper of a brothel, she is the opposite of that heavenly office.
103–4	**Nor answers have ... what should go by water:** Desdemona cannot give any answers that will not be accompanied by tears.
111–14	**Those that do teach ... a child to chiding:** People who teach babies do it gently with easy tasks. Desdemona speculates that Othello might rebuke her in the same way, as she is unaccustomed to censure.
115	**Bewhored her:** Made her out to be a whore.
121	**Callat:** Prostitute.
131–33	**Some busy and insinuating ... not devised this slander:** Emilia suggests someone is telling Othello lies and slandering Desdemona ('cogging' = deceiving; 'cozening' = cheating).
136	**A halter pardon him:** Emilia is not as forgiving as Desdemona, asserting that hanging would be an appropriate punishment for such a liar.

Questions

1 What does Emilia report about Cassio and Desdemona at the beginning of this scene?

2 Draw up a table similar to previous examples (e.g. page 32) to demonstrate your understanding of the way in which Shakespeare conveys Othello's extreme agitation in this scene.

3 Many critics have suggested that Othello's downfall is caused by his immense concern with his own honour. Find a quote that suggests Othello's main concern is for his reputation.

4 Find a simile Othello uses to illustrate Desdemona's lack of 'honesty' or her infidelity.

5 Quote and explain a metaphor Othello employs to describe Desdemona.

6 Why does Iago command Emilia to 'speak within door'?

7 Read Desdemona's speech (from line 148 onwards). Summarise her opinion of Othello at this stage of the play.

8 What does Iago give as an explanation for Othello's current mood?

Extend

1 How does Othello interpret Desdemona's kneeling and praying (line 22)? How is this particularly unfair?

2 After Othello accuses Desdemona of being 'false', in line 39 she asks, 'With whom? How am I false?' Why do you think Othello does not tell her?

3 Emilia poses the question, 'Hath she forsook so many noble matches, / Her father and her country and her friends, / To be called whore?' (lines 125–27). Explain how this statement is ironic in the context of the entire play. Hint: Think of how a different character used this same information.

4   How does Emilia describe the person who has deceived Othello, and in what way(s) is this ironic? Include quotes in your response.

5   In this scene, there is frequent repetition of two groups of words: 'eyes' / 'see' and 'true' / 'truth' / 'honest'. What do you think Shakespeare might be drawing our attention to by repeating these two particular groups of words?

Discuss

1   Why do you think Desdemona does not react more forcefully to Othello's accusations? Do you agree with some critics who insist she is too passive?

2   If you were to direct this scene, how would you portray the character of Desdemona? Would you emphasise her passivity? Quietness? Determination? Anything else? What dramatic devices would you use to emphasise this aspect of her character? Consider techniques such as the actor's voice, body language, position and movement on the stage, as well as theatrical components such as music and lighting.

Press
PLAY   **Oliver Parker: DVD Chapter 19 (Othello accuses Desdemona)**

1   In this scene, Parker uses a number of devices to build tension or a sense of frightening expectation in the viewer. How does he use aspects such as camera work, music, voiceover, pauses and props to do this?

2   Othello looks directly at the camera in this scene. Who is the only other character to have done so previously? What do you think Parker might be suggesting about the character of Othello?

Act 4 Scene 2 (Part 2)

Characters   In a nutshell

Iago
Roderigo

A furious and frustrated Roderigo complains that he is almost bankrupt and feels that he does not have any hope with Desdemona. Iago quickly persuades Roderigo to calm down, after which he tells him that, to prevent Desdemona and Othello leaving the island, he must murder Cassio.

Before you read

• Roderigo complains that the jewels he has given to Desdemona through Iago would have been enough to corrupt a votarist (a nun). The audience can guess that these jewels have never reached Desdemona. At this stage in the play, Roderigo is like a desperate gambler, who, having gambled nearly everything away, cannot easily walk away and cut his losses.

Daffest me:	Evades me
Fobbed:	Attempted to satisfy someone with lies or excuses
Solicitation:	A request
Mettle:	Character or spirit
Harlotry:	Prostitution (in this case it is used to describe the person, not the profession)

Act 4 Scene 2 (Part 2) A room in the castle.

[RODERIGO enters]

IAGO	How now, Roderigo!	
RODERIGO	I do not find that thou dealest justly with me.	
IAGO	What in the contrary?	
RODERIGO	Every day thou daffest me with some device, Iago, and rather, as it	175
	seems to me now, keepest from me all conveniency than suppliest	
	me with the least advantage of hope. I will indeed no longer endure	
	it, nor am I yet persuaded to put up in peace what already I have	
	foolishly suffered.	
IAGO	Will you hear me, Roderigo?	180
RODERIGO	'Faith, I have heard too much, for your words and performances are	
	no kin together.	
IAGO	You charge me most unjustly.	
RODERIGO	With nought but truth. I have wasted myself out of my means. The	
	jewels you have had from me to deliver to Desdemona would half	185
	have corrupted a votarist. You have told me she hath received them	
	and returned me expectations and comforts of sudden respect and	
	acquaintance, but I find none.	
IAGO	Well; go to; very well.	
RODERIGO	Very well? Go to? I cannot go to, man; nor 'tis not very well.	190
	By this hand, I think it is scurvy, and begin to find myself fobbed in it.	
IAGO	Very well.	
RODERIGO	I tell you 'tis not very well. I will make myself known to Desdemona.	
	If she will return me my jewels, I will give over my suit and repent my	
	unlawful solicitation; if not, assure yourself I will seek satisfaction	195
	of you.	
IAGO	You have said now.	
RODERIGO	Ay, and said nothing but what I protest intendment of doing.	
IAGO	Why, now I see there's mettle in thee, and even from this instant do	
	build on thee a better opinion than ever before. Give me thy hand,	200
	Roderigo. Thou hast taken against me a most just exception; but yet,	

	I protest, I have dealt most directly in thy affair.
RODERIGO	It hath not appeared.
IAGO	I grant indeed it hath not appeared, and your suspicion is not without wit
	and judgement. But, Roderigo, if thou hast that in thee indeed, 205
	which I have greater reason to believe now than ever – I mean purpose,
	courage and valour – this night show it: if thou the next night following
	enjoy not Desdemona, take me from this world with treachery and
	devise engines for my life.
RODERIGO	Well, what is it? Is it within reason and compass? 210
IAGO	Sir, there is especial commission come from Venice to depute Cassio in
	Othello's place.
RODERIGO	Is that true? Why, then Othello and Desdemona return again to Venice.
IAGO	O, no; he goes into Mauritania and takes away with him the fair
	Desdemona, unless his abode be lingered here by some accident, 215
	wherein none can be so determinate as the removing of Cassio.
RODERIGO	How do you mean, removing of him?
IAGO	Why, by making him uncapable of Othello's place, knocking out
	his brains.
RODERIGO	And that you would have me to do? 220
IAGO	Ay, if you dare do yourself a profit and a right. He sups tonight with
	a harlotry, and thither will I go to him. He knows not yet of his
	honourable fortune. If you will watch his going thence, which I will
	fashion to fall out between twelve and one, you may take him at your
	pleasure. I will be near to second your attempt, and he shall fall 225
	between us. Come, stand not amazed at it, but go along with me; I will
	show you such a necessity in his death that you shall think yourself
	bound to put it on him. It is now high suppertime, and the night grows
	to waste. About it!
RODERIGO	I will hear further reason for this. 230
IAGO	And you shall be satisfied.

[Both exit]

Text notes

181–82   **For your words … no kin together:** Roderigo states that Iago's words seem completely
      unrelated to his actions ('performances').

191   **Scurvy:** Miserable or contemptible.

208–9   **Devise engines for my life:** Use instruments of torture on me to the point of death.

210   **Is it within reason and compass?** Is it a credible, achievable plan?

214   **Mauritania:** A territory in western Africa.

215   **His abode be lingered:** His stay be lengthened.

Questions

1 What do we discover about Roderigo's situation from his speeches in this scene?

2 With what does Roderigo threaten Iago?

3 How does Iago pacify Roderigo?

4 Who speaks the majority of the dialogue at the beginning of this scene? Who dominates the dialogue by the end? What does this tell the audience about their relationship?

Extend

1 Some of Iago's initial replies to Roderigo's desperate complaints seem flippant and designed to infuriate him (see lines 189 and 192). Can you think of a reason he might have for employing this tactic?

2 The way Shakespeare ends this scene suggests that Iago and Roderigo's dialogue will continue beyond this scene. In this way, the scene can be described as elliptical.

   a Give at least two reasons why Shakespeare might have used the dramatic device of hinting at further dialogue but not including it.

   b Do you think the audience is supposed to assume that Roderigo will be convinced and carry out Iago's instructions?

   c Why does Shakespeare's decision to suggest more conversation offstage make Roderigo's character appear more credible?

Discuss

1 If Roderigo could think clearly at this stage of the play, what evidence does he have that Iago is not to be trusted?

2 Besides the proportion of dialogue (see Question 4 above), what dramatic devices would you use to show the changing nature of the relationship between Iago and Roderigo in this scene? Consider techniques such as body language, tone of voice and blocking (movement and position on the stage).

Thinking about the conflict between illusion and reality

We have already observed that the essence of Shakespeare's *Othello* is conflict, demonstrated by a series of sustained oppositions or antitheses: black / white, male / female, civilised Venetians / barbaric Turks, night / day, man / beast, and love / jealousy, to name but a few.

A thematic undercurrent that runs throughout the entire play is the conflict between illusion and reality, between what *seems* to be true and what is *actually* true. In short, the characters are deceived when the reality of Iago's lies is hidden beneath words and appearances that only seem to be true. The audience, however, is always in the privileged position of being able to see the illusion that Iago creates, the reality behind his illusion and the conflict that occurs when reality and illusion collide.

REALITY	Iago hates Othello (1.3.363) and seeks to destroy him by poisoning him with jealousy (2.3.318; 3.3.329–33).

ILLUSION	Iago pretends to love and respect Othello (3.3.216), with 'visages of duty' (1.1.50), 'shows of service' (1.1.52) and outward 'flags' or 'signs of love' (1.1.154). Consequently, Iago is seen by all other characters (except his wife; see 4.2.130–140) as 'good' (2.1.97), 'full of love' (3.3.121) and 'of exceeding honesty' (3.3.262).
	Q How does Iago's statement in Act 1 Scene 1, line 65 relate to this important theme? **Q** How is Iago described by other characters in Act 5 Scene 1, lines 31–32 and Act 5 Scene 2, line 151?

DRAMATIC IRONY	**Q** A key device employed by Shakespeare is **dramatic irony** (see page 81). How does the audience's knowledge of the conflict between Iago's illusion and reality create dramatic tension in the play?

Throughout *Othello*, we see Iago, the 'hellish villain' of the play, lurking in the background like the secret director of a sinister play, manipulating the other characters for his own selfish gain. Note how Iago uses the following devices to pour the pestilence of jealousy into the ears of Roderigo and Othello, deceiving them into believing his lies, so that they 'see' things that are not true:

Asides

Q How does Shakespeare show Iago's deceptive character in his asides to Roderigo in Act 2 Scene 3, lines 116 and 135?

Q Read Act 2 Scene 1, lines 163–64, 190–92. Despite Iago's deception of other characters, how do his asides assist the audience to see the reality of his lies?

Hiding / Spying

Q In Act 4 Scene 1, Iago encourages Othello to hide while Iago speaks with Cassio. How does Iago use Othello's hiding and spying to deceive Othello?

Ellipsis

Q In Act 4 Scene 1, lines 32–34, how does Iago use unfinished sentences to manipulate Othello or to manufacture a false reality?

In *Othello*, Shakespeare's powerful and sustained opposition of words such as 'true', 'truth', 'truly' and 'honest' against phrasing such as 'lie', 'lies', 'liar' and 'false' provides substantial illustration of the conflict between illusion and reality. Act 4 Scene 2 is dominated by the antithesis between truth and falsehood. Ironically, and with most tragic consequences, Iago deceives Othello into believing that Desdemona is 'false' (sexually unfaithful – Act 4 Scene 2 lines 37–39 and Act 5 Scene 2, line 63), yet the audience is always fully aware that she is 'honest, chaste and true' (Act 4 Scene 2, line 16).

Q How does the antithesis between Othello and Emilia's view of Desdemona in Act 5 Scene 2, lines 127, 133–34 reinforce this irony?

In the tragic conclusion of the play, watch for how all characters finally see the truth of Iago's deception, albeit too late. In particular, take note of the following:

- How Shakespeare employs Iago's wife (Emilia) to highlight the reality of Iago's villainous character (Act 4 Scene 3, lines 81–100; Act 5 Scene 2, lines 133–34, 152–64, 219–21)
- The way in which various characters describe Iago once they see him for who he really is: Roderigo (Act 4 Scene 2, lines 181–82; Act 5 Scene 1, line 41), Othello (Act 5 Scene 2, line 234), Montano (Act 5 Scene 2, line 238) and Lodovico (Act 5 Scene 2, lines 285 and 369)
- Roderigo and Lodovico's appropriate description of Iago as an 'inhuman dog' or 'Spartan dog' respectively (Act 5 Scene 1, line 62 and Act 5 Scene 2, line 362)
- Othello's assessment of himself once he finally sees the truth (Act 5 Scene 2, line 324).

Act 4 Scene 3

Characters

Desdemona
Emilia
Othello
Lodovico

In a nutshell

Othello orders Desdemona to go directly to bed and to dismiss her attendant, Emilia. As Emilia prepares Desdemona for bed, the women discuss Othello's recent behaviour and Desdemona insists that, despite Othello's anger, she still loves him. She then tells Emilia the tale of her mother's maid, Barbara, who was abandoned by her mad husband, and Desdemona sings the song Barbara used to sing. The two women discuss infidelity and Emilia asserts that when women stray, it is often their husbands' fault.

Before you read

- Note that while you will probably read the Willow Song in class, it is sung in stage productions. The Willow Song was sung by Desdemona's mother's maid, Barbara, whose lover went mad and left her. There are obvious parallels between the situations of Desdemona and Barbara, and Desdemona looks for comfort in the song. This is also an ominous example of foreshadowing of Desdemona's end, as the maid, Barbara, died singing it.

- Emilia is outspoken about the sexual desires of women and their need for justice in this scene. Her dialogue is radical for a character created in the seventeenth century, especially a female character, and many critics have described her as a feminist before her time. Look out for her strength of conviction in this scene as well as in the final act.

Incontinent:	Unchaste or immoral
Prithee:	Used to introduce a request (short for 'I pray thee')
Forsake:	Abandon
Dispatch:	Deal with something quickly
Anon:	Soon
Scorn:	Bitter feelings
Bode:	Be an omen of something (good or bad)
Troth:	Truth or good faith
Peevish:	Perverse or irritable
Sport:	Recreation or entertainment

Act 4 Scene 3   Another room in the castle.

[OTHELLO, LODOVICO, DESDEMONA, EMILIA and Attendants enter]

LODOVICO	I do beseech you, sir, trouble yourself no further.	
OTHELLO	O, pardon me: 'twill do me good to walk.	
LODOVICO	Madam, good night; I humbly thank your ladyship.	
DESDEMONA	Your honour is most welcome.	
OTHELLO	Will you walk, sir?	
	O, Desdemona –	5
DESDEMONA	My lord?	
OTHELLO	Get you to bed on the instant. I will be returned	
	forthwith. Dismiss your attendant there. Look't be done.	
DESDEMONA	I will, my lord.	

[OTHELLO, LODOVICO and Attendants exit]

EMILIA	How goes it now? He looks gentler than he did.	10
DESDEMONA	He says he will return incontinent;	
	He hath commanded me to go to bed,	
	And bade me to dismiss you.	
EMILIA	Dismiss me?	
DESDEMONA	It was his bidding; therefore, good Emilia,	
	Give me my nightly wearing, and adieu.	15
	We must not now displease him.	
EMILIA	I would you had never seen him!	
DESDEMONA	So would not I. My love doth so approve him,	
	That even his stubbornness, his checks, his frowns	
	Prithee, unpin me – have grace and favour in them.	20
EMILIA	I have laid those sheets you bade me on the bed.	
DESDEMONA	All's one. Good faith, how foolish are our minds!	
	If I do die before thee, prithee, shroud me	
	In one of those same sheets.	

EMILIA	Come, come, you talk.
DESDEMONA	My mother had a maid called Barbara: 25
	She was in love, and he she loved proved mad
	And did forsake her. She had a song of 'willow';
	An old thing 'twas, but it expressed her fortune,
	And she died singing it. That song tonight
	Will not go from my mind; I have much to do, 30
	But to go hang my head all at one side,
	And sing it like poor Barbara. Prithee, dispatch.
EMILIA	Shall I go fetch your night-gown?
DESDEMONA	No, unpin me here.
	This Lodovico is a proper man.
EMILIA	A very handsome man. 35
DESDEMONA	He speaks well.
EMILIA	I know a lady in Venice would have walked barefoot to Palestine for a
	touch of his nether lip.
DESDEMONA	*[Singing]*

> *The poor soul sat sighing by a sycamore tree,*
> > *Sing all a green willow;* 40
> *Her hand on her bosom, her head on her knee,*
> > *Sing willow, willow, willow.*
> *The fresh streams ran by her, and murmured her moans;*
> > *Sing willow, willow, willow;*
> *Her salt tears fell from her, and softened the stones —* 45

Lay by these —
> > *Sing willow, willow, willow —*

Prithee, hie thee; he'll come anon —
> *Sing all a green willow must be my garland.*
> *Let nobody blame him; his scorn I approve —* 50

Nay, that's not next — Hark! Who is't that knocks?

EMILIA	It's the wind.
DESDEMONA	*I called my love false love; but what said he then?*

> > *Sing willow, willow, willow.*
> *If I court more women, you'll couch with more men!* 55

So, get thee gone; good night. Mine eyes do itch:
Doth that bode weeping?

EMILIA	'Tis neither here nor there.
DESDEMONA	I have heard it said so. O, these men, these men!
	Dost thou in conscience think — tell me, Emilia — 60
	That there be women do abuse their husbands
	In such gross kind?
EMILIA	There be some such, no question.
DESDEMONA	Wouldst thou do such a deed for all the world?
EMILIA	Why, would not you?

DESDEMONA	No, by this heavenly light!
EMILIA	Nor I neither by this heavenly light; 65
	I might do't as well i' the dark.
DESDEMONA	Wouldst thou do such a deed for all the world?
EMILIA	The world's a huge thing: it is a great price
	For a small vice.
DESDEMONA	In troth, I think thou wouldst not.
EMILIA	In troth, I think I should, and undo't when I had done. Marry, I would 70
	not do such a thing for a joint-ring, nor for measures of lawn, nor for
	gowns, petticoats, nor caps, nor any petty exhibition; but for the whole
	world – who would not make her husband a cuckold to make him a
	monarch? I should venture purgatory for't.
DESDEMONA	Beshrew me, if I would do such a wrong 75
	For the whole world.
EMILIA	Why, the wrong is but a wrong i' the world; and having the world for
	your labour, 'tis a wrong in your own world, and you might quickly
	make it right.
DESDEMONA	I do not think there is any such woman. 80
EMILIA	Yes, a dozen; and as many to the vantage as would store the world
	they played for.
	But I do think it is their husbands' faults
	If wives do fall: say that they slack their duties,
	And pour our treasures into foreign laps, 85
	Or else break out in peevish jealousies,
	Throwing restraint upon us; or say they strike us,
	Or scant our former having in despite.
	Why, we have galls; and though we have some grace,
	Yet have we some revenge. Let husbands know 90
	Their wives have sense like them: they see and smell
	And have their palates both for sweet and sour,
	As husbands have. What is it that they do
	When they change us for others? Is it sport?
	I think it is. And doth affection breed it? 95
	I think it doth. Is't frailty that thus errs?
	It is so too. And have not we affections,
	Desires for sport, and frailty, as men have?
	Then let them use us well, else let them know,
	The ills we do, their ills instruct us so. 100
DESDEMONA	Good night, good night. God me such uses send,
	Not to pick bad from bad, but by bad mend!

[Exit]

38	**I know a lady in Venice ... Nether lip:** Emilia jokes that she knows a woman who would undertake a gruelling pilgrimage to touch Lodovico's lower lip.
49	**Garland:** Wreath.
55	**Couch:** Go to bed with someone.
71	**Joint-ring:** A ring with two connecting halves, often given as a love token.
72	**Petty exhibition:** Small gift.
74	**Purgatory:** Catholics believed that some people went to purgatory for their sin to be purged so that they could enter heaven.
81–82	**Yes, a dozen ... the world they played for:** Emilia claims she knows of about a dozen women who would cheat on their husbands to gain the world and who would, in the process, populate the world.
89	**We have galls:** Emilia asserts that, like men, women have feelings (that can be bitter). The implication is that women are not necessarily permitted to voice their discontent in a male-dominated society.
95–96	**And doth affection ... I think it doth:** Emilia's opinion is that desire causes men to stray.
96	**Is't frailty that thus errs?** Is it a weakness that causes this mistake?

Questions

1 How would you describe Lodovico's speech and behaviour?

2 Describe Othello's speech in this scene. Does he seem calmer? Why do you think this might be?

3 How differently do Desdemona and Emilia discuss Othello and Lodovico in this scene? What does this tell us about the women's characters?

4 How is Barbara's situation similar to Desdemona's?

5 How would you describe the tone of Desdemona's speeches in this scene?

6 How do Desdemona's views on infidelity provide a contrast to Emilia's views? Why do you think Shakespeare places this dialogue here, shortly before Desdemona is murdered?

7 What elements make this scene emotive?

Extend

1 How does Desdemona, in this scene, provide a contrast to Iago's portrayal of her in his conversations with Othello?

2 This scene could be described in some ways as warmly domestic. Quote a line or phrase that contributes to the naturalistic setting.

3 Read the Willow Song again (lines 39–55).

   a What poetic devices does Shakespeare employ in this song? Quote examples in your answer.

   b How would you describe the tone of this song?

   c What words do you find particularly emotive?

   d Quote and explain a line in the song that reflects Desdemona's attitude to Othello.

4 Emilia uses a great deal of antithesis in lines 65–93.

    a List several examples of paired opposites from these lines.

    b What might Shakespeare's purpose be in saturating Emilia's dialogue with antitheses?

Discuss

1 What is your assessment of Emilia's character at this point in the play? How do you think your attitude would be different if you were viewing the play in Shakespeare's time?

2 Do you think Desdemona sees her death as something inevitable? Present one argument for, and one against this view.

Press PLAY **Oliver Parker: DVD Chapter 21 (the Willow Song)**

In this scene, shots of Desdemona singing the Willow Song are juxtaposed with shots of Othello.

1 How do the shots of Othello show him to be isolated and distressed?

2 How does Parker's use of back-lighting (presenting Othello as a **silhouette**) emphasise the contrast between Othello and Desdemona?

3 How effective do you think Parker's use of juxtaposition is in this scene? Could this have been done differently?

A word about repetition in *Othello*

Repetition is a salient feature of Shakespeare's *Othello*, used effectively to emphasise the central themes of the play. While earlier acts and scenes certainly show evidence of repetition, the sheer volume of repeated phrases in the next and final Act is staggering. Even the characters themselves notice the overwhelming use of duplication in other characters' dialogue, so much so that Othello reprimands Emilia, 'What needs this iterance, woman?' (Act 5 Scene 2, line 147). The heaping on of words and images to saturation point has an accumulative effect, called **cumulation**.

    Echoing is a specific example of repetition in *Othello*, and is particularly obvious in the exchange between Othello and Iago in Act 3.

Q Re-read Act 3 Scene 3, lines 102–11.

    a Quote various words and phrases that Iago repeats back to Othello during their exchange.

    b How does this language device of echoing draw our attention to the manipulative character of Iago?

Look up the following scenes, then construct and complete a table in your note book like the one overleaf to demonstrate your understanding of the types and purposes of repetition used throughout *Othello*, which climax in Act 5.

Repeated words, phrases or ideas	Textual reference	Intended effect
Repetition of words in a short section of text:		
'Thieves' *(5 times)*	1.1.79–81	To emphasise the perceived place of women as property
'Money' *(8 times)*	1.3.324–50	
_____ *(8 times)*	2.3.241–47	To highlight Cassio's humiliation
'Handkerchief' *(11 times)*	3.3.309–11; 3.4.82–93; and 4.1.35–41	
'L_____' *(13 times)*	3.4.1–9; 4.1.34–35	To emphasise the conflict between illusion and reality
'Whore' *(10 times)*	4.2.72–162	
'It is the_____' *(3 times)*	5.2.1–3	To slow the action and dialogue down, and to justify Othello's murder of Desdemona
'My wife' or 'wife' *(5 times)*	5.2.95–96	
_____ *(9 times)*	5.2.136–54	To emphasise Emilia's shock and horror
'Villain' or 'villainy' *(many times!)*	Throughout 5.2	
Consecutive repetition of words:		
'Strange / pitiful' (x2)	1.3.159–60; 4.1.178–79	To emphasise Othello's tenderness and gentleness
'And this' (x2)	2.1.189	
_____ (x3)	3.3.455	
'Cassio!' (x3)	5.1.83	To highlight Bianca's grief
'O!' (x3)	5.2.196	
_____ (x3)	5.2.324	
Frequent repetition of antithesis between 'honest' / 'lie' & 'heaven' / 'hell'	Throughout the entire play	To emphasise the conflict between reality and illusion
Abundant repetition of imagery relating to: Animals	Throughout the entire play	(Refer to box **More about imagery**, page 127)
Poison / Disease		

Act 5 Scene 1

Characters

Iago
Cassio
Othello
Lodovico
Roderigo
Gratiano
Bianca
Emilia
Narrator (optional, to read stage directions)

In a nutshell

As Iago and Roderigo wait in the street to ambush Cassio, Iago advises the uncertain Roderigo how to carry out his task. Roderigo fails to injure Cassio but is himself badly wounded in the ambush. Iago sneaks up behind Cassio, wounds him in the leg and exits. In the confusion that follows, Cassio's cries for help attract the attention of Gratiano and Lodovico, and Othello briefly enters and approves Iago's actions. Iago re-enters and, after a brief conversation with Gratiano and Lodovico, goes to investigate the situation. He then stabs and kills the defenceless Roderigo. While Iago is attending to Cassio's wounds, Bianca enters and cries out when she sees the wounded Cassio. As Roderigo and Cassio are carried offstage, Iago accuses Bianca of plotting to kill Cassio.

Before you read

- When approaching this scene, it is interesting to consider the staging at the Globe Theatre, where the play was originally performed (see the picture of the New Globe on page 7). When Iago commands Roderigo to 'stand behind this bulk', he is probably referring to one of the pillars onstage. The stage direction for Othello to enter and approve Iago's actions may seem strange but Othello probably would have entered on the balcony above.

- There is something darkly comical about the confusion of this scene. Make sure you read the stage directions carefully so you don't share the confusion of the characters onstage.

- This scene contains a moment of terrible insight for Roderigo, when he suddenly sees Iago for what he truly is. This foreshadows a number of horrible realisations by the other characters in the final scene.

Rapier: Light, sharp-pointed sword
Resolution: Determination or certainty
Restitution: Recovery, restoration or retrieval

Gait: (The manner of someone's) walk

Slain: Killed

Direful: Disastrous or terrible

Garter: A band used to hold up socks or stockings

Prithee: Used to introduce a request (short for 'I pray thee')

Fie: An exclamation of annoyance, disapproval or disgust

Act 5 Scene 1   Cyprus, a street.

[IAGO and RODERIGO enter]

IAGO	Here, stand behind this bulk; straight will he come.	
	Wear thy good rapier bare, and put it home.	
	Quick, quick; fear nothing; I'll be at thy elbow.	
	It makes us, or it mars us; think on that,	
	And fix most firm thy resolution.	5
RODERIGO	Be near at hand; I may miscarry in't.	
IAGO	Here, at thy hand; be bold, and take thy stand.	

[IAGO hides]

RODERIGO	I have no great devotion to the deed,	
	And yet he hath given me satisfying reasons;	
	'Tis but a man gone. Forth, my sword: he dies.	10
IAGO	I have rubbed this young quat almost to the sense,	
	And he grows angry. Now, whether he kill Cassio,	
	Or Cassio him, or each do kill the other,	
	Every way makes my gain. Live Roderigo,	
	He calls me to a restitution large	15
	Of gold and jewels that I bobbed from him,	
	As gifts to Desdemona.	
	It must not be. If Cassio do remain,	
	He hath a daily beauty in his life	
	That makes me ugly; and, besides, the Moor	20
	May unfold me to him: there stand I in much peril.	
	No, he must die. But so, I hear him coming.	

[CASSIO enters]

RODERIGO	I know his gait: 'tis he – Villain, thou diest!	

[RODERIGO tries to stab CASSIO]

CASSIO	That thrust had been mine enemy indeed,	
	But that my coat is better than thou know'st,	25
	I will make proof of thine.	

[CASSIO draws and wounds RODERIGO]

RODERIGO	O, I am slain!

[IAGO sneaks up behind CASSIO, wounds him in the leg, and then exits]

CASSIO	I am maimed for ever. Help, ho! Murder! Murder!

[CASSIO falls, as OTHELLO enters]

OTHELLO	The voice of Cassio: Iago keeps his word.	
RODERIGO	O, villain that I am!	
OTHELLO	It is even so.	
CASSIO	O, help, ho! Light! A surgeon!	30
OTHELLO	'Tis he – O brave Iago, honest and just,	
	That hast such noble sense of thy friend's wrong!	
	Thou teachest me – Minion, your dear lies dead,	
	And your unblest fate hies – Strumpet, I come.	
	Forth of my heart those charms, thine eyes, are blotted;	35
	Thy bed, lust-stained, shall with lust's blood be spotted.	

[OTHELLO exits, then LODOVICO and GRATIANO enter]

CASSIO	What, ho! No watch? No passage? Murder! Murder!	
GRATIANO	'Tis some mischance; the cry is very direful.	
CASSIO	O, help!	
LODOVICO	Hark!	40
RODERIGO	O wretched villain!	
LODOVICO	Two or three groan: it is a heavy night;	
	These may be counterfeits: let's think't unsafe	
	To come in to the cry without more help.	
RODERIGO	Nobody come? Then shall I bleed to death.	45
LODOVICO	Hark!	

[IAGO re-enters, with a light]

GRATIANO	Here's one comes in his shirt, with light and weapons.	
IAGO	Who's there? Whose noise is this that cries on murder?	
LODOVICO	We do not know.	
IAGO	Did not you hear a cry?	
CASSIO	Here, here! For heaven's sake, help me!	
IAGO	What's the matter?	50
GRATIANO	This is Othello's Ancient, as I take it.	
LODOVICO	The same indeed, a very valiant fellow.	
IAGO	What are you here that cry so grievously?	
CASSIO	Iago? O, I am spoiled, undone by villains!	
	Give me some help.	55
IAGO	O me, Lieutenant! What villains have done this?	
CASSIO	I think that one of them is hereabout,	
	And cannot make away.	

| IAGO | O treacherous villains! | |

[To LODOVICO and GRATIANO]

	What are you there? Come in, and give some help.	
RODERIGO	O, help me here!	60
CASSIO	That's one of them.	
IAGO	O murderous slave! O villain!	

[Stabs RODERIGO]

RODERIGO	O damned Iago! O inhuman dog!	
IAGO	Kill men i' the dark! – Where be these bloody thieves? –	
	How silent is this town! – Ho! Murder! Murder! –	
	What may you be? Are you of good or evil?	65
LODOVICO	As you shall prove us, praise us.	
IAGO	Signior Lodovico?	
LODOVICO	He, sir.	
IAGO	I cry you mercy. Here's Cassio hurt by villains.	
GRATIANO	Cassio!	70
IAGO	How is't, brother!	
CASSIO	My leg is cut in two.	
IAGO	Marry, heaven forbid!	
	Light, gentlemen; I'll bind it with my shirt.	

[BIANCA enters]

BIANCA	What is the matter, ho? Who is't that cried?	
IAGO	Who is't that cried?	
BIANCA	O my dear Cassio!	75
	My sweet Cassio! O Cassio, Cassio, Cassio!	
IAGO	O notable strumpet! Cassio, may you suspect	
	Who they should be that have thus mangled you?	
CASSIO	No.	
GRATIANO	I am sorry to find you thus; I have been to seek you.	80
IAGO	Lend me a garter – So – O, for a chair,	
	To bear him easily hence!	
BIANCA	Alas, he faints! O Cassio, Cassio, Cassio!	
IAGO	Gentlemen all, I do suspect this trash	
	To be a party in this injury –	85
	Patience awhile, good Cassio – Come, come;	
	Lend me a light – Know we this face or no? –	
	Alas! My friend and my dear countryman,	
	Roderigo! No! Yes, sure! O heaven, Roderigo!	
GRATIANO	What, of Venice?	90
IAGO	Even he, sir. Did you know him?	
GRATIANO	Know him? Ay!	

IAGO	Signior Gratiano? I cry you gentle pardon;
	These bloody accidents must excuse my manners
	That so neglected you.
GRATIANO	I am glad to see you.
IAGO	How do you, Cassio? O, a chair, a chair! 95
GRATIANO	Roderigo!
IAGO	He, he, 'tis he. *[A chair is brought in]* O, that's well said, the chair!
GRATIANO	Some good man bear him carefully from hence;
	I'll fetch the general's surgeon. *[To BIANCA]* For you, mistress,
	Save you your labour. He that lies slain here, Cassio, 100
	Was my dear friend: what malice was between you?
CASSIO	None in the world, nor do I know the man.
IAGO	*[To BIANCA]* What, look you pale? – O, bear him out o' the air.

[CASSIO and RODERIGO are carried off]

	Stay you, good gentlemen – Look you pale, mistress? –
	Do you perceive the gastness of her eye? – 105
	Nay, if you stare, we shall hear more anon –
	Behold her well; I pray you, look upon her.
	Do you see, gentlemen? Nay, guiltiness will speak,
	Though tongues were out of use.

[EMILIA enters]

EMILIA	'Las, what's the matter? What's the matter, husband? 110
IAGO	Cassio hath here been set on in the dark
	By Roderigo and fellows that are 'scaped.
	He's almost slain, and Roderigo dead.
EMILIA	Alas, good gentleman! Alas, good Cassio!
IAGO	This is the fruit of whoring. Prithee, Emilia, 115
	Go know of Cassio where he supped tonight.
	[To BIANCA] What, do you shake at that?
BIANCA	He supped at my house, but I therefore shake not.
IAGO	O, did he so? I charge you, go with me.
EMILIA	Fie, fie upon thee, strumpet! 120
BIANCA	I am no strumpet, but of life as honest
	As you that thus abuse me.
EMILIA	As I? Foh! Fie upon thee!
IAGO	Kind gentlemen, let's go see poor Cassio dressed –
	Come, mistress, you must tell's another tale –
	Emilia, run you to the citadel, 125
	And tell my lord and lady what hath happed –
	Will you go on afore? *[Aside]* This is the night
	That either makes me or fordoes me quite.

[All exit]

2 **Put it home:** Direct it to the target (in this case, probably the heart).

4 **It makes us, or it mars us:** We will be successful (made) or ruined (marred) by this action.

11 **I have rubbed this young quat almost to the sense:** Iago admits that, in using Roderigo, he has probably got away with all he can, and Roderigo is on the verge of seeing sense ('quat' = pimple).

24–26 **That thrust had been mine … I will make proof of thine:** Roderigo's sword would have killed Cassio but his armour (or possibly his leather jerkin) protected him. Now he threatens to test his attacker's armour.

33–34 **Minion, your dear lies … unblest fate hies:** A paraphrase might read: Desdemona, your love (i.e. Cassio) lies dead, and soon you will also be dead. 'Minion' could mean darling (a term of affection) or slave (a term of abuse) and is, therefore, appropriate to the situation.

34 **Strumpet:** Prostitute.

43 **Counterfeits:** Tricks (they are fearful that the cries might be leading them into a trap).

84–85 **Gentlemen all … party in this injury:** Iago accuses Bianca of having a share in a plan either to injure or murder Desdemona.

105 **Gastness:** Ghastliness (horror).

Questions

1 What is Roderigo's state of mind at the beginning of this scene? How does Shakespeare make this clear?

2 What are Iago's reasons for wanting Roderigo and Cassio dead?

3 Summarise the events and identify the results of the fighting in one or two sentences.

4 Choose two examples in which characters wrongly describe Iago in this scene (e.g., Othello calls him 'brave') and explain how these descriptions are ironic.

5 Iago identifies Roderigo with the words, 'Alas! My friend and my dear countryman'. How are his words particularly ironic?

6 What details in this scene might cause the audience to be sympathetic to Roderigo?

7 What does Iago suggest about Bianca in this scene? How is this a further example of dramatic irony?

8 How is the language Iago employs when talking to Cassio ironic?

9 Quote a line that shows Iago is aware of the risks he is taking.

Extend

1 Iago has been compared to a play's director or stage-manager by various critics: how true is this of his behaviour in this scene and elsewhere?

2 Iago says that he would like Cassio killed because 'He hath a daily beauty in his life / That makes [him] ugly.' What you do think this tells us about Iago's personality?

3 The original performances of *Othello* at the Globe Theatre would have taken place during the day. How does Shakespeare create the effect of darkness and confusion through the characters' dialogue and actions?

4 Why do you think Iago decides to accuse Bianca of conspiring against Cassio's life? How does Bianca's situation parallel Desdemona's?

5 Does the literal darkness of this scene have any metaphorical significance? Explain your answer.

Discuss If you were given the task of directing this scene, what dramatic devices would you use (besides the characters' dialogue and actions) to reinforce the sense of darkness and confusion?

Props as symbols in *Othello*

Shakespeare's plays depend on the interplay between the characters' dialogue and the audience's imagination for the presentation of ideas. In this sense, the audience agrees to suspend its disbelief, as opposed to expecting dramatic realism, especially in regard to setting and stage props. For instance, in the Prologue to *Henry V*, the audience is encouraged to 'Think, when we talk of horses, that you see them / Printing their proud hoofs i'th'receiving earth' (lines 27–28).

The use of stage props in Shakespearean theatre is relatively infrequent, but when they are used, they carry with them a significant interpretive weight. For example, consider the dagger in *Macbeth* or Yorick's skull in *Hamlet*, both of which have become powerful symbols of multi-generational and cross-cultural ideas. Thus, when the script of *Othello* repeatedly mentions two particular props we can assume they are central to our understanding of the play. In Act 5 Scene 2, Shakespeare merges parallel visual representations of Desdemona's purity: her handkerchief ('spotted with strawberries') and her 'blood … spotted' wedding sheets.

1 Desdemona's handkerchief
Throughout the play, frequent reference is made to Desdemona's silk handkerchief, a treasured gift from Othello that is embroidered with decorative strawberries.

In Shakespeare's time, handkerchiefs were elaborate and expensive symbols of love, especially between upper-class couples. Moreover, the strawberry motif was one of the most popular embroidery designs in Elizabethan and Jacobean England, and was a visual and metaphorical emblem associated with the Virgin Mary, hence virginal blood or purity.

Specifically, Desdemona's handkerchief becomes a potent symbol of her sexual purity, especially her faithfulness to Othello in their marriage union. In fact, the elaborately narrated history of the handkerchief (see Act 3 Scene 4, lines 49–69) is steeped in references to magic and poetic legend associated with virgins and purity, further reinforcing the mystical union between Othello and Desdemona.

Iago deliberately transforms the handkerchief from a symbol of purity to one that is 'stained' with 'lust'. He uses it to manipulate Othello's perception of reality, convincing him with 'ocular proof' that his wife is playing the 'whore' with Cassio. Other characters who come into contact with Desdemona's handkerchief become victims of destructive jealousy (e.g. Bianca in Act 4 Scene 1, lines 139–45). Finally, we see Othello's obsessive repetition of the word 'handkerchief' (Act 3 Scene 3, lines 309–11, Act 3 Scene 4, lines 82–93 and Act 4 Scene 1, lines 35–41) and the merging in Act 5 Scene 2 of this important emblem with the play's other major symbol of Desdemona's purity: her wedding sheets.

2 Desdemona's wedding sheets

The other major stage prop in *Othello* is Desdemona's marriage bed, and the associated 'wedding sheets', mentioned 25 times throughout the play.

Following Othello's vicious verbal attack, in which he repeatedly calls her a 'whore' (Act 4 Scene 2, lines 24–90), Desdemona asks Emilia to lay her wedding sheets on the bed (Act 4 Scene 2, line 105), perhaps as a reminder of her faithfulness to Othello. Some critics alternatively suggest that Desdemona uses her sheets here as a 'shroud' (Act 4 Scene 3, lines 23–24) in preparation for her death, which she assumes from Othello's threats is imminent.

a Symbols of virginal purity

Dating back to ancient Greek and Hebrew cultures (e.g. see *Deuteronomy* 22:13–22), it was customary in Renaissance Europe for husbands (and even fathers) to demand to see bloodstained wedding sheets as visual proof of a bride's virginity. Unfortunately for Othello, his mind has been so 'poisoned' by Iago, that what should have been seen as proof of Desdemona's fidelity is falsely perceived: 'Thy bed, lust-stained, shall with lust's blood be spotted' (Act 5 Scene 1, line 36).

b Parallel symbols

Desdemona's handkerchief, 'spotted with strawberries', is visually echoed on a larger scale in Act 5 by her bloodstained wedding sheets: both are powerful symbols of Desdemona's purity, of her sexual faithfulness to Othello. However, Othello cannot see this important truth.

3 Light

We have previously noted that *Othello* abounds in references to 'eyes' or 'seeing' (see **More about imagery**, page 127). In Act 5 Scene 2, Shakespeare makes brief but effective use of one further symbolic reference, this time to 'light'.

Q What literal light is present in Desdemona's bedchamber (see stage direction before line 1)?

Q When Othello says, 'Put out the light, and then put out the light' (line 7), how is this repetition to be interpreted literally but also metaphorically?

Q Make a list of other words and phrases in this scene that refer to light.

Q What important theme or idea might Shakespeare be suggesting about Othello through the cumulation of these words and phrases?

Q Read lines 96–100, which are spoken by Othello after he kills Desdemona.

  a What effect does Shakespeare create by having Othello repeat 'My wife'?

  b Othello speaks of putting out the light on a grand scale. What image does he use?

  c What might Shakespeare be demonstrating about Othello by this hyperbolic image?

Act 5 Scene 2 (Part 1)

Characters

Othello
Emilia
Desdemona
Narrator (optional, to read stage directions)

In a nutshell

Set on murdering Desdemona, Othello enters her bedchamber. His farewell kisses awaken her, and she asks him to come to bed. Amid Desdemona's protests of innocence, Othello speaks of his sorrow at her unfaithfulness, and when he reveals that Iago has killed Cassio, Desdemona's shock at this further confirms her guilt in his mind. Despite her cries for mercy, Othello suffocates Desdemona with a pillow, but he is interrupted by Emilia, who knocks at the door. When Othello lets Emilia in, she tells of recent events and Othello notes with disapproval that Cassio has not been killed. Just before she dies, Desdemona denies to Emilia that Othello murdered her. When Othello reveals how Iago told him of Desdemona's infidelity, Emilia insists that it is her husband who is a liar and, after insulting Othello, cries out for help.

Before you read

- Othello's opening soliloquy in this scene includes some of the play's most beautiful language. One particular detail worth noting is that, as Othello goes to kill Desdemona, he repeats the phrase 'it is the cause'. Although he cannot bear to name Desdemona's sin, he insists that he has good reason for killing her and that, rather than being vengeful, this killing is sacrificial. The audience is also aware that Othello is still fascinated with Desdemona, describing her skin as 'monumental alabaster': a translucent white stone, used to make statues and tombs. Additionally, Othello compares her to the burning torch he is carrying, musing that once he puts out the light of Desdemona's life he cannot relight it, as he can a torch. Othello then compares Desdemona's life to a rose, which once plucked cannot be reattached, and he continues the analogy by breathing in her scent, as if he were smelling a sweetly perfumed flower. Finally, despite the sin Othello believes Desdemona has committed, he cannot resist kissing her, and these kisses awaken her.

- The stage direction *[within]* occurs throughout this scene. It means the line is delivered from somewhere offstage.

Balmy:	Pleasant or gentle
Forfend:	Forbid
Portents:	Signs of a future event

Perjury: Dishonesty
Yonder: Over there
Folly: Stupidity
Iterance: Repetition
Pernicious: Destructive, dangerous or evil
Coxcomb: Idiot or fool
Malignant: Evil or spiteful

Act 5 Scene 2 (Part 1) A bedchamber in the castle.

[DESDEMONA is in bed asleep; a light burning. OTHELLO enters]

OTHELLO	It is the cause, it is the cause, my soul –	
	Let me not name it to you, you chaste stars! –	
	It is the cause. Yet I'll not shed her blood,	
	Nor scar that whiter skin of hers than snow,	
	And smooth as monumental alabaster.	5
	Yet she must die, else she'll betray more men.	
	Put out the light, and then put out the light.	
	If I quench thee, thou flaming minister,	
	I can again thy former light restore,	
	Should I repent me; but once put out thy light,	10
	Thou cunning'st pattern of excelling nature,	
	I know not where is that Promethean heat	
	That can thy light relume. When I have plucked the rose,	
	I cannot give it vital growth again;	
	It must needs wither. I'll smell it on the tree.	15

[Smelling her, then kissing her]

| | Ah balmy breath, that dost almost persuade | |
| | Justice to break her sword! One more, one more. | |

[He kisses her]

| | Be thus when thou art dead, and I will kill thee, | |
| | And love thee after. One more, and this the last. | |

[He kisses her]

	So sweet was ne'er so fatal. I must weep,	20
	But they are cruel tears. This sorrow's heavenly;	
	It strikes where it doth love. She wakes.	
DESDEMONA	Who's there? Othello?	
OTHELLO	Ay, Desdemona.	
DESDEMONA	Will you come to bed, my lord?	
OTHELLO	Have you prayed tonight, Desdemona?	
DESDEMONA	Ay, my lord.	25

OTHELLO	If you bethink yourself of any crime	
	Unreconciled as yet to heaven and grace,	
	Solicit for it straight.	
DESDEMONA	Alas, my lord, what do you mean by that?	
OTHELLO	Well, do it, and be brief; I will walk by:	30
	I would not kill thy unpreparèd spirit;	
	No, heavens forfend! I would not kill thy soul.	
DESDEMONA	Talk you of killing?	
OTHELLO	Ay, I do.	
DESDEMONA	Then heaven	
	Have mercy on me!	
OTHELLO	Amen, with all my heart!	
DESDEMONA	If you say so, I hope you will not kill me.	35
OTHELLO	Hum!	
DESDEMONA	And yet I fear you, for you are fatal then	
	When your eyes roll so. Why I should fear I know not,	
	Since guiltiness I know not; but yet I feel I fear.	
OTHELLO	Think on thy sins.	
DESDEMONA	They are loves I bear to you.	40
OTHELLO	Ay, and for that thou diest.	
DESDEMONA	That death's unnatural that kills for loving.	
	Alas, why gnaw you so your nether lip?	
	Some bloody passion shakes your very frame:	
	These are portents; but yet I hope, I hope,	45
	They do not point on me.	
OTHELLO	Peace, and be still!	
DESDEMONA	I will so. What's the matter?	
OTHELLO	That handkerchief, which I so loved and gave thee,	
	Thou gav'st to Cassio.	
DESDEMONA	No, by my life and soul!	
	Send for the man and ask him.	
OTHELLO	Sweet soul, take heed;	50
	Take heed of perjury: thou'rt on thy deathbed.	
DESDEMONA	Ay, but not yet to die.	
OTHELLO	Yes, presently.	
	Therefore, confess thee freely of thy sin,	
	For to deny each article with oath	
	Cannot remove nor choke the strong conception	55
	That I do groan withal. Thou art to die.	
DESDEMONA	Then Lord have mercy on me!	
OTHELLO	I say, amen.	
DESDEMONA	And have you mercy too! I never did	
	Offend you in my life; never loved Cassio	
	But with such general warranty of heaven	60
	As I might love. I never gave him token.	

OTHELLO	By heaven, I saw my handkerchief in's hand.
	O perjured woman! Thou dost stone my heart,
	And makest me call what I intend to do
	A murder, which I thought a sacrifice.	65
	I saw the handkerchief.
DESDEMONA	He found it then;
	I never gave it him. Send for him hither;
	Let him confess a truth.
OTHELLO	He hath confessed.
DESDEMONA	What, my lord?
OTHELLO	That he hath used thee.
DESDEMONA	How? Unlawfully?	70
OTHELLO	Ay.
DESDEMONA	He will not say so.
OTHELLO	No, his mouth is stopped.
	Honest Iago hath ta'en order for't.
DESDEMONA	O! My fear interprets. What, is he dead?
OTHELLO	Had all his hairs been lives, my great revenge
	Had stomach for them all.	75
DESDEMONA	Alas! He is betrayed and I undone.
OTHELLO	Out, strumpet! Weep'st thou for him to my face?
DESDEMONA	O, banish me, my lord, but kill me not!
OTHELLO	Down, strumpet!
DESDEMONA	Kill me tomorrow. Let me live tonight!	80
OTHELLO	Nay, if you strive –
DESDEMONA	But half an hour!
OTHELLO	Being done, there is no pause.
DESDEMONA	But while I say one prayer!
OTHELLO	It is too late.

[He suffocates her with a pillow]

EMILIA	*[Within]* My lord, my lord! What, ho! My lord, my lord!
OTHELLO	What noise is this? Not dead? Not yet quite dead?	85
	I that am cruèl am yet merciful;
	I would not have thee linger in thy pain:

[He smothers her again]

	So, so.
EMILIA	*[Within]* What, ho! My lord, my lord!
OTHELLO	Who's there?
EMILIA	*[Within]* O, good my lord, I would speak a word with you!
OTHELLO	Yes, 'tis Emilia – By and by – She's dead.	90
	'Tis like she comes to speak of Cassio's death.
	The noise was here. Ha! No more moving?
	Still as the grave. Shall she come in? Were't good?

	I think she stirs again. No. What's best to do?	
	If she come in, she'll sure speak to my wife.	95
	My wife! My wife! What wife? I have no wife.	
	O insupportable! O heavy hour!	
	Methinks it should be now a huge eclipse	
	Of sun and moon, and that the affrighted globe	
	Should yawn at alteration.	
EMILIA	*[Within]* I do beseech you,	100
	That I may speak with you, O, good my lord!	
OTHELLO	I had forgot thee. O, come in, Emilia.	
	Soft, by and by. Let me the curtains draw.	
	Where art thou?	

[OTHELLO unlocks the door to allow EMILIA to enter]

	What's the matter with thee now?	
EMILIA	O, my good lord, yonder's foul murders done!	105
OTHELLO	What, now?	
EMILIA	But now, my lord.	
OTHELLO	It is the very error of the moon;	
	She comes more nearer earth than she was wont,	
	And makes men mad.	110
EMILIA	Cassio, my lord, hath killed a young Venetian	
	Called Roderigo.	
OTHELLO	Roderigo killed!	
	And Cassio killed!	
EMILIA	No, Cassio is not killed.	
OTHELLO	Not Cassio killed? Then murder's out of tune,	
	And sweet revenge grows harsh.	115
DESDEMONA	O, falsely, falsely murdered!	
EMILIA	O Lord! Alas, what cry is that?	
OTHELLO	That? What?	
EMILIA	Out and alas! That was my lady's voice.	
	Help! Help, ho! Help! O lady, speak again!	
	Sweet Desdemona! O sweet mistress, speak!	120
DESDEMONA	A guiltless death I die.	
EMILIA	O, who hath done this deed?	
DESDEMONA	Nobody; I myself. Farewell.	
	Commend me to my kind lord. O! Farewell!	

[She dies]

OTHELLO	Why, how should she be murdered?	
EMILIA	Alas, who knows?	125
OTHELLO	You heard her say herself it was not I.	
EMILIA	She said so; I must needs report the truth.	
OTHELLO	She's like a liar, gone to burning hell!	
	'Twas I that killed her!	

EMILIA	O, the more angel she,
	And you the blacker devil! 130
OTHELLO	She turned to folly, and she was a whore.
EMILIA	Thou dost belie her, and thou art a devil.
OTHELLO	She was false as water.
EMILIA	Thou'rt rash as fire, to say
	That she was false. O! She was heavenly true!
OTHELLO	Cassio did top her; ask thy husband else. 135
	O, I were damned beneath all depth in hell,
	But that I did proceed upon just grounds
	To this extremity. Thy husband knew it all.
EMILIA	My husband?
OTHELLO	Thy husband.
EMILIA	That she was false to wedlock?
OTHELLO	Ay, with Cassio. Nay, had she been true, 140
	If heaven would make me such another world
	Of one entire and perfect chrysolite,
	I'd not have sold her for it.
EMILIA	My husband?
OTHELLO	Ay, 'twas he that told me first:
	An honest man he is, and hates the slime 145
	That sticks on filthy deeds.
EMILIA	My husband?
OTHELLO	What needs this iterance, woman? I say thy husband.
EMILIA	O mistress, villainy hath made mocks with love.
	My husband, say that she was false?
OTHELLO	He, woman;
	I say thy husband. Dost understand the word? 150
	My friend, thy husband: honest, honest Iago.
EMILIA	If he say so, may his pernicious soul
	Rot half a grain a day! He lies to the heart.
	She was too fond of her most filthy bargain.
OTHELLO	Ha! 155
EMILIA	Do thy worst:
	This deed of thine is no more worthy heaven
	Than thou wast worthy her.
OTHELLO	Peace, you were best.

[OTHELLO moves threateningly toward EMILIA]

EMILIA	Thou hast not half that power to do me harm
	As I have to be hurt. O gull! O dolt! 160
	As ignorant as dirt! Thou hast done a deed

[OTHELLO draws his sword]

	I care not for thy sword; I'll make thee known,
	Though I lost twenty lives – Help! Help, ho! Help!
	The Moor hath killed my mistress! Murder! Murder!

Text notes

8	**Thou flaming minister:** You burning torch (here 'minister' = servant or instrument).
12	**Promethean:** Prometheus defied the gods to bring fire to mankind.
13	**Relume:** Relight or rekindle.
20	**So sweet was ne'er so fatal:** Othello states that nothing was ever so sweet and deadly at the same time. This use of antithesis perhaps illustrates his internal conflict.
26–28	**If you bethink … Solicit for it straight:** Othello tells Desdemona to seek forgiveness for her sins immediately.
40	**They are loves I bear to you:** The only sin Desdemona can think of is her love for Othello that caused her to deceive her father.
54–56	**For to deny each article … I do groan withal:** Othello asserts that Desdemona's denials do not convince or sway him and that, even should she deny every point, he would still be suspicious. He compares his pain to that of giving birth.
108–10	**It is the very error … makes men mad:** When the moon comes too near to the earth, it makes men mad. The moon was widely associated with madness. Lunacy is derived from the Latin word for moon, 'luna'.
114–15	**Then murder's out of tune … grows harsh:** Othello is saying that the wrong man has been murdered and what should be sweet revenge is instead harsh.
132	**Thou dost belie her:** You tell lies about her.
133	**She was false as water:** Othello compares Desdemona with water, possibly because water was considered proverbially unreliable; hence, this is a metaphor for Desdemona's supposed infidelity.
135	**Cassio did top her:** Cassio had sex with her. It is interesting to note that Othello uses the word 'top', which has been used twice previously by Iago to describe Othello and Desdemona's sexual union in vulgar terms.
136–38	**O, I were damned beneath … To this extremity:** Othello concedes that his actions would bring damnation, if he had not had such sound reasons for this extreme course of action (murdering Desdemona).
141–43	**If heaven would … sold her for it:** Othello claims that, if Desdemona had been faithful, he would not have traded her for a world made out of chrysolite or topaz (a precious stone). According to legend, topaz would crack if it had any flaws and it was therefore believed to be an appropriate symbol for purity. Shakespeare probably chooses to name this particular stone for its exotic sound.
152–53	**If he say so … Rot half a grain a day:** Emilia asserts that, if Iago is telling a lie like this, she wishes him a slow death (she is possibly referring to damnation here).
156–58	**Do thy worst … thou wast worthy of her:** Emilia contradicts Othello's self-proclaimed heavenly mission by stating that the gap between his action (Desdemona's murder) and heavenly (moral) action is as wide as the gap between Desdemona's goodness and Othello's depraved character.
159–60	**Thou hast not half … have to be hurt:** Emilia says she can endure a lot more pain than Othello has the ability to inflict.
160	**Gull:** Fool (equivalent to a sucker today); **dolt:** idiot.

1 What devices or particular words do you think give an emotional intensity to Othello's opening soliloquy?

2 Why does Othello want Desdemona to pray? What does this tell us about his attitude towards her?

3 What is Desdemona's reaction to Cassio's murder? How does Othello react to this?

4 Quote a line or phrase that suggests Desdemona struggles or tries to fight against Othello.

5 How does Desdemona show her loyalty to Othello until the end?

6 How is Othello's statement in line 128 about Desdemona ('she's like a liar, gone to burning hell!') ironic?

7 What effect does Emilia's repetition of the phrase 'my husband' (lines 139–49) produce in this scene? How does this dialogue reinforce her disbelief?

8 Why do you think Shakespeare has Othello identify Iago as 'honest, honest Iago' (line 151)?

1 Othello says in his opening speech, 'Put out the light, and then put out the light' (line 7). What do you think he means by this? Explain the two lights and the poetic device he is using.

2 How does Desdemona's presence (although asleep) add a tension and a resonance to Othello's soliloquy (lines 1–22)?

3 What do you notice about the pace of the dialogue in this scene (especially lines 23–84)? How does this contribute to the action?

4 When Othello tells Desdemona to think of her sins, she responds, 'They are loves I bear to you' (line 40). To what extent do you find this to be true? Do you think this statement resonates with something Iago said at the end of Act 2?

5 What can we tell about Desdemona from her final words? How are they ironic?

6 Create a table to demonstrate your understanding of how Othello's language changes immediately after he murders Desdemona (focus on lines 90–158). Consider aspects such as hyperbole, antithesis, imagery, repetition, sentence length and punctuation.

7 Some critics accuse Emilia of being particularly racist toward Othello beginning at line 160. What is your opinion?

8 Can you find any evidence in this section of Act 5 Scene 2 that Emilia has a better opinion of Iago than he deserves?

1 Before being murdered, Desdemona says, 'That death's unnatural that kills for loving' (line 42). To what extent would you call Othello's feelings for Desdemona love?

2   Many modern performances of *Othello* omit the lines where Desdemona revives and speaks her final words, because a contemporary audience generally likes naturalistic (or realistic) theatre. If you were directing a modern production of the play, which keeps these lines, describe how you would direct this part of the scene. Include aspects such as lighting, music, blocking and location of the bed on stage.

Press PLAY **Oliver Parker: DVD Chapters 25–26 ('Put out the light')**

1   Parker has Othello break his 'put out the light' soliloquy into smaller sections with many pauses and actions. Do you find this effective? Why or why not?

2   How does Parker convey Othello's reluctance to murder Desdemona?

3   Discuss how Parker uses costume to contrast the characters of Desdemona and Othello.

4   Parker omits the dialogue when Desdemona revives to clear Othello's name. Why do you think Parker makes this decision? Do you agree with it?

Performing Act 5 Scene 2

Othello's murder of Desdemona has provoked no small stir amongst audiences, critics, directors and actors since its first performance in 1604:

- Dr Samuel Johnson (1765) writes, 'This dreadful scene … is not to be endured'.
- H. H. Furness (1886) describes 'the unutterable agony of this closing scene'.
- A. C. Bradley (1905) argues that, of all Shakespeare's tragedies, '*Othello* is the most painfully exciting and the most terrible'.

Similar views are expressed today:

- Edward Pechter (1999) labels this scene as 'most appalling'.
- Michael Neill (2002) contends, 'The ending of *Othello* is … disturbing [and] brutal … perhaps the most shocking in Shakespearean tragedy.'
- Clare R. Kinney (2007) finds the 'claustrophobic horror' of *Othello*'s final scene 'the most unbearable to watch'.

As an audience, we are fully aware that Iago has cruelly deceived Othello, and that Desdemona is indeed innocent. Thus, Othello's violent language in this scene (repeatedly calling Desdemona a liar and a 'strumpet' or whore), and his brutal act of smothering her with a pillow, are agonising to watch.

This disturbing spectacle is crucial to our understanding of the characters portrayed and the ideas presented, and raises numerous questions about how to perform the scene, both in terms of theatrical devices and characterisation.

1 **Technical aspects of directing the scene**

According to Shakespeare's script, Othello murders Desdemona in her bed. Discuss the following questions in groups or as a class to decide how you would stage this scene.

a **Props**

Q Where should the bed be positioned? Upstage? Downstage?

Q Could Othello murder her offstage, leaving the grizzly details to the audience's imagination?

Q Should Desdemona be hidden behind curtains, like in many productions of the nineteenth century?

b **Positioning**

Q Should Othello face the audience? Have his back to the audience?

Q Is it necessary to see the characters' facial expressions?

c **Lighting**

Q Desdemona is asleep, so should the stage be darkened?

Q How might this affect the visibility of the characters' actions?

d **Sound**

Q Should Othello whisper his opening lines?

Q When Othello and Desdemona interact, should their voices be raised?

Q Is music appropriate for this scene? If so, what music would be suitable?

Q Would music interfere with the actors' delivery of their dialogue?

2 **Portraying Desdemona**

a **Passive silence?**

Q Should Desdemona be characterised as passive? A sacrificial victim?

Q Is it appropriate to cast Desdemona as silently passive for today's audience?

Q Are there any indications in the text that she should be portrayed this way?

b **Angry assertion?**

Q Should Desdemona be angry when protesting her innocence (Act 5 Scene 2, lines 58–61, 66–68)?

Q In Act 1, Desdemona boldly speaks before the Senate, so wouldn't she be equally vigorous now?

Q Read lines 79–82. What can be said of Desdemona's interruption of Othello?

Q There are implied or embedded stage directions when Othello states 'Down strumpet!' and 'Nay, if you strive'. What is implied about Desdemona's actions here?

Act 5 Scene 2 of *Othello* is arguably the most intense scene in all of Shakespeare's tragedies. Consequently, a director's decisions on the use of technical features, combined with choices about how to portray Desdemona, are paramount.

Othello's final speech

In Othello's final speech (lines 339–57), he requests that he be remembered accurately and asks that the extremity of his circumstances be taken into account. As a Venetian General he was, in effect, the defender of Christian civilisation against the barbarian Turks. Now he recognises the barbarian in himself and, again as the defender of civilisation, carries out a judgement and execution upon himself. Critics hotly debate the purpose of Othello's final speech. Is Othello merely self-deluded and trying to comfort himself by putting a favourable slant on his actions? Has he learned anything? How much dignity does he, in fact, regain?

Read Othello's final speech out aloud a few times, then read the notes and answer the questions. You might like to read the speech by going around the class, with each student reading up to the next punctuation mark:

e.g.   Student 1: *Soft you;*

   Student 2: *a word or two before you go.*

   Student 3: *I have done the state some service*, etc.

In your reading, try to preserve the rhythm (iambic pentameter).

Individually, or in small groups, answer the following questions and come to your own conclusions. Discuss your answers with the rest of the class.

Q What role do Othello's military accomplishments play in this speech? Does he want to be remembered for these actions?

Q Were Othello's deeds 'unlucky' in your opinion?

Q What does Othello say in defence of his actions?

Q How accurate are Othello's descriptions of himself as:

- 'one that loved not wisely but too well'?
- 'one not easily jealous'?

Q To what extent is Othello like the 'base Indian'?

Q Does it make any difference whether a 'Judean' or an 'Indian' throws away the pearl (line 348)? Explain which reading you prefer and why.

Q Othello does not mention any other characters by name: what does his omitting them suggest?

Q Is Othello's decision to carry out judgement and execution on himself noble and dignified? Does it in any way vindicate his past actions or set anything right? Do you think Othello regains any dignity in his dying speech?

Q List the exotic words and images employed in this speech. To what extent is this a return to the language Othello uses in Act 1 (before the destructive effects of jealousy transformed him)?

Q Do you think Othello gains new insight through his tragic circumstances?

Q Annotate the soliloquy with your own notes and comments, using the annotated soliloquy on page 92 as a model.

Act 5 Scene 2 (Part 2)

Characters

Othello
Emilia
Lodovico
Iago
Montano
Cassio
Gratiano
Narrator (optional, to read stage directions)

In a nutshell

The noise of Emilia's cries brings Gratiano, Montano, Iago and others into the room. When the truth about the handkerchief comes to light, Othello rushes at Iago, who stabs Emilia before escaping. Emilia dies singing the Willow Song and asks to be laid by Desdemona's side. Iago is captured and, after the plots are discovered, he vows never to speak again. In the full realisation of what he has done, Othello commits suicide, after which Iago is led away to be tortured.

Before you read

- Tragedy in general, and Shakespearean tragedy in particular, provides characters onstage with some space for reflection. This is not the case in *Othello*, as it is not until the middle of the final scene that Othello discovers the truth about Iago, a character who, in turn, refuses to reveal his motivations. A mere twelve lines are spoken after Othello's dying words, leaving the audience, like the central characters, in a state of shock.

Odious:	Hateful
Go to:	Go away or get moving
Perforce:	By force
Perchance:	By chance, or maybe
Zounds:	God's Wounds (a violent oath)
Impediments:	Obstructions or obstacles
Fie:	Expression of annoyance, disapproval or disgust
Fable:	Story
Upbraids:	Tells someone off
Censure:	Severe criticism

Act 5 Scene 2 (Part 2)   A bedchamber in the castle.

[OTHELLO and EMILIA stand near the bed on which DESDEMONA lies, murdered; MONTANO, GRATIANO, IAGO and others enter]

MONTANO	What is the matter? How now, General!	165
EMILIA	O, are you come, Iago? You have done well,	
	That men must lay their murders on your neck.	

GRATIANO	What is the matter?	
EMILIA	Disprove this villain, if thou be'st a man.	
	He says thou told'st him that his wife was false.	170
	I know thou didst not; thou'rt not such a villain.	
	Speak, for my heart is full.	
IAGO	I told him what I thought, and told no more	
	Than what he found himself was apt and true.	
EMILIA	But did you ever tell him she was false?	175
IAGO	I did.	
EMILIA	You told a lie: an odious, damnèd lie;	
	Upon my soul, a lie, a wicked lie.	
	She false with Cassio? Did you say with Cassio?	
IAGO	With Cassio, mistress. Go to; charm your tongue.	180
EMILIA	I will not charm my tongue; I am bound to speak:	
	My mistress here lies murdered in her bed –	
ALL	O heavens forfend!	
EMILIA	And your reports have set the murder on.	
OTHELLO	Nay, stare not, masters; it is true, indeed.	185
GRATIANO	'Tis a strange truth.	
MONTANO	O monstrous act!	
EMILIA	Villainy, villainy, villainy!	
	I think upon't, I think I smell't. O villainy!	
	I thought so then – I'll kill myself for grief.	190
	O villainy! Villainy!	
IAGO	What, are you mad? I charge you: get you home.	
EMILIA	Good gentlemen, let me have leave to speak.	
	'Tis proper I obey him, but not now.	
	Perchance, Iago, I will ne'er go home.	195
OTHELLO	O! O! O! *[He falls on the bed]*	
EMILIA	Nay, lay thee down and roar,	
	For thou hast killed the sweetest innocent	
	That e'er did lift up eye.	
OTHELLO	*[Rising]* O, she was foul!	
	I scarce did know you, uncle. There lies your niece,	200
	Whose breath, indeed, these hands have newly stopped.	
	I know this act shows horrible and grim.	
GRATIANO	Poor Desdemona! I am glad thy father's dead:	
	Thy match was mortal to him, and pure grief	
	Shore his old thread in twain. Did he live now,	205
	This sight would make him do a desperate turn,	
	Yea, curse his better angel from his side,	
	And fall to reprobation.	
OTHELLO	'Tis pitiful, but yet Iago knows	
	That she with Cassio hath the act of shame	210
	A thousand times committed. Cassio confessed it,	

And she did gratify his amorous works
With that recognizance and pledge of l
Which I first gave her. I saw it in his han
It was a handkerchief, an antique token
My father gave my mother.

EMILIA   O heaven! O heavenly po

IAGO   Zounds, hold your pea

EMILIA

No, I will speak as liber
Let heaven and men an
All, all, cry shame agai

IAGO   Be wise, and get you ho

[IAGO threatens to stab EMILIA]

EMILIA	I will not.
GRATIANO	Fie! Your swo
EMILIA	O thou dull Moor! That handkerchief thou speak'st of
	I found by fortune and did give my husband;
	For often, with a solemn earnestness,
	More than indeed belonged to such a trifle,
	He begged of me to steal it.
IAGO	Villainous whore!
EMILIA	She give it Cassio? No, alas! I found it,
	And I did give't my husband.
IAGO	Filth, thou liest!
EMILIA	By heaven, I do not; I do not, gentlemen.
	O murderous coxcomb! What should such a fool
	Do with so good a wife?
OTHELLO	Are there no stones in heaven
	But what serve for the thunder? Precious villain!

                    225
                    230

[He runs at IAGO, who stabs EMILIA from behind and runs off]

GRATIANO	The woman falls; sure, he hath killed his wife.	235
EMILIA	Ay, ay. O, lay me by my mistress' side.	
GRATIANO	He's gone, but his wife's killed.	
MONTANO	'Tis a notorious villain. Take you this weapon,	
	Which I have here recovered from the Moor.	
	Come, guard the door without; let him not pass,	240
	But kill him rather. I'll after that same villain,	
	For 'tis a damnèd slave.	

[MONTANO and GRATIANO exit]

OTHELLO	I am not valiant neither,	
	But ever puny whipster gets my sword.	
	But why should honour outlive honesty?	245
	Let it go all.	

EMILIA   What did thy song bode, lady?
Hark, canst thou hear me? I will play the swan,
And die in music: *[Singing]Willow, willow, willow* —
Moor, she was chaste; she loved thee, cruel Moor;
So come my soul to bliss, as I speak true;   250
So speaking as I think, I die, I die.

[She dies]

OTHELLO   I have another weapon in this chamber:
It is a sword of Spain, the ice-brook's temper.
O, here it is – Uncle, I must come forth.

GRATIANO   *[Within]* If thou attempt it, it will cost thee dear: 255
Thou hast no weapon, and perforce must suffer.

OTHELLO   Look in upon me then and speak with me,
Or, naked as I am, I will assault thee.

[GRATIANO re-enters]

GRATIANO   What is the matter?
OTHELLO   Behold, I have a weapon;
A better never did itself sustain   260
Upon a soldier's thigh. I have seen the day,
That, with this little arm and this good sword,
I have made my way through more impediments
Than twenty times your stop. But, O vain boast!
Who can control his fate? 'Tis not so now.   265
Be not afraid, though you do see me weaponed:
Here is my journey's end, here is my butt,
And very sea-mark of my utmost sail.
Do you go back dismayed? 'Tis a lost fear;
Man but a rush against Othello's breast,   270
And he retires. Where should Othello go? –

[OTHELLO looks towards DESDEMONA on the bed]

Now, how dost thou look now? O ill-starred wench!
Pale as thy smock! When we shall meet at compt,
This look of thine will hurl my soul from heaven,
And fiends will snatch at it. *[He touches her]*   275
Cold, cold, my girl! Ev'n like thy chastity. –
O cursèd, cursèd slave! Whip me, ye devils,
From the possession of this heavenly sight!
Blow me about in winds! Roast me in sulphur!
Wash me in steep-down gulfs of liquid fire!   280
O Desdemona! Desdemona! Dead!
Oh! Oh! Oh!

[LODOVICO, MONTANO, CASSIO carried in a chair, and Officers with IAGO as prisoner, enter]

LODOVICO	Where is this rash and most unfortunate man?	
OTHELLO	That's he that was Othello; here I am.	
LODOVICO	Where is that viper? Bring the villain forth.	285
OTHELLO	I look down t'wards his feet; but that's a fable.	
	If that thou be'st a devil, I cannot kill thee.	

[He wounds IAGO]

LODOVICO	Wrench his sword from him.	
IAGO	I bleed, sir, but not killed.	
OTHELLO	I am not sorry neither; I'd have thee live,	
	For, in my sense, 'tis happiness to die.	290
LODOVICO	O thou Othello, that wert once so good,	
	Fall'n in the practice of a damnèd slave.	
	What shall be said to thee?	
OTHELLO	Why, anything;	
	An honourable murderer, if you will,	
	For nought I did in hate, but all in honour.	295
LODOVICO	This wretch hath part confessed his villainy;	
	Did you and he consent in Cassio's death?	
OTHELLO	Ay.	
CASSIO	Dear General, I never gave you cause.	
OTHELLO	I do believe it, and I ask your pardon.	300
	Will you, I pray, demand that demi-devil	
	Why he hath thus ensnared my soul and body?	
IAGO	Demand me nothing: what you know, you know.	
	From this time forth I never will speak word.	
LODOVICO	What? Not to pray?	
GRATIANO	Torments will ope your lips.	305
OTHELLO	Well, thou dost best.	
LODOVICO	Sir, you shall understand what hath befall'n,	
	Which, as I think, you know not. Here is a letter	
	Found in the pocket of the slain Roderigo,	
	And here another: the one of them imports	310
	The death of Cassio to be undertook	
	By Roderigo.	
OTHELLO	O villain!	
CASSIO	Most heathenish and most gross!	
LODOVICO	Now here's another discontented paper,	315
	Found in his pocket too; and this, it seems,	
	Roderigo meant to have sent this damnèd villain;	
	But that belike Iago in the interim	
	Came in and satisfied him.	
OTHELLO	O the pernicious caitiff!	
	How came you, Cassio, by that handkerchief	320
	That was my wife's?	

CASSIO	I found it in my chamber,
	And he himself confessed but even now
	That there he dropped it for a special purpose
	Which wrought to his desire.
OTHELLO	O fool! Fool! Fool!
CASSIO	There is besides in Roderigo's letter	325
	How he upbraids Iago, that he made him
	Brave me upon the watch; whereon it came
	That I was cast; and even but now he spake,
	After long seeming dead, Iago hurt him,
	Iago set him on.	330
LODOVICO	[To OTHELLO] You must forsake this room and go with us.
	Your power and your command is taken off,
	And Cassio rules in Cyprus – For this slave,
	If there be any cunning cruelty
	That can torment him much and hold him long,	335
	It shall be his. You shall close prisoner rest,
	Till that the nature of your fault be known
	To the Venetian state – Come, bring him away.
OTHELLO	Soft you; a word or two before you go.
	I have done the state some service, and they know't;	340
	No more of that. I pray you, in your letters,
	When you shall these unlucky deeds relate,
	Speak of me as I am; nothing extenuate,
	Nor set down aught in malice. Then must you speak
	Of one that loved not wisely but too well;	345
	Of one not easily jealous, but being wrought
	Perplexed in the extreme; of one whose hand,
	Like the base Indian, threw a pearl away
	Richer than all his tribe; of one whose subdued eyes,
	Albeit unusèd to the melting mood,	350
	Drop tears as fast as the Arabian trees
	Their medicinal gum. Set you down this,
	And say besides, that in Aleppo once,
	Where a malignant and a turbaned Turk
	Beat a Venetian and traduced the state,	355
	I took by the throat the circumcisèd dog,
	And smote him, thus.

[OTHELLO stabs himself]

LODOVICO	O bloody period!
GRATIANO	All that's spoke is marred.
OTHELLO	I kissed thee ere I killed thee. No way but this:
	Killing myself, to die upon a kiss.	360

[He kisses DESDEMONA, and dies]

CASSIO	This did I fear, but thought he had no weapon,
	For he was great of heart.
LODOVICO	*[To IAGO]* O Spartan dog,
	More fell than anguish, hunger, or the sea!
	Look on the tragic loading of this bed:
	This is thy work. The object poisons sight;
	Let it be hid – Gratiano, keep the house,
	And seize upon the fortunes of the Moor,
	For they succeed on you. To you, lord governor,
	Remains the censure of this hellish villain:
	The time, the place, the torture. O, enforce it!
	Myself will straight aboard, and to the state
	This heavy act with heavy heart relate.

365

370

[All exit]

Text notes

180   **Charm your tongue:** Hold your tongue.

204–8   **Thy match was mortal … fall to reprobation:** Gratiano reports that Desdemona's father died because of her decision to elope with Othello. He thinks that if Desdemona's father were still alive, the sight of Desdemona's corpse would cause him such shock and misery that he would curse the angel at his side (his guardian angel) and commit suicide, thus falling into eternal damnation ('reprobation').

212–14   **And she did gratify … Which I first gave her:** Othello asserts that Desdemona rewarded Cassio's lovemaking with the gift of the handkerchief.

215   **An antique token:** An old gift.

219   **No, I will speak as liberal as the north:** I will speak as freely at the north wind blows.

247–48   **I will play the swan, / And die in music:** The swan was believed to sing only once in its lifetime. Today, someone's final performance is known as his or her 'swan song'.

253   **It is a sword of Spain, the ice-brook's temper:** There is a type of Spanish sword that was made by plunging hot steel into a cold river.

260–61   **A better never did … a soldier's thigh:** A soldier carried his sword in a sheath by his side. Othello says that there is no better sword than his.

263–64   **I have made my way … twenty times your stop:** Othello claims that, in battle, he has cut through more than twenty times the number of the men in front of him with the sword he is holding.

267–68   **Here is my journey's end … my utmost sail:** Othello has come to the end of his journey, and the beacon marks his entrance to the final harbour ('butt' = target).

269–71   **'Tis a lost fear … And he retires:** Othello tells the other men that they have nothing to fear. If they attack him with as much as a rush (a long, thin leaf), he will retreat.

272   **Ill-starred wench:** Unlucky (or doomed) girl. The name Desdemona means 'ill-starred' in Greek; here, Othello is blaming fate (the stars) rather than himself.

273 **Compt:** The final account or judgement day.

286–87 **I look down t'wards … I cannot kill thee:** In stories, the Devil often comes in disguise but cannot cover up his hooves. Othello refers here to the cloven hooves that would prove Iago to be a devil, but acknowledges that these are only in stories.

314 **Most heathenish:** Barbaric and ungodly.

315 **Discontented paper:** A discontented letter (another piece of evidence).

316–19 **It seems Roderigo … in and satisfied him:** It seems that Roderigo was going to send this letter to Iago but Iago stopped his complaints by killing him, just before he could deliver it.

319 **Pernicious caitiff:** Destructive wretch.

343 **Extenuate:** Tone down or reduce.

344 **Aught:** Anything.

346 **Wrought:** Worked (manipulated by Iago).

348–49 **Like the base Indian … all his tribe:** Early explorers of America noted the Indians' ignorance of the value of the precious stones they would throw away. Othello, likewise, has thrown away Desdemona's love without realising its true value. While most contemporary editions use the word 'Indian', the First Folio text has the word 'Judean', which may be an allusion to Judas who betrayed Jesus for thirty pieces of silver. There is also an allusion to 'the pearl of great price', in Matthew's Gospel, where it is used as a metaphor for heaven.

349–52 **Of one whose subdued eyes … Their medicinal gum:** Othello claims that he is usually restrained, being unused to these kinds of emotional situations, but is now overwhelmed with grief and shedding tears as fast as Arabian trees produce their fragrant juices (these juices were associated with healing).

353 **Aleppo:** A Muslim city in modern-day Turkey.

354 **Malignant:** Evil or spiteful.

355 **Traduced:** Slandered or dishonoured.

356 **Circumcisèd:** Young Muslim boys have their foreskins removed in a religious ceremony.

357 **Smote him:** Struck him (down).

362–63 **O Spartan dog … or the sea:** Spartan hounds were famous for their vicious nature. Lodovico accuses Iago of being cruel ('fell') as anguish, hunger or the sea.

Questions

1 What do you think Othello means by the term 'puny whipster' (line 244)? Make sure you read this phrase in context.

2 How does Shakespeare use language to convey Emilia's shock and terror when she discovers that Desdemona's handkerchief has been used in Iago's scheme?

3 Is Emilia wholly honest when she claims to have 'found by fortune' Desdemona's handkerchief (line 225)?

4 What does Othello feel is the condition of his soul?

5 Find a line that suggests Othello is particularly concerned about his honour. Do you feel this is Othello's greatest concern?

6 Emilia sings a snatch of the Willow Song as she is dying. What purpose do you think this serves? That is, why does Shakespeare include the song here?

7   Create and complete a table like the one to demonstrate your understanding of the ways in which Shakespeare uses various language devices to show Othello's despair, in the speech beginning, 'Now, how dost thou look now?' (see lines 272–82).

Language device	Example(s) from Othello's speech
Repetition of words and phrases	
Antithesis (clash of opposites)	
Violent imagery	
Sentence length	
Punctuation	
Sentence fragments	

8   One of the most striking features of the final scene of *Othello* is Iago's decision never to speak again (line 304).

   a   How do you think he should deliver these final lines?

   b   Why do you think Iago makes the decision never to speak again?

   c   Do you think the audience already knows enough about his motivations?

   d   Do you find this feature of the play's ending unsatisfying or do you find it appropriate?

9   Othello asks to be remembered as 'an honourable murderer' and as someone 'who loved too well'. Is he deceiving himself in your opinion?

10   Why do you think the word 'heart' is repeated throughout this scene? What effect does this create? What do you think are Shakespeare's reasons for doing this?

Extend

1   What does Emilia mean when she says, ''Tis proper I obey him, but not now' (line 194)?

2   To what extent is Emilia's decision to align herself with Desdemona rather than her husband to be expected from what we know of Emilia before Act 5?

3   Towards the end of this scene, Othello makes the statement 'Cassio hath the act of shame / A thousand times committed.' How do these lines highlight Othello's delusion? How else might these lines be interpreted?

4   Othello asks the rhetorical question, 'Who can control his fate?' (line 265).

   a   Do you think this statement has a resonance and poignancy when considering the play as a whole?

   b   Do you think Othello is attempting to avoid responsibility for his actions?

5   When Othello looks on Desdemona towards the end of this scene, he makes the comment, 'When we shall meet at compt, / This look of thine will hurl my soul from heaven ...' (lines 273–74). What do these lines suggest about how well Othello knows Desdemona?

6   Shakespeare considers it necessary that a series of letters be discovered in Roderigo's pockets towards the end of the play (lines 308–19). Is this necessary in your opinion? Is it an effective device for resolving the narrative tension and structure of the play?

7   Throughout the play, Iago is presented as someone unable to understand virtuous and selfless qualities. For example, he sees love merely as lust and dismisses concepts such as generosity and heroism (see **Iago and the Devil**, page 98). How is this character flaw Iago's undoing in this scene? Hint: Iago should have followed the advice he gave to Othello, 'Look to your wife.'

8   Do you think the play ends with a sense that things have been put right, that order has been restored?

9   Look up the box on page 79 entitled **Thinking about characters' fatal flaws**. Draw the diagram once again in your note book, this time writing as many details as you can next to each section: examples of jealousy, acts of deception, occurrences of misunderstanding and the ultimate results of death and destruction.

Discuss

1   How much responsibility does Emilia bear for Desdemona's death? Do her actions in the final scene vindicate or redeem her in your opinion? Is she the hero of the play?

2   In Lodovico's closing speech, he looks at Desdemona's bed and says, 'The object poisons sight; / Let it be hid' (lines 365–66). What do you think he means by this statement?

3   If you were given the role of directing a performance of this final scene, how would you advise an actor to play either Emilia or Cassio? Consider especially the devices of voice (e.g. volume, pace, pauses) and body language (e.g. facial expressions, gestures and blocking).

Press PLAY **Oliver Parker: DVD Chapters 28–29 (the closing scenes)**

1   Parker omits Desdemona's final words and Othello's extended speech that demonstrates his extreme grief (lines 259–82), choosing also to have the characters speak in calm and subdued voices throughout the scene. Do you find these to be effective directorial decisions? How else might he have directed the scene? What would you have done? Think in terms of lighting, camera work, music and blocking.

2   What do you think was Parker's aim in directing Iago to climb onto the bed, lie on top of Othello and look directly at the camera? What interpretation of Iago and Othello's roles in the play might Parker be implying?

3   What effect is created by Cassio's opening the window to let the light flood into the room? How does this light contrast to the rest of the film and what themes or ideas does it therefore reinforce?

4   In the final scene of the film, the bodies of Desdemona and Othello are buried at sea. Write a short paragraph that justifies either the view that this is an honourable burial or, alternatively, that it lacks any dignity. In your answer, consider cinematic devices such as lighting, colour, music (the Willow Song), diegetic sound and props, and discuss what you think it adds to Parker's interpretation of the play.

This heavy act with heavy heart relate
Othello as tragedy

What we now call the First Folio was published in 1623, a thick book entitled *Mr William Shakespeare's Comedies, Histories and Tragedies. Othello* was included in the section marked *Tragedies*, along with such famous plays as *Romeo and Juliet*, *Hamlet*, *Macbeth* and *King Lear*. The book did not offer a definition of tragedy; many of its Histories include tragic elements and many of the tragedies include plenty of historical detail, and all of Shakespeare's plays include some comic elements. So, what did the editors mean by tragedy?

The term tragedy generally suggests an unhappy ending, while comedy suggests a happy ending. Although it could be argued that some Shakespearean tragedies such as *Macbeth* and *Hamlet* are not merely tragic (with the respective kingdoms of Scotland and Denmark being liberated from a rule of a usurping tyrant), *Othello* is far less ambiguous. In fact, it has often been said that *Othello* is a tragedy built on a comedy. In the first one and a half acts, the lovers (Othello and Desdemona) overcome obstacles in Venice and pass through a storm to arrive in Cyprus as a happily married couple, and the same storm also defeats the Turkish enemy. This is the stuff of Shakespearean comedy. Even by the conclusion of Act 4, nothing irreversible has happened, no one has been murdered and Othello could still discover the truth. Tragedy only strikes at the end of *Othello*, leaving the characters virtually no time for reflection.

The term tragedy was first used in ancient Greece. The Greek philosopher Aristotle asserted the following things about tragedy in his work *Poetics*:

1 It should be serious, dignified and written in a language more elevated than everyday speech.

2 It should focus on a hero or heroes, usually distinguished by their rank or ability.

3 The tragic hero should make some error in action, causing suffering for himself and those around him.

4 The tragic hero should arrive at some sort of profound moment of recognition, which Aristotle called *anagnorisis*.

5 The audience should feel sympathy for this tragic hero.

6 Tragedy should evoke feelings of pity and fear, leading the audience to question their assumptions about human experience and finally bringing about a release from tension (*catharsis*).

7 The plot should involve dramatic reversals or ironies.

In Shakespeare's day the term tragedy was used more loosely, but some elements are common to the majority of Shakespeare's tragedies:

1 Shakespeare's tragic heroes (generally men) tend to be elevated above the common man by rank or ability.

2 The tragic hero is generally alienated from his own society through his experiences or the choices he has made.

3 The fall of the hero tends to affect the whole community.

4 The tragic hero comes to recognise the flaws in his judgements and the consequences of his destructive actions, and from this he draws some meaning of potentially universal significance.

Q To what extent does *Othello* adhere to Aristotle's model for tragedy?

Q To what extent does *Othello* adhere to the Shakespearean model for tragedy proposed above?

Q Do you think Othello recognises his destructive actions for what they are? Does he draw from them any meaning of universal significance?

General activities

Oral presentations / performance

1 Make your own CD soundtrack for a film version of *Othello*. Choose at least eight songs that you feel are appropriate for different scenes (or excerpts from scenes) in the film. Specify which eight scenes you have chosen and write at least 50 words on each song to explain why it is appropriate for the particular scene you have chosen. Include at least four of the following scenes:

> Act 1 Scene 1 (Iago & Roderigo wake Brabantio)
> Act 1 Scene 2 (Introducing Othello)
> Act 2 Scene 1 (Desdemona arrives in Cyprus to Cassio's praises)
> Act 2 Scene 2 ('A night of revels')
> Act 2 Scene 3 ('Divinity of hell')
> Act 3 Scene 3 ('Beware, my lord, of jealousy!')
> Act 4 Scene 1 (Othello spies on Cassio)
> Act 4 Scene 3 (The Willow Song)
> Act 5 Scene 2 (Othello's soliloquy 'Put out the light')
> Act 5 Scene 2 (Othello's final speech)

You may choose to perform this as an oral presentation, playing short excerpts from each song and explaining your choices.

2 Explain what your emphasis would be if you were given the opportunity to direct your own version of *Othello*. Cover, in particular, your choice of costume for five of the main characters. Explain what sort of atmosphere you would look to create through your set design.

3 Record a scene (or an excerpt from a scene) from the play as part of a radio play.

4 Perform a scene from the play as a group, or perform one of the soliloquies or monologues on your own.

5 Produce a one-minute trailer advertising your film version of *Othello*. This can take the form of either a television, film or radio advertisement. Make sure you consider music, sound effects and voiceover.

6   Set up a chat-show style interview with one or more of the characters from the play where you discuss what happened to the character(s).

Make sure you stay in character for the entire length of the interview.

7   Cover one of the following scenes as a news report (minimum length of two minutes) based on:

- Cassio being chosen as Othello's Lieutenant (Act 1, Scenes 1 and 2)
- Desdemona and Othello's marriage (Acts 1 and 2)
- The brawl, followed by Cassio losing his position as Lieutenant (Act 2 Scene 3)
- Cassio the new Governor of Cyprus (Act 4 Scene 1)
- Desdemona's murder and the horrible truth (Act 5 Scene 2)

This can take the form of either a video or a radio news story. Make sure you capture and maintain your audience's attention, and that you include some interviews.

8   Memorise a passage from *Othello* and perform it for your class. Briefly place it in context before you deliver the lines, and explain your interpretation after your performance.

9   Present a talk to your classmates entitled, 'What's so great about Shakespeare?' In your talk, you might like to discuss elements of *Othello* such as the characters, themes and language features.

Questions for debate

Debate <u>one</u> of the following questions. The Affirmative Team will agree with the statement, while the Negative Team will disagree. Both teams should consist of three members who each speak for two minutes.

1   The female characters bear no responsibility for the tragedy that occurs in *Othello*.

2   Othello is a noble, dignified character.

3   The central character of *Othello* is, in fact, Iago.

Creative writing

1   Try writing part of one of the scenes as a chapter from a modern novel. This will mean that you will have to fill in some details of the setting, incorporate dialogue into the flow of your writing, and give some idea of what characters are thinking, even in places where they do not use a soliloquy. Make sure you use modern language, and that you keep elements such as narrative voice and verb tense consistent.

2 Write a letter in prose from Lodovico to the Senate, at the conclusion of Act 5, explaining recent events and the course of action you chose to take. Make sure you use correct letter writing conventions; you can use Shakespearean language or modern English.

3 Write an email from a modern Roderigo to Iago, at the conclusion of Act 4, explaining your grievances. Make sure you use current email conventions; you can use Shakespearean language or Modern English.

4 Write a 300–500 word newspaper article on one of the following events from the play.

- Cassio being chosen as Othello's Lieutenant (Act 1, Scenes 1 and 2)
- Desdemona and Othello's marriage (Acts 1 and 2)
- The brawl, followed by Cassio losing his position as Lieutenant (Act 2 Scene 3)
- Cassio the new Governor of Cyprus (Act 4 Scene 1)
- Desdemona's murder and the horrible truth (Act 5 Scene 2)

Make sure your headline and your opening sentence grab the reader's attention. Also, include some quotes from the actual play or fictitious interviews with characters. You might like to present this using ICT (PowerPoint, Flash, or create a website).

5 Write a 400 word psychiatric report about Iago at the conclusion of Act 5. Use modern language to write your report.

6 Think of three alternative titles for *Othello* and write a few sentences (between 80 and 100 words on each) explaining why each alternative title would effectively market the play or film to a modern audience.

7 Script an additional conversation between Iago and Roderigo to take place sometime between Act 4 Scene 2 and Act 5 Scene 1, where Iago persuades Roderigo to kill Cassio. Use the same conventions you have observed Shakespeare using throughout the play. Make sure, for example, that you begin a new line each time a different character speaks, and try to write in character.

8 Script an additional conversation between Iago and Emilia, to take place in the middle of Act 4, concerning Desdemona and Othello's situation. Use the same conventions you have observed Shakespeare using throughout the play. Make sure, for example, that you begin a new line each time a different character speaks, and try to write in character.

9 Give Iago or Desdemona a dying speech or monologue (10–20 lines). Make sure you employ Shakespearean language and try to write in character.

10 Create a blog (web log) in which you write some entries from one character's point of view at different stages in the play, responding to the events that have occurred. Add other characters' comments to your character's log.

Illustration

1 Design a poster for your own film or stage version of *Othello*. Include quotes, some phrases that will catch the viewer's attention and a list of the cast for your film.

2 Present one of the scenes from *Othello* as a comic book or comic strip (e.g. manga).

3 Create a PowerPoint or Flash presentation on five characters in the play; include key quotes, a background that you feel is representative of each character, an appropriate symbol for them, and some background music. Write 50 words on each character, explaining why you made these creative choices.

4 Create a Facebook or MySpace page for one of the characters in *Othello*. Make sure you include your character's interests, their interpretation of some of the events of the play, comments from friends and so on. See if you can include some links to appropriate music.

Questions for discussion

Discuss the following questions in a group or as a class.

1 Does Shakespeare portray Othello sympathetically?

2 Does Shakespeare portray Emilia sympathetically?

3 'Iago is the real star of *Othello* and the play should be named after him.' Do you agree with this statement?

4 What do you consider is Iago's principal motivation for bringing about Othello's destruction?

5 Can Desdemona be considered wholly innocent? Does she in any way contribute to her own destruction?

6 To what extent does Othello's imagination ruin him?

7 Why do you think Iago is so successful in his schemes?

8 The poet W. H. Auden made this comment about Othello's final speech: 'Othello learns nothing, remains in defiance, and is damned' (*Lectures on Shakespeare*, Princeton University Press, 2000). To what extent do you agree with this statement?

9　Could *Othello* be in any way considered a racist play?

10　Can a modern-day audience learn anything from *Othello*?

11　Some critics have said that the central conflict in *Othello* is between male and female. To what extent do you believe this is true?

Essay questions

1　How do symbolism and imagery reinforce the main themes of *Othello*?

2　How does Shakespeare use language to define character and heighten the drama of certain situations in *Othello*?

3　To what extent is Othello presented as noble and heroic in Shakespeare's play?

4　'*Othello* is a play of violent contrasts'. Discuss this statement with reference to Shakespeare's play.

5　Discuss the ways in which Shakespeare explores the themes of pride and jealousy in *Othello*.

6　Who or what is to blame for the tragedy of *Othello*?

7　How important are soliloquies in *Othello*?

8　To what extent are the female characters in *Othello* victims of a sexist and patriarchal society?

9　'The tragedy of *Othello* has nothing to do with race.' Discuss.

10　To what extent does *Othello* fit Aristotle's model of tragedy?

11　Show how Shakespeare uses one or more of the following techniques to present his main ideas in *Othello*:

- imagery
- repetition
- setting
- props
- dramatic irony.

12　'Hiding the truth has tragic consequences in *Othello*.' Discuss.

13　Discuss the importance of Shakespeare's use of antithesis in *Othello* to explore the central ideas of the play.

Appendix 1

To the teacher

It will not be possible for your students to attempt every activity in this book, but we have given you a wide range of activities and questions in order for you to determine what best suits the particular needs of your class. Listed below are some of the features of this edition of *Othello* and a brief explanation of how they might be useful in your lessons. We have used a range of icons to help you and your students identify different parts of the text.

1   Understanding the narrative

Before you begin reading the text, it is important that your students have a sound grasp of the story. It is a good idea for the class to read through the **Act summaries** on pages 19–20, and complete the **Quick questions** and **Freeze-frames** activity on pages 21–22.

At the beginning of each scene, we have given a brief outline of what happens, called **In a nutshell**.

2   Reading the text

While it is likely you will read most of the play as a class, you should also read some scenes in smaller groups, and you might like to perform some as well.

At the beginning of each scene we have listed the **Characters** in order of importance. It is advisable that, as the teacher, you take a major role and delegate the other major parts to your most confident readers. It is also helpful if one student reads the stage directions for some scenes; we have indicated where this might be helpful by listing 'Narrator' among the characters.

Where possible, try to allocate parts the day before you perform a scene so that students have an opportunity to look over and perhaps practise their parts. Encourage students to read loudly and clearly, and be forthcoming with your praise where you can.

Shakespeare's language (see pages 10–16) provides some basic reading tips and explanations of key language features. We recommend that you look at the reading tips before you begin reading, and then explain them to your class. This section also includes a list of key words that recur frequently throughout the play. You might like to familiarise your students with this before you begin reading the play.

It is important that you do not overwhelm your students with too many concepts in a short period of time. Introduce concepts such as iambic pentameter after your students have begun to gain an intuitive feeling for the language.

We have also provided general introductions on **Jacobean England**, **Shakespeare** himself, and **Sources** and **Settings** for *Othello*. These will provide some background and a context in which to read the play. The notes on Jacobean England and the theatre are the most important of these introductions. You could read these as a class or ask students to read them in their own time.

There is, of course, no substitute for seeing the text performed as a live production, and we recommend you have actors or performance companies, such as Bell Shakespeare, visit your school.

3   Understanding the text

We have included a short **Vocabulary list** at the beginning of each scene. All of these words, plus some others from the text and the **Text notes**, are printed at the back of the book so you can find a word without having to remember where it was first introduced.

The **Before you read** section, at the beginning of every scene, provides reading tips and anticipates problems students may have. Phrases and words that are more secondary to the understanding of a scene are printed as **Text notes** at the end of each scene or part of a scene. In most cases, these notes provide an interpretation of a specific word or phrase and, in this way, can be limiting. We would encourage students not to make these their first point of reference but rather to use them, where necessary, after they have read through the scene and thought about it themselves.

Finally, a number of **History boxes** provide useful historical information on Jacobean England. Most of this information we have included to give an historical context for specific scenes. Other information has been provided to fire the students' curiosity.

4   Analysing the text

Questions

In ordering the **Questions**, we have attempted to balance chronology against degree of difficulty. For some scenes you might look to save time by dividing the questions among different groups in the class, or you may simply use them as a springboard for discussion. It is not necessary to use every question in the book.

Extend

We have also included more challenging **Extend** questions that will allow some students, or the entire class, to analyse a scene in greater depth. It is important that all students engage with the technical aspects of the play, and, for this reason, we have also included questions relating to theatrical and language technique among the general questions.

Discuss
Finally, some questions have been designed for general discussion of personal responses to the text, as well as possible interpretations for performance. These are indicated by the **Discuss** icon.

A word about …

Shakespeare's themes and techniques highlight particular ideas and devices used by Shakespeare throughout this play. We recommend that students first read these boxes themselves and that you then explain the concept using the examples.

5   The films (Press play)

Press
PLAY

Oliver Parker's 1995 film of *Othello* is easily the most accessible, exciting version of the play. It is useful to show excerpts from the film as your class studies the play to reinforce your students' understanding of key scenes, and it may serve as an alternative to reading some scenes. The **Press play** activities provide opportunities for further analysis and discussion.

6   General activities

There is deliberate overlap between the **Questions for debate, Questions for discussion** and **Essay questions** (pages 205–208). How you use these will depend largely on the type of class you have. We have generally found that it is better to read through the play in its entirety before beginning debates, essays or creative activities. Again, this will depend on your personal preference. You might like to break up your reading of the play after Act 2 or 3 with one of the **Oral presentations / performance** or **Creative writing** activities on pages 204–207.

7   Further reading

We have provided **A Shakespeare reading list** on page 213, in case you wish to read more on Shakespeare and Elizabethan or Jacobean England. We also highly recommend any of the Bell Shakespeare Company's short courses for teachers.

8   A note about the text

We have based this edition of *Othello* on the First Folio and Quarto, generally conforming to standard modern editions. We have divided some of the longer scenes into two parts to make them more digestible for your students, but you may choose to ignore these divisions. Some of the stage directions and the spelling have been modernised, in line with standard editorial practices for preparing editions of Shakespeare's plays. Modern punctuation conventions are followed, with the exception of the dash (–), which we have used to indicate an interruption in the flow or the direction of the conversation; for example, when a character switches from soliloquising to addressing another character on stage, or when a character switches from speaking to one character to addressing another (see **Shakespeare's language** on pages 10–16 for a more detailed explanation).

9   Finally ...

No one could reasonably expect to understand every phrase or allusion in Shakespeare's plays and your students should not expect to either. Making this clear from the outset will foster the confidence in students to talk about what they do understand and what they do know: to see the text as a glass half full, rather than a glass half empty. Moreover, this will encourage students to appreciate the subtleties and resonances of the language and to truly understand that there are more things in heaven and earth than are dreamt of in our pedagogy.

Appendix 2

A Shakespeare reading list

Alexander, Catherine M. S., *Shakespeare: The Life, the Works, the Treasures*, Allen & Unwin, Sydney, 2007.

Bate, Jonathan, *The Genius of Shakespeare*, Picador, London, 1997.

Crystal, David & Ben, *Shakespeare's Words*, Penguin, London, 2002.

Greenblatt, Stephen, *Will in the World: How Shakespeare Became Shakespeare*, Norton, London, 2004.

Greer, Germaine, *Shakespeare: A Very Short Introduction*, Oxford University Press, Oxford, 2002.

Gurr, Andrew, *The Shakespearean Stage*, Cambridge University Press, Cambridge, 1992.

Hussey, S. S., *The Literary Language of Shakespeare*, Longman, Harlow, 1982.

Kay, Dennis, *Shakespeare: His Life, Work and Era*, Sidgwick & Jackson, London, 1991.

Kermode, Frank, *Shakespeare's Language*, Penguin, London, 2001.

Kermode, Frank, *The Age of Shakespeare*, Phoenix, London, 2005.

Rodenburg, Patsy, *Reading Shakespeare*, Methuen, London, 2002.

Sandler, Robert (ed.), *Northrop Frye on Shakespeare*, Yale University Press, New Haven, 1986.

Shapiro, James, *1599: A Year in the Life of William Shakespeare*, Faber & Faber, London, 2005.

Tillyard, E. M. W., *The Elizabethan World Picture*, Vintage Books, New York, 1960.

Wells, Stanley, *A Dictionary of Shakespeare*, Oxford University Press, Oxford, 1998.

Wells, Stanley, *Shakespeare & Co.*, Penguin, London, 2007.

Wilson, Jean, *The Shakespeare Legacy*, Bramley Books, Godalming, 1995.

Wood, Michael, *In Search of Shakespeare,* directed by David Wallace, Maya Vision International, 2004.

Vocabulary list

Abhor: Hate
Abroad: About the place; freely at large
Adieu: Goodbye
Affined: Bound to
Affliction: Suffering
Alacrity: Speed
Amiable: Loving and tender
Ancient: The standard-bearer, third-in-command (Iago's position for most of the play)
Anon: Soon
Assails: Attacks
Assay: Attempt
Aught: Anything
Avaunt: Be gone
Ay: Yes

Bark: Ship
Base: Immoral; common
Beguile: Deceive; charm
Bereft: Without or lacking
Beseech: Beg; forcefully request (entreat)
Beshrew: Curse
Bestial: Animal-like, as opposed to human
Betimes: At an early hour; speedily
Betwixt: Between
Bode / Boding: Acts as an omen of something (good or bad)
Boon: A request or petition
Bootless: Useless
Bounteous: Generous
Brace: Two
By'r Lady: A mild oath, swearing by the Virgin Mary, or 'By Our Lady'

Caitiff: Wretch
Cashiered: Dismissed or sacked

Censure: Blame and judgement; severe criticism
Charter: Permission
Chaste: Sexually pure
Check / Cheque: Rebuke; interruption
Chide / chid: To criticise or tell someone off
Citadel: City

Civility: Manners or proper behaviour
Clamour: Noise
Clime: Country
Coffers: Boxes or chests
Complexion: Skin colour
Conceit: Thought, idea or imagination; also a technical term for an extended metaphor
Consuls: Ancient Roman heads of state (rhymes with *tonsils*)
Converse: Engage in conversation
Coxcomb: Idiot or fool
Credit: Reputation; credibility
Credulous: Gullible
Cuckold: A man whose wife has been sexually unfaithful
Cudgelled: Beaten

Diablo: Italian for Devil
Direful: Disastrous or terrible
Discourse: Conversation
Discretion: Sound judgement or tact
Dispatch: To deal with something or get it done quickly
Disposition: Arrangements
Disproportioned: Inconsistent
Dissemble: Deceive
Divinity: Theology; relating to the divine
Dotes: Loves obsessively; becomes infatuated with someone

Egregiously: Extraordinarily; very badly
Eminent: Important
Ensign: The standard-bearer, third-in-command (Iago's position for most of the play)
Ensue: To happen next; to occur or follow as a consequence
Entreats: Strongly requests or begs
Ere (pronounced *air*): Before
Err: Make an error
Expostulate: Argue at length or plead

Fable: Story
Fie: An exclamation of annoyance, disapproval or disgust
Filch: Steal

Folly: Stupid or improper behaviour
Fond: Foolish; loving
Forbear: Tolerate; put up with
Forfend: Forbid
Forsake: Reject; leave
Fortitude: Strength (and in this case, the fortifications)
Frank: Generous; honest and up-front
Fulsome: Distasteful or repulsive

Gait: (The manner of someone's) walk
Gallants: Members of the gentry (the upper class)
Galleys: Venetian ships
Garter: A band used to hold up socks or stockings
Go to: Get moving; get to work; come on
Governor: The person in charge of a colony, in this case Cyprus
Green: Naive
Hallowed: Regarded as holy or sacred
Haste: Great speed
Hence: From here
Hither: Here; to this place
Hitherto: Up until now
Homage: Submission; respectful acknowledgement
Honest: Honourable or chaste (sexually pure); also means truthful
Humour: Mood (the humours were bodily fluids that were believed to control someone's personality)

Imminent: About to happen
Impediments: Obstructions or obstacles
Imperious: Kingly; powerful
Import: Of importance
Importune: Beg someone forcefully
Imposition: Burden
Imputation: Reputation; prestige
Incense: Anger or cause to be angry
Incontinent: Immoral or unchaste; lacking self-control
Indiscreet: Lacking tact or discretion
Infirmity: Weakness
Iniquity: Wrongdoing

Jove: The Roman god Jupiter

Kindred: Matching character
Kinsmen: Relatives
Knave: Troublemaker or trickster

Languishes: Suffers; wastes time
Lascivious: Vulgar or lustful
Lechery: Lustful behaviour
Lewd: Rude or vulgar
List: Listen

Magnifico: A Venetian nobleman (Brabantio)
Manifest: Show
Malignant: Evil; spiteful
Mark: Pay attention
Marry: An exclamation of surprise or frustration; a mild oath referring to the Virgin Mary
Meet: Appropriate or fitting
Mere: Nothing more than
Mettle: Character or spirit
Minx: A bold, flirtatious girl
Moor: Someone of north African origin (Othello is a Moor)
Mutiny: A rebellion against proper or legal authority

Negligence: Neglect or carelessness
Noble: Dignified and brave; of the upper-class
Nuptial: Wedding

Office: Duty; position
Oft: Often
Overt: Open and obvious

Pagan: Anyone who is not Christian (in Shakespeare's time)
Palpable: Obvious; able to be touched or felt
Parley: Talk
Peevish: Perverse or irritable
Peradventure: Perhaps
Perchance: Perhaps; by chance
Perdition: Destruction; ruin
Perforce: By force
Perjury: Dishonesty
Pernicious: Destructive or dangerous; evil
Physician: Doctor
Pilot: Captain of a ship

Pish: An exclamation expressing contempt or annoyance
Pith: Vigour or strength
Pliant: Suitable, favourable
Portent: A sign of a future event
Potent: Powerful
Prate: Prattle or talk nonsense
Prithee: Used to introduce a request (short for 'I pray thee …')
Procure: Obtain (something)
Profane: Insulting or worldly (opposite to sacred)
Profess: Declare publicly
Promulgate: Make something widely known
Propriety: Normal peaceful state
Prosperous: Wealthy (perhaps also generous)

Quillets: Quibbles or hair-splitting distinctions

Rapier: Light, sharp-pointed sword
Rebuke: Criticism or insult
Relish: Appreciate or savour
Remorse: Strong feelings of regret and repentance
Reproach: Criticism or insult
Restitution: Recovery; restoration; retrieval
Revels: Celebrations
Ruminate: Ponder or thoughtfully consider

Sagittary: The name of an inn or pub
Sanctified: Set apart to God; made holy
Sans: without (a French word, pronounced *sohn*)
Sated: Satisfied
Satiety: Excess
Saucy: Insolent; insulting
'Sblood: God's blood (an oath appropriate for a rough soldier)
Segregation: Shattering
Senate: The government
Servitor: Servant
Shrift: Confession
Signior: Sir (friendly)
Signiory: Venetian government
Sirrah: Similar to 'Sir' but used to address social inferiors

Slain: Killed
Slanderer: Someone who insults people
Solicitation: A request
Sooth: Truth; truly
Spinster: An old woman
Sport: Recreation or entertainment
Strumpet: Prostitute
Suffice: Satisfy
Suit: A petition or request to someone in authority
Suitor: Someone making a request

Taper: Candle
Tempest: Storm
Thence: From that place (or time)
Thou: You
Thy: Your
Topped / Tupped: A vulgar term to describe sex
Traverse: Take aim; stab
Trifle: Unimportant things
Troth: Truth; good faith
Tush: A mild exclamation meaning 'rubbish'

Valiant: Brave or heroic
Veritable: Rightly named
Vexation: Exasperation or worry
Vices: Morally bad qualities (opposite of virtues)
Virtue: Goodness
Visage: Face
Vouch: Guarantee or warrant

Wanton: Carefree; unrestrained; with no boundaries
Whence: From what place, cause or origin
Wherefore: Why
Wit: Good sense; cleverness or intelligence
Withal: In addition; with this
Woo: Win someone over romantically
Works: Fortification or defences
Wrought: Worked (on)

Yonder / yond: Over there

Zounds: God's Wounds (a violent oath)

Image credits

A number of images in the public domain have been sourced from the Wikimedia Commons website, commons.wikimedia.org/wiki/Main_Page. Copyright owners are identified where known. Every effort has been made to source the owners of copyright of images used in this book; the publishers welcome any information pertaining to unacknowledged work.

Cover image: Lenny Henry and Conrad Nelson in the 2009 Northern Broadsides'
    production of *Othello* / Nobby Clark/ArenaPAL
Page 1 source: Wikimedia Commons
Page 3 source: Wikimedia Commons
Page 4 source: Wikimedia Commons
Page 5 photo © Lance Bellers, source: iStockphoto
Page 6 source: Wikimedia Commons
Page 7 photo © Tohma, source: Wikimedia Commons
Page 63 photo © University of Birmingham, source: The University of Birmingham
    Research and Cultural Collections
Page 105 sources: Wikimedia Commons; Wikipedia

Index

Page references to images are indicated by italics.

H

handkerchief, 118, 172, 179–80
hyperbole, 116–17, 146

I

iambic pentameter, 12–16, 60, 146
imagery
    of animals, 33–4, 127, 146, 172
    of darkness, 24
    of poison or disease, 79–80, 92,
        128, 146, 165, 172
    of seeing, 128
    of violence, 128, 146

J

Jacobean England, 3–5, 24, 63, 152–3
Journey of the Magi, use of
    foreshadowing in, 74

K

Kemp, William, 100–1

M

metaphors, 62
Moorish ambassador to Elizabeth I,
    63, *63*

N

Nineteen Eighty-Four, use of
    foreshadowing in, 74

P

Paradise Lost, 98
Parker, Oliver, film of *Othello* directed
    by, 32–3, 40, 61, 73, 98, 116, 127,
    137, 145, 161, 171, 189, 201–2
Paterson, Don, use of conceits by, 62
pathetic fallacy, 74
prose, 14, 60, 146
punctuation in Shakespeare, 10–11
    see also contractions; dashes
puns, 103

R

race and racism, 24–5, 33, 42
repetition, 92, 146, 171–2, 179–80
rhyme, 13–14

S

Saint Augustine, 99
Shakespeare's life and work, *1*, 1–2
similes, 62
soliloquies, 51–2, 92
songs, 13–14, 82
    see also Willow Song, the
stichomythia, 146

T

tragedy, 79–80, 192, 202–3

V

Vice, character of, 99

W

Willow Song, the, 14, 166, 171